Assessment in Social Work

Assessment in Social Work

Second Edition

Judith Milner

and

Patrick O'Byrne

Consultant editor: Jo Campling

Contents

List of Tables and Figures

Tables

Figures

Acknowledgements

There are many people who deserve our thanks for their help in the revision of this book, not least being Jo Campling for prompting us to prepare the second edition and Catherine Gray and Alison Caunt at Palgrave Macmillan. Their support and guidance has been much appreciated.

As usual, the staff at Northorpe Hall Child and Family Trust, Mirfield, have been unstinting in their support, encouragement and the provision of opportunities to test out our ideas. A special thanks to Maureen Gibbons who provided us with an ex-student's view of omissions in the first edition.

We also thank Suki Desai of the University of Wolverhampton, Verrol Liverpool of the University of North London and Ian Warwick of the University of Huddersfield for their helpful comments on how anti-oppressive and evidence-based practice could be better incorporated in this edition.

Lastly, we are grateful as ever to Mary O'Byrne and Judith's dachsund, Rosie, who bore our strange working hours with their customary good humour and stoic patience.

JUDITH MILNER
PATRICK O'BYRNE

1

Introduction

The revisions in this book reflect the revisions in government guidance covering the legislation outlined in the first edition, and the impact of these revisions on assessment practice. Largely these are to do with an increasing emphasis on ensuring that assessments are evidence-based, consider risk more comprehensively in all its contexts, and accountability. We introduce these issues in Chapter 2, continue them throughout the 'maps' chapters and include the *Signs of Safety* approach to child protection practice outlined by Turnell and Edwards (1999) in Chapter 11. In order to emphasise further the links between assessment and interventions, we have added information on outcomes research into the effectiveness of particular interventions at the end of each 'maps' chapter. This, we hope, will enable social workers to consider whose needs are best met by their chosen methods of assessing and intervening.

Social workers have traditionally drawn mainly on psychosocial theory as their preferred framework for understanding the nature of service users and their problems. We draw attention to the limitations of this theory in partnership approaches which aim to respect more fully service users' own theories about the nature of their difficulties, and have expanded the chapter on solution focused approaches. Additionally we include a separate chapter on narrative approaches in order to offer another approach to empowering assessment practice, broadening also our discussion of the various 'isms'.

Finally, we remedy a serious omission in the first edition by including more material on mental health assessments; and include a wider range of case examples to avoid the previous heterosexist bias. Thus we hope that this edition of the book will strengthen still further the possibility of more constructive assessments.

We seek new ways to bring clarity to this complex subject of assessment by addressing the shifts in social work theory. Probably the greatest of these shifts is the growing awareness of the uses of power, particularly the impact of powerlessness and oppression. At the

1

same time, there has been a greater move towards constructionist thinking. Indeed, social constructionism has a great deal to say about power (see, for example, Burr, 1995; Parton, 1996). These writers also demonstrate that, as various ideas are being developed about post-modern approaches to social work and re-evaluating earlier theory, there is movement towards greater respect for service users' views. This involves entering much more into dialogue with service users, adopting a stance of uncertainty, and a willingness to listen to their accounts and co-construct more helpful accounts with them. Parton and Marshall (1988) described the process as one of co-creating a sense of harmony with marginalised people, developing both reflexivity and action, rather than knowledge as such: in short, becoming aware of the socially constructed nature of social work itself (see also Parton and O'Byrne, 2000).

Although there is no single definition of social constructionism, Burr (1995) provides a helpful explanation that takes the approach of listing the main things one would have to accept in order to be described as a constructionist. These include:

- taking a critical stance towards many taken-for-granted ways of understanding the world;
- viewing various ways of understanding the world as relative to periods in history and to culture;
- seeing knowledge not as being determined by the nature of things, but as constructed between people as they talk and interact;
- an awareness that social action is driven by the social constructions of the time;
- since the social world is made up of people's interactions, believing that there are no essential 'given' natures to be discovered in the psycho-social world;
- a questioning of realism and the idea of objective truth and an awareness that the language we use determines the meaning of things, rather than vice versa. Language, rather than being just a medium for expressing ideas, actually determines thought to the extent that truth is the product of language: language constructs social reality.

From time to time through this book, we adopt a constructionist stance, particularly in our use of terms and phrases such as uncertainty, dialogue, language as crucial, partnership, participation, reinterpretation, people as essentially subjective, narrative, co-constructing meaning and reflexivity. Space does not permit a full analysis of this approach here, and the reader who needs such an analysis is recommended to use the work of the writers mentioned above. What we will be doing is drawing on this approach to present current ideas in such a way that they can be used in a practical framework. Here we are merely saying where many of our ideas on assessment are rooted, and we raise this to help the reader make sense of what may appear to be conflicting theories. For example, essentialist theory, as we outline in our presentation of Freudian theory in Chapter 6, does, we suggest, reflect no more than a particularly persistent social construction that is 'out of step' with other theories. Later theories such as cognitive psychology and solution-focused and narrative theory reflect much more recent social constructions that emphasise collaboration with service users, open-mindedness and uncertainty. Throughout, we stress the importance of assessment being rooted in usable theory in the sense that it leads to helpful action, as evaluated by *both* social workers and service users.

Having survived the experience of discovering how inadequate our earlier ideas were in terms of promoting anti-oppressive practice, we have been struck by the lack of any comprehensive framework for assessment in social work. There are, however, only too many linear, prescriptive and stylised assessment formats that come nowhere near meeting the complexities, uncertainties and ambiguities of current social work practice. The lack of a conceptual framework was reflected in the literature, where it tended to be dismissed in a few pages of advice to the practitioner on the need to be objective and thorough. Closer examination of prescriptions on assessment activity revealed that techniques of assessment activity had developed from an unquestioned use of knowledge about the nature of people, which had been extensively borrowed from the disciplines of psychiatry and psychology and which was preoccupied with individual casework.

This did not seem to us to be a sound base for focusing on the task in hand, that is social work, especially in the new climate of *social* work following wide-ranging legislative changes. The new legislation defined assessment as a separate activity that was to be simple, speedy and informal, although the task was complicated by the need to provide value for money, involve the consumer and coordinate the efforts of a vast range of allied services. Social workers found themselves deluged with government advice on how to undertake assessments via a series of checklists for different sorts of service user.

There appeared to be no easily accessible pool of wisdom on which social workers could depend in their efforts to meet the new demands and little evidence of the existence of well-developed skills in involving service users in the assessment process. The research into the effectiveness of social work assessments made depressing reading, especially when measured by service user satisfaction with assessment outcomes. Additionally, we found that, although most writers commented that assessment was a continuous process, there was little evidence that social workers did in fact re-evaluate their assessments. Indeed, there was a good deal of evidence that they sought to confirm rather than disconfirm their initial assessments, often shaping information to fit favoured theoretical models and concentrating on risks rather than needs. Most worrying of all was the realisation that a social worker's initial assessment took on the status of 'truth' and became the key determinant to future action and outcomes.

Therefore we attempt to examine the dominant concerns of social work in the new climate of empowerment, partnership, choice and value for money, and present an overarching framework for assessment work. Because social work assessments are essentially social studies of situations, we suggest that the tenets of sound qualitative research can be applied to this area. Our framework will emphasise the need for assessing social workers to make a clear statement of intent, be actively accountable for their values and take a systematic approach to data collection. At various points the book will draw a parallel between good assessment work and participatory research. Everitt *et al.* (1992) also make this point and stress the value of the spirit of enquiry, making assumptions explicit, thinking through theoretical perspectives, clarifying hypotheses and testing them while engaging and listening to people's worlds and remaining conscious 'of the pervasiveness of ideology in the way we see the world' (p. 4). We suggest the development of multiple and testable hypotheses about the nature of people's problems and solutions, and making decisions that lead to measurable outcomes and are subject to consumer feedback.

Developing multiple hypotheses means that social workers will be faced with the need to find their way through the thicket of concepts and theories current in social work, so we have provided a series of 'maps' that suggest ways in which social workers can find their way through the complex terrain of human situations. We do not suggest that there is any single correct way to analyse human situations but encourage social workers to be reflexive and develop a pragmatic truth that fits social work situations in a way which is most satisfying for service users, the end product being a story that is *helpful* to all concerned. We see assessment as a journey for which social workers need to select the most appropriate map if they are to get to their destinations quickly and efficiently. We do not believe that assessment can be easily separated from intervention – change happens at all stages of the social work process – but we do think it dangerous to read a map while driving, so we recommend that social workers familiarise themselves with a range of maps before planning the assessment journey. Should they get lost on the way or should the service user not meet them at the destination, they will then need to consult the maps again. Uncertainty is, we suggest, the beginning of hopefulness.

Essentially, the structure of this book presents a comprehensive framework for assessment that includes a set of maps to guide social workers towards helpful analyses. First, however, Chapter 2 considers carefully the contradictions of traditional assessment work, the problematic role of psychology and other social work knowledge, and the impact of recent legislation and guidance.

As the values climate of social work assessments has changed, we include an early chapter, Chapter 3, to help clear up this area before selecting an appropriate map. Any assessment must, therefore, be prefaced by a consideration of the power elements in social worker–service user relationships. Service user rights and responsibilities can best be understood in terms of equal opportunities and facilitated by social workers seeking to bridge the gaps between themselves and service users. Accommodating and being sensitive to all the 'isms' can seem a daunting task, but they can be conflated so that the task becomes more manageable and competition between various 'isms' reduced. We see gender issues as central in this process because men who suffer oppression because they are old, disabled, homosexual or children, become 'unmanned'; black men become 'ultra-manned'; and most carers are women. We will argue that men need to be brought more clearly into the assessment process if it is to be both truly anti-oppressive and effective.

Chapter 4 examines the evaluation of assessment and considers how far assessment can be viewed as a process rather than an event. Here our preferred framework is introduced fully, but, in order to prepare readers, we briefly mention below what that framework is and suggest that they will find this comprehensive framework useful irrespective of social workers' tasks and practice settings.

Map selection and the question of seeking the truth are dealt with in Chapter 5. We aim to demonstrate the breadth of the subject from which better analyses of situations can be arrived at by selecting from the five different 'maps'. Social workers will be able to select those maps that are more in line with their personal views of human difficulties and with their values (*their* constructions) and that are the most helpful for their individual practice.

The framework has five stages, which we list briefly here:

1 *Preparation*. Deciding who to see, what data will be relevant, what the purpose is and what the limits of the task are.
2 *Data collection*. People are met and engaged with, difference gaps are addressed, and empowerment and choice are safeguarded as we come to the task with respectful uncertainty and a research mentality.
3 *Weighing the data*. Current social and psychological theory and research findings that are part of every qualified worker's learning are drawn on to answer the questions 'Is there a problem?' and 'How serious is it?' (Existing theories are listed in Chapter 5; however, it is not the purpose of this book to discuss them at length.)
4 *Analysing the data*. One or more of the analytical maps are then used to interpret the data and to seek to gain an understanding of them in order to develop ideas for intervention. Five maps will be introduced in Chapter 5, each one being fully presented in Chapters 6–10; we hope that their novel names will aid understanding as well as recall.
5 *Utilising the analysis*. This is the stage in which judgments are finalised. The difficulties of this stage are elaborated upon in Chapter 11, where we acknowledge the stressful nature of this stage of assessment, the issue of risk-taking and the importance of language.

Because we devote five chapters to the analytical maps, it will be clear that stage 4 is a major concern of ours. We hope that our presentation of these maps will encourage students and colleagues in practice to draw on or select from these chapters to arrive at deeper and more action-orientated analyses of situations, thereby creating more useful interventions. We are suggesting that this is best done from the humble co-constructivist stance mentioned earlier. While practitioners need to be clear about what they are doing, as Everitt *et al.* (1992, p. 33, emphasis added) point out, 'it needs to be stated that *clarity is not the same as certainty*. Certainty in theory leads to dogma and blinkered practices. Clarity opens it up for scrutiny'.

We wish to stress the central importance of assessment for effective social work, not only for planning interventions, but also for reviews, for deciding when to end interventions and for the evaluation of interventions after they have ended. As will become clear in later chapters, the search for a good assessment is not seen by us as a search for the truth or a diagnosis, but rather in terms of building a more helpful set of meanings and a more creative account that will assist service users in moving on. Central to this is 'talk', reflective discussion that helps to reframe difficulties and mobilise people's own potentialities.

Finally, we suggest that this book takes an approach that will be helpful in promoting anti-oppressive practice, and that it will encourage practitioners to be 'concerned with developing knowledge in ways which will enable service users... to become "knowers" (and have) their understandings of their experiences of inequality acknowledged as legitimate' (Everitt *et al.*, 1992, p. 3).

2

From Traditional Practice to New Complexities

In this chapter we outline some historical difficulties with assessment and its preoccupation with problem narratives and clientism. Various pressures on social workers are considered, as are the consequences of the special role of psychology in defining 'normality'. We then address shifts in the focus of assessments arising from an emphasis in more recent legislation on accountability, value for money, and service user perspectives as well as the added complexities arising from a preoccupation with risk assessment and evidence-based practice in government guidance. Finally, we identify ways in which social workers can manage the increasingly complex demands of assessment work.

The history of assessment

Traditionally, social work texts have expressed agreement that assessment is a key element in social work practice because, without it, workers would be left to react to events and intervene in an unplanned way (see, for example, Davies, 1981; Coulshed, 1988; Reder *et al.*, 1993). Having agreed on the centrality of assessment in the social work process, texts then dismiss the subject in a few pages. Apart from some brief homilies on counterchecking facts and hypotheses and the necessity of reassessing wherever appropriate, most writers make a list of information-yielding sources and then depart from the subject to other aspects of the social work process.

However, gathering information, sifting it carefully and coming to an 'objective' and 'accurate' conclusion is by no means as unproblematic as this suggests; assessment has never been the scientific activity that many writers pretended. For example, Coulshed (1988) compared assessment with a social study that 'avoids labels and is reached as a result of logical analysis of data which has been carefully and

systematically collected'. (Coulshed, 1988, p. 3). She implied that editing needed to be done but made no suggestion on how this skill could
be acquired, although editing shapes the way information is collected
and selected for the initial assessment (Sheldon, 1995) and later information is processed selectively and discretely if it fails to confirm the
initial hypothesis (Reder *et al.*, 1993). Viewing assessment as unproblematic and unbiased in itself created a gap between theories of
problem causation and intervention, a gap in which the client was
often squeezed to fit the social worker's ideas about the nature of
people and how best their problems could be addressed. Denney
(1992), for example, found in his study of probation reports that
many of the assessments seemed to contradict the form of work
advocated. The most commonly used interventions were largely individual rather than social, although there have been some protests:

> If we are to maintain the integrity of 'community' care, 'social'
> service and 'social' work, we have to confront the constant tendency
> that we all have to *regress to the individualisation of individual prob-
> lems*. (Smale and Tuson, 1993, p. 30)

Similarly, Barber (1991) also expressed dismay at the tendency
towards 'reductionism' in which social work became equated with
casework and individual solutions were found within the psychopathology of individuals and their interpersonal relations. He traces this
development back to Mary Richmond's work in the USA, in which
she identified two central themes: that clients and problems have to be
individualised, and that successful casework requires careful diagnosis
(Richmond, 1917). These themes, along with Freudian theorising,
underpinned the vastly influential work of Hollis (1964). Yet Barber
comments that, even earlier, C. Wright Mills was complaining about
the limitations of such an approach:

> Present institutions train several kinds of persons – such as judges
> and social workers – to think in terms of situations. Their activities
> and mental outlook are set within the existing norms of society; in
> their professional work they tend to have an occupationally trained
> incapacity to rise above 'cases'. (Mills, 1943, p. 171)

Harrison (1995a) refers to this as the 'forensic gaze', suggesting
that it gives rise to 'placebo solutions'. He illustrates his point with
the example of a refugee mother of five children (Mrs A), who lost half
her family, struggled through a civil war, fought her way to England,

studied in the evenings for a decent job and then popped out to the shop, leaving a 10-year-old in charge of the family. She was then 'threatened' with parenting skills training, a solution firmly embedded in a belief that family pathology is the key to much abuse and neglect rather than one, minority, analysis of the context of abuse (see, for example, Hearn, 1995a). Why the preoccupation with individual casework? Barber (1991) complains that the problem with much casework theory is that the sole unit of concern and the focus of all analysis is the individual. The research by Sinclair *et al.* (1995) into assessments of young people accommodated by a local authority also expressed concern about the tendency of 'traditional' assessments to concentrate on searching for the origins of past problems. They comment: 'However it is defined, assessment was commonly associated with identifying a problem, the purpose of which was to find an appropriate resource or solution' (Sinclair *et al.*, 1995, p. 130).

Given that resources available to social workers have always been restricted, it is not surprising that they have been lured into locating the solution within the individual. There are several reasons why social workers find a broad, social assessment particularly difficult to undertake and present successfully to their managers. Assessment of individual need is affected by expediency because there is pressure on workers to construct their assessments so that they fit into existing resource provision (Neill, 1989), although this is not quite what is envisaged in the original DoH guidance (1990a). The pressures of expediency may mean that it is easier as a consequence to subsume some individual needs under more general family needs when faced with uncooperative family members. For example, Bebington and Miles (cited in DoH, 1990b, p. 6) found that a combination of poverty and lack of available social support led to children being accommodated, and: 'Most people enter residential care because of the relationships they have, or do not have, in their social circumstances and not just because of their individual characteristics' (Smale and Tuson, 1993, p. 26). Similarly mental health problems are more likely to result from a range of adverse factors associated with social exclusion than individual characteristics (DoH, 1998, p. 6).

When faced with the miseries of poverty, inadequate housing and poor employment conditions, it is easier to seek psychological explanations for events than to explore complex interactions between the social and psychological dimensions of problems. The 'psychologising' of social problems in this way has been referred to as 'therapy to help you come to terms with your rats' by practitioners who are only too aware of the fate of an accurate assessment. Agency function rarely permits social workers to address major problems rooted in social deprivation, while, at the same time, holding them responsible for attempting to operationalise a care plan that is not founded on a realistic social assessment.

Equally damaging is sociological reductionism, as the report into Paul's death through neglect (The Bridge, 1995) most vividly demonstrated. Indeed, research shows that a different approach to child protection assessments is taken depending upon whether the subject of inquiry is a case of physical or sexual abuse; the former tends to focus on parents, the latter on children (Corby, 2000). There remains a rightful place for psychological explanations in assessments; the real issue is to remain cautious (Sutton, 2000) and avoid blaming or pathologising individuals by ascribing to them the cause of their difficulties that stem from injustice, disadvantage and deprivation. Barber (1991) clearly argues that external difficulties cause and interact with internal difficulties. The 'social' frequently becomes 'psychological' and vice versa; the disempowered develop 'learned helplessness', for example, and resource improvement may not be a helpful solution on its own. Many service users either 'lack the purchasing power to seek solutions to their problems or are constrained by the courts to submit to social work' (Barber, 1991, p. 29). Common to both instances is a lack of control over some of the important events in their lives, and therefore a 'psychology of empowerment' is useful. Powerlessness generates despair, listlessness and lethargy, people internalising the views of oppressors, blaming themselves and developing dysfunctional self-defeating thought processes and behaviours so that, in Freire's (1972) terms, 'the oppressor lives inside'.

Helpful assessments retain a careful balance of the social and psychological as 'social work theories which seek to avoid or deny the need for individual change are likely to be as inadequate as approaches which reduce all human problems to the level of psychopathology' (Barber, 1991, p. 31). We will address this balance in later chapters, but here we turn to some serious problems with the 'psy complex' and how it has been developed in related social work knowledge.

What is normal?

When Rose (1985) developed the concept of the 'psy complex', he argued that, during and after the Second World War, the proliferation of clinics and nurseries for children made it possible to collect comparable information on a large number of subjects, and that subsequent analyses led to the construction of norms. Developmental norms not only represented what was normal for children at any given age, but also enabled the normality of *any* individual child to be assessed by comparison with this norm. Thus there came into existence a 'psychology' – a complex of discourses, practices, agents and techniques through which applied and clinical psychology could define 'normal' children and, by this definition, 'happy' families, 'good enough' parents and even social 'tranquillity'. At the same time, psychology claimed an ability to deal with the problems posed for society by dysfunctional, abnormal conduct. However, Rose suggests that there has been a bit of fast footwork here, 'normal' (a value-laden term) being substituted for 'normative'. In theory, both words are adjectives meaning according to rule, establishing a standard or average. But 'abnormal', which is no more than a deviation from a standard or average, has come to mean undesirable.

That *normative* is regularly translated into *normal* is illustrated daily in television weather reports. Monthly totals of rainfall or sunshine are shown by comparison with previous seasons' averages. Although the previous averages will be altered by the addition of the current season's weather patterns, thus providing a new average, the old figure is regarded as a *normality* with which to contrast the current trends. The leap from normative to normal means, then, that there is some expect- ation of what sort of weather we can reasonably expect, and the weather forecaster is not infrequently heard to comment on how much sunshine we *should* have had – and, in the case of rain, how much we *ought not* to have had. By changing what is normative to what is normal, we then come to define the weather states that we regard as *desirable*. This does not matter very much in the case of the weather, but when we operate these processes in the case of human behaviour, it can be stigmatising to groups of people whose behaviour is only a variation of the normative, thus limiting the assessment process.

That assessments are neither neutral nor individualised is perhaps most obvious when we examine Mental Health Act assessments. These vividly demonstrate the adult, white, Eurocentric bias in the develop- ment of concepts of risks and needs (Braye and Preston-Shoot, 1995). Young, single people (particularly men) are many more times likely to be admitted to hospital formally than are their married counterparts, especially if they are black:

The most striking finding is the extent of over-representation of Black people, compared with the background population, among those who are admitted under Part 11 of the Act. Black people, and those from other ethnic minorities, also appear to be over-represented in the group of people detained under Section 136. (Audini and Lelliott, 2001, p. 5).

Traditionally social work attitudes towards assessment are based on an individual dependency-led model (Dalrymple and Burke, 1995), leading to what Lindow (2000) refers to as 'clientism'; that is, simply by *being* a client of social services, people's judgements about themselves and their differences are seen as inferior to those of social workers; who become the experts in problem solving. Thus service users' potential and possible solutions are often ignored. This leads to social workers clinging onto their hypotheses and interventions in the face of considerable failure. For example, child protection social workers who hold strong beliefs about the importance of attachments in health personality development undertook lengthy assessments consisting of ten sessions with parents discussing their attachment experiences, without ever once observing the parents parenting their children. The results were that mothers not uncommonly were prescribed counselling to come to terms with previous experiences of sexual abuse before their children could be returned home, despite the mothers exhibiting many mothering skills and capacities (for a fuller discussion, see Milner, 2001). Similarly Dobash *et al.* (2000) base their understanding of domestic violence on a concept of male abuse of power, with interventions predicated on the principle of challenging abusive men in groups. Their research into the men's analyses of their behaviour revealed that the men located their violence in domestic discord and desperately wished to stop arguing with their partners; and that their narratives were so impoverished that they did not understand the concepts of male power underpinning the prescribed group 'challenging'. Dobash *et al.* (2000) reframe these findings as more 'denial' in need of further challenging. The group work interventions researched had a high drop out rate, but rather than reassess in the light of service user views, the authors recommend more of the same, but backed up by a court mandate.

Lindow (2000) suggests that this pessimism and persistence with the original planned intervention is partly caused by the compartmentalised thinking that characterises much service delivery; imposed largely by legislation which is based on preventing something rather than enabling independence – a shift towards risk assessment. Furthermore, treating people in separate groups according to age, impairment or defined status can powerfully enhance stereotyping. People's life situations are actually much more complex than this; they can occupy several social work 'categories' simultaneously. For example, Jeff was a young man who physically abused his partner but had also been sexually abused by his foster father and was about to lose his job; so should he be the subject of a risk assessment or a needs assessment? Similarly, fifteen-year-old Cassy was her disabled mother's primary carer but was being physically abused by her alcoholic father; so should she be assessed as a young carer or as a child at risk of significant harm? A risk assessment would probably mean that neither of their own descriptions of themselves would be considered: Jeff viewed himself as a child in need whilst Cassy viewed herself as an adult with responsibilities. If they were to be appropriately compartmentalised for service assessment and delivery, Jeff would be best served by a children and families team and Cassy by an adult care team; although their particular risks and needs do not actually compartmentalise neatly.

Whilst social workers remain within a problem solving narrative which pays little attention to the complexities of assessment, it is very difficult for them to make social rather than individual assessments, as the former would highlight what is currently well hidden; that is, the moral issues involved in making judgements about what is and what is not desirable social behaviour. It is not surprising, therefore, that social workers tend to drift towards psychological reductionism, to analysing and working on the individual client: this client was for a long time most likely to be a woman. Despite client compartmentalisation, the bulk of carers are women (for an overview, see Williams, 1993), as are clients (for an overview, see Braye and Preston-Shoot, 1995).

The impact of legislation in the early 1990s

Traditionally, social work became more and more bound up with psychologising the family, locating the roots of social problems within the family, and prescribing solutions largely within women's capacities to take responsibility for any changes that need making – whether this was within the context of husband–wife or mother–child relationships. The sweeping reforms embodied in the welfare and education legislation enacted in the early 90s, with the emphasis on the family and its informal networks as an essentially private arena for the provision of care – a new view of the family as an independent economic unit – clarified the distinction between assessment and intervention but added a new set of values for social workers. These included partnership, empowerment, multi-agency co-operation, and value for money. Assessment was separated from interventions, which became 'care planning': 'the former being focused on the identification of the object-ives of care and the problems which are to be tackled, and the latter being focused on the actual selection of appropriate means to meet these needs, such as negotiating and co-ordinating services' (Challis and Davies, 1986, p. 43).

However broadly welcome the new legislation was to social workers, it had two major influences on assessment practices. First, by separat-ing assessment from intervention, and social workers from much 'hands-on' intervention, it removed them from the source of their prac-tice theory. Second, it made their values explicit. It did not increase resources, suggest new interventions or state how the people social workers traditionally 'individualised' were to be increasingly valued by society. While providing much-needed definitions of assessment, the new legislation had the effect of leaving social workers in a vacuum between the old and new styles of working and/or encouraging a checklist mentality. Some of the blame for the vacuum, however, lay with agency management, whose role was to equip staff for change; the law itself cannot directly govern practice.

Although all the major pieces of legislation (the Education Reform Act 1988, the Education Act 1993, the Children Act 1989, the National Health Service and Community Care Act 1990, and the Criminal Justice Act 1991) emphasised assessment as a separate and important activity, with both the Children Act and the National Health Service and Community Care Act having the same ideological underpinnings, it was the latter which most clearly spelled out precisely what is meant by assessment: 'there has clearly been detailed thinking on the purpose and nature of assessment activity and this is reflected in the impressive range of documents which have been produced by the SSI on this topic.' (Sinclair *et al.*, 1995, p. 42)

If social workers adopted a discrete approach to each client group, they could develop an expertise in a particular model of assessment, but there was no overarching framework. The following brief list of assessment definitions contained in the legislation illustrates the com-plexities introduced:

Although assessment is a service in its own right it can be distin-guished from the services that are arranged as a consequence. The needs-led approach pre-supposes a progressive separation of assess-ment from service provision. Assessment does not take place in a vacuum: account needs to be taken of the local authority's criteria for determining when services should be provided, the types of services they have decided to make available and the overall range of services provided by other agencies, including health authorities. (DoH, 1990a, 3.15).

Assessment arrangements should normally include an initial screening process to determine the appropriate form of assessment. Assessment: The process of objectively defining needs and determining eligibility for assistance against stated policy criteria. It is a participative process involving the applicant, their carers and other relevant agencies. (DoH, 1990a, Appendix B/1).

The PSR [pre-sentence report] should therefore be impartial, balanced and accurate... The purpose of the PSR is to provide a professional assessment of the nature and the causes of a person's offending behaviour and the action which can be taken to reduce re-offending. (Home Office, 1995, p. 7).

An initial investigation will clearly be needed in cases involving direct allegations or other reasonable grounds for suspecting abuse. The social worker must decide, in accordance with agency policy and in consultation with the professional network, whether or not a comprehensive assessment is needed at the next stage. (DoH, 1988, p. 20).

Although Section 17 of the Children Act gave local authorities a general duty to safeguard and promote the welfare of children in need, there was little reference to the assessment of children 'in need' in the guidance accompanying the Children Act (Tunstill, 1993). As a consequence, women, who were most likely to be on the receiving end of assessments, were subject to a bewildering variety of formats depending on the location of the social worker within a specific specialisation with its own particular assessment definition. Take, for example, the following hypothetical scenario:

Mrs Edwards is a depressed black woman living in poor material circumstances with three children, two of whom have problems at school, and a partner who is due to be paroled from prison where he is serving a sentence for aggravated burglary. She has no near relatives, although she is a regular church-goer.

By 1996, Mrs Edwards could have found herself subjected to several varied and contradictory assessment formats depending upon which part of the welfare services first came into contact with her. For example, her mental health needs might have been assessed under the provisions of the NHS and Community Care Act 1990 but, equally, she may have received a risk assessment under the provisions of the Mental Health Act 1983. Similarly, the needs of her children could have been assessed in terms of either Section 17 or the risks to them estimated under Section 8 of the Children Act 1989. Additionally, there was the possibility that her children would be assessed under the provisions of either the Education Act 1981 or the Education Act 1993, depending largely on whether their special educational needs were determined to be worthy of specialist educational support or whether they fell into an exclusion from school category. Being black children, they would be particularly likely to be subject to racist assessments in either case (see, for example, Blyth and Milner, 1996). Mrs Edwards might well have been assessed under the provisions of the Criminal Justice Act 1991 to determine whether she was able to reduce the risk of her partner re-offending. She was also entitled to an assessment of her own needs under the Carers (Recognition and Service) Act 1995. Not only was our hypothetical woman likely to be bewildered by the complexities of welfare assessments, but so too were the hypothetical probation officer, approved social worker, child protection social worker, education welfare officer and community care manager. Despite their differing assessment briefs, they were all exhorted to underpin their efforts with the same principles.

These principles were set out in most detail in guidance relating to the NHS and Community Care Act 1990 and the hypothetical Mrs Edwards' first assessment was probably undertaken by a care manager. This assessor is charged with aiding her empowerment through the rights of citizenship, the right to self-determination, dignity and individualisation. Her limited choices must be maximised and her individual aspirations and abilities realised (DoH, 1990a, p. 23), and the 'assessment process should be as simple, speedy and informal as possible' (DoH, 1990a, 3.3). Additionally, Mrs Edwards should have extended choices as a potential service user and be involved in a participatory assessment process (Social Services Inspectorate, 1991). Baldwin (1993) argues that choice is defined as knowledge and experience of three or more options.

And the care manager would have to work in an entirely participatory manner:

Assessment is a participatory process. It necessarily involves establishing trust and understanding if meaningful information is to be obtained. The most effective way of achieving understanding may be to enable people to describe their situations in their own words, using their preferred language and at their own pace. Assessment should be a process of working alongside people. They should not be the passive recipients of a potentially humiliating service. (Social Services Inspectorate, 1991, p. 14).

After assessing Mrs Edwards' needs according to these principles, the care manager would come up against the reality that community care in the form of, say, respite or domiciliary care was in short supply and probably only available for 'deserving' or 'high-risk' cases. So this woman would have a high probability of facing child protection case conference scrutiny of her mothering as a means of converting her into a high enough risk case to obtain access to scarce resources (Denman and Thorpe, 1993; Milner, 1993), an experience which could hardly be anything but 'humiliating'. In this assessment arena, despite the parental partnership prescription of the Children Act 1989, the development of participation would be restricted and ambiguous, and its focus limited and not always welcomed by families (Thoburn *et al.*, 1995).

The reality of providing resources in this scenario means that it is unlikely that 'Packages of care should be designed in line with individual needs and preferences' (Meredith, 1993, p.41) or that 'Authorities are aware that assessment systems must centre on the needs of users and carers rather than the requirements of services' (Audit Commission, 1992, p. 36). This latter would be particularly difficult to achieve in our scenario because of the prescription not to discriminate on the grounds of cultural needs (see, for example, Home Office, 1995, p. 5). Interventions and assessments for black people are particularly underdeveloped and inappropriate for these potential service users (see, for example, Ahmad, 1990; Denney, 1992).

Despite these potential problems for a community care manager, the Audit Commission (1992) expected an assessment to pull together the multiplicity of workers and assessment formats to create: 'a seamless service; agree distinction and responsibility between health and social care, liaison with housing agencies, independent organisations involved in planning' (Audit Commission, 1992, p. 64). The creation of a 'seamless service' has become even more difficult with the 'discovery' of new abuses to prevent; particularly the identification of men as more significant in risk assessments, and an increasing emphasis on evidence-based practice. These added complexities are discussed below.

New complexities

Although gender is discussed more fully in Chapter 3, the influence of feminist theorising is evident in much recent government guidance. The way in which subjects of social interventions have been re-constructed has re-focused assessment work. The previously unquestioned underpinnings of social work assessments in which women were held responsible for the emotional well-being of the family by nature of their roles as wives and mothers (for a fuller discussion of women's powerless responsibility, see Rich, 1977), enabling them to become both clients and workers by nature of their potential as well as their actual status in the family, has shifted as the abusive nature of male power has been highlighted. Broadly welcome though this re-analysis is in placing responsibility for violence on to the people who mostly perpetrate it, it has merely shifted the 'blame', retaining a problem focus within the individual, and emphasising risk, rather than creating a safety focus.

This is most obvious in the changes in probation practice where the protection of the public from harm takes precedence over the needs of the individual in any planned intervention (see, for example, Chapman and Hough, 2001, Chapter 2). The key features of offender assessment include not only the appropriate identification of risk but also criminogenic factors, motivation to change, and responsiveness (Kemshall, 1996), involving the probation officer in assessments over and above the pre-sentence report. All offenders supervised by the probation service must have a written assessment addressing all the points listed above, a written supervision plan must be completed within 15 working days of an order being made, or the date of release (Home Office, 2000, C10), the offender must be involved in its formulation and it has to be reviewed every four months (Home Office, 2000, C11). Additionally an offender may need multi-agency assessment as a potentially dangerous offender (Home Office, 1997). Thus Mrs Edwards' husband would now face assessment as a potentially dangerous offender on his release from prison, possibly obscuring further her mental health needs, despite her now being entitled to a safe, sound, supportive service (DoH, 1998).

Similar shifts in focus are evident in government guidance; for example, the responsibility of social workers to identify cases of adult abuse and children involved in prostitution and assess their needs (DoH, 2000a and b). As with the National Standards, the assessment procedures emphasise the importance of establishing the 'facts' as though they are unproblematic, despite an acknowledgement elsewhere in these documents that the issues are actually extremely complex. For example, the assessing social worker is charged with the responsibility for 'identifying, investigating and responding to allegations of abuse' (DoH, 2000a, 3.10) but the guidance cautions whether intervention is in the best interests of the vulnerable adult or in the public interest (2.20) as 'Personal and family relationships within domiciliary locations may be equally complex and difficult to assess and intervene in'. (2.15).

The most obvious complexity is that the abuser is often the main carer. For example, a needs assessment of Lynne's mental and physical frailty cast her as needy (deserving), vulnerable, dependent and incompetent. The influence of scarce resources meant that when her son lost his flat through unpaid rent and moved in with her, he was recruited as her main carer. She then had several hospital admissions following overdoses and facial bruising which she told neighbours were caused by her son but which she vigorously denied in hospital. A reassessment of her as victim of adult abuse floundered on the possibility of further risk to Lynne of reabuse and the loss of her main carer. In actual fact this family's relationships were more complex than carer and cared for. They were interconnected in that they both were grieving the recent deaths of Lynne's husband and older son; they were interdependent in that the son needed a home with his mother and she depended on him to pick her up after falls and arrange medical treatment; and neither of them had any other close emotional contact. Thus they were simultaneously vulnerable and competent and their desires for independence and choice were stifled by assessments which were framed in the either/or of needs/risk.

There are also particular problems of resource provision for physically vulnerable adults. For example, Hanson and Maroney (1999) point out that partner abuse is not an uncommon experience of people in an advanced stage of HIV infection but that neither wheelchairs nor intravenous drips are available in refuges. Equally, residential homes can be inhospitable because of homophobic attitudes on the part of other residents.

The resource issue is even more prominent in the identification of the needs of children involved in prostitution. The guidance (DoH, 2000b) recommends that children involved in prostitution be regarded as children in need of protection rather than young offenders but any assessment of risk is complicated by the fact that there are multiple abusers. Not only is the young person at risk from pimps but the punters constitute a large body of men, few of whom would see themselves as child sex offenders. The research shows that child prostitution is not a discrete entity, being integrated into the mainstream prostitution market serving all prostitution users, with users being prostitute users who become child sex abusers through their prostitute use rather than the other way round (Barrett and Mullenger, 2000). Furthermore, the young people involved do not always see their needs in the same way as adults, there being important elements of network belongingness and economic survival involved (for a fuller discussion of these complexities, see Kelly *et al.*, 1995). The 'best interests of the child', says Mullender (1999) can be a suspiciously catch-all phrase, implying an inability to spell out what children's needs actually are; and those best interests are based on adultocentric notions of need (Braye and Preston-Shoot, 1995).

A further complication in assessment work is the growing trend to promote evidence-based practice. There are two strands to this; the first being research evidence into problem causality, evaluation for knowledge as opposed to accountability (for a fuller discussion of the purposes of evaluation research, see Lewis and Utting, 2001). This 'evidence' influences the 'facts' selected during the assessment process, determining whether the focus is on needs, risks or resources. For example, the evidence from attachment studies provides an explanation for dysfunctional behaviour at any stage of the life span (for an overview, see Howe, 1995) and is widely used in assessments, particularly in adoption, guiding and informing a range of interventions aimed at fulfilling attachment *needs*. Other evidence provides possible indications of increased *risk*; for example, the link between early cruelty to animals and subsequent abusive behaviour in adulthood (for an overview, see Lockwood and Ascione, 1998). In the case of the former, biases necessarily creep in – mainly to do with neglecting the wider social context of families as intra-personal relationships are explored; whilst in the latter, a checklist mentality is encouraged – despite prediction checklists being shown to be crude and unreliable measures of risk (for an overview, see Corby, 2000, pp. 186–9). Thus simpler diagnosis is achieved at the expense of false certainty; a certainty that is hidden as social workers rarely make clear their preferred theories about the nature of people to the service users they are assessing. This denies the service user the possibility of participating fully in an assessment. When given this opportunity, they often define themselves differently. For example, when we advertised a domestic violence service for adults who wished to change their abusive behaviour, we found that three of the first ten adults to avail themselves of the service were women in same-sex relationships. As programme design was underpinned by 'evidence' that domestic violence is the result of the abuse of male power, interventions consisted of groups for heterosexual men and refuges/support services for heterosexual women. This effectively denied resources to lesbian, gay and bisexual people.

The second strand of evidence-based practice takes a more pragmatic view, being primarily concerned with effective practice. Chapman and Hough (2001) see this concern as arising partly from an increase in the probation service's caseload which coincided with pressures of cash limits and partly as a reverse of the 'Nothing Works' pendulum. Outcome research indicates that some probation interventions are more effective than others (see, for example, McGuire, 1995) and this shifts the focus of assessment work away from needs in favour of extensive assessments of risk of harm, offender motivation, and the targeting of effectiveness-based work using specific models such as that devised by Kemshall (1998). Similarly outcome research indicates particular intervention effectiveness in other areas of social work; for example, Macdonald, 1998 (child protection), Macdonald, 1997 (mental health), Buchanan, 1999 (young people with behavioural disorders). (Comment on outcome research into the effectiveness of particular social work methods is included at the end of 'map' Chapters 6 to 10.)

Evaluation research undertaken to establish accountability (did it work?) is often regarded as particularly sound research because of the impartiality of the 'stand aloof' researcher (Lewis and Utting, 2001; Newburn, 2001) but biases still exist. Macdonald (2000) suggests that synthesising the effectiveness literature is fraught with difficulties in that literature reviews often contain biased summaries, much of the research is out of date by the time of publication, and it is rarely updated in the light of new evidence. Moreover, as Webb (2001) points out, evidence-based practice is limited by the complex phenomena involved; for example, much decision making is not rationally determined or subject to control. There is also 'a degree of ambiguity over the extent to which "what works" for children is the same as "what works" for families and "what works" for society as a whole' (Glass, 2001, p. 17). How, for example, would a researcher set out to evaluate the effectiveness of mental health services under the new framework? This lists a broad range of clinical and practice interventions:

● evaluating the effectiveness and cost-effectiveness under usual service conditions of psychological and psychosocial interventions;
● comparing the outcomes for self harm between different types of services;
● assessing relative cost-effectiveness, service user satisfaction and concordance rates of atypical antipsychotic drugs, newer

antidepressants, complementary therapies compared to standard management;

- evaluating the better management of antisocial attitudes/behaviours that attract the label of severe personality disorder and service user involvement;
- developing and evaluating a range of occupational activities to maximise social participation, enhance self-esteem and improve clinical outcomes;
- developing research tools with service users to assess their view on how services can best meet their needs (DoH, 2001, pp. 19–20).

Where does this leave the assessing social worker?

For the busy social worker, trying desperately to keep up to date with all the new information contained in the research literature and the procedures and responsibilities laid down in government guidance, selecting what information is relevant to them remains the biggest problem in assessing for a specific purpose (either risk or needs) and being fair. The social work literature, research evidence and government guidance remains vague about how this task is to be undertaken, yet it is central because the process controls the nature, direction and scope of social work intervention; an intervention that may well affect a service user's entire life.

It is rarely possible to have a single purpose when dealing with families in trouble. Their real-life situations involve the assessing social worker in attempts to achieve a satisfactory balance between diverse needs, recognised risks and restricted resource provision. There is always also the tendency to drift not only towards psychological reductionism as a placebo solution to inadequate resources, but also towards risk assessments as a response to continuous public castigation of social work efforts. Despite the principle that individuals should be allowed to assess the risks to themselves (Social Services Inspectorate, 1991; DoH, 2000a), should an elderly person be found to have died alone at home it is likely that social work will be found culpable. A study of care provided for elderly people (Sinclair *et al.*, 1990, p. 176) found that:

social workers were predominantly concerned with the degree to which clients were 'at risk'. So in order to assist decisions about staying at home or moving to residential care, workers examined depression, mental confusion, the client's failure to behave prudently, the effects of living alone whilst being physically ill or disabled, and environmental factors such as trip hazards or poor heating.

Risk predominates in the assessments of elderly people being discharged home from hospital. Clark *et al.* (1996) found that older people were less concerned about their safety than professional assessments indicated, and were more concerned with coming to terms with their disabilities and retaining some control over their lives. This in no way follows the recommendations for comprehensive assessment outlined by Challis *et al.* (1990), which included physical and mental health, attitude and outlook, environmental and social circumstances, views of their most pressing problems and desired solutions, and identification of retained abilities and strengths.

There are, however, some welcome trends in all these added complexities. The revised assessment framework for children in need and their families (DoH, 2000c) shifts the focus of assessment away from deficit identification by recommending that the assessing social worker builds on family strengths as well as identifies difficulties (1.33). It also explicitly encourages assessment of family *and* environmental factors; for example, exploration of the wider context of the local neighbourhood and community and its impact on children and their parents, and identification of community resources (2.16). This hopefully will counter the tendency to psychologise families; at the very least, the potential value of church attendance for our hypothetical Mrs Edwards would be seriously considered in the assessment process, whilst, optimally, her poor material circumstances would be addressed. Similarly, guidance on care leavers now stresses that assessment is a process requiring continual planning (DoH, 1999a).

Whatever the difficulties with the effectiveness research, it has at least identified the core skills of successful assessment work. These include being punctual, reliable, courteous, friendly, honest and open: 'Staff who lack integration between their values and behaviour lose credibility with the people with whom they are working' (Chapman and Hough, 2001, 1.53). Similarly, the DoH (1999b) identifies listening, being non-judgemental, having a sense of humour, straight talking, and being trustworthy as essential elements of good professional practice (3.40). This brings assessment work back to basic social work principles and considerably simplifies the task.

Being straightforward with people and embracing the complexities of their lives actually helps make sense of the sometimes competing requirements in assessment activity. Despite their similarities, people are actually very different in how they deal with their difficulties and so do not fit neatly into existing categories of service provision. Nor do they define themselves as carer or cared for, or abused or abuser, or competent or vulnerable. These categories are more blurred in the everyday realities of their lives. They are capable of making assess-ments about their own needs, risks, and the resources they would find useful; thus being potentially able to do much of the work for the assessor – even where risk factors are high, such as cases where child abuse is strongly suspected but denied (Essex *et al.*, 1996). This is recognised in the guidance on adult abuse (DoH, 2000a) where it is recommended that social workers assess their assessments by learning from experience – including user/carer views on how interventions have worked for *them* (3.19), reflecting what Lymbery (2001) refers to as the breaking down of barriers between service users and social workers to create a 'new professionalism' that encompasses values of empowerment, advocacy and antioppressive practice as part of every-day social worker thinking. We examine antioppressive practice more fully in the following chapter.

Summary

- Traditionally, assessment activity has not been well defined in the social work literature.
- A preoccupation with individual casework has inhibited the development of 'social' assessments.
- Assessments have tended to locate the problems of family dysfunc-tion not only in individuals, but also in individual mothers.
- 'Borrowed' knowledge from psychiatry and psychology has been the major influence on social work assessments.
- Where there is an obvious psychological dimension, the balance between internal and external factors needs careful consideration.
- Legislation defines assessment as an activity separate from inter-vention.
- Assessment activity is defined differently in each new piece of legislation.
- Differing emphases on risk, needs and resources make it difficult for social workers to develop an overarching framework for all their assessments.
- Assessment practice is beginning to move towards a balance of interests and external factors and more respect for service users' attitudes and views.

- A dual focus on risk and safety is easier to accommodate in assessment frameworks than needs and risk.
- Assessments need to be evaluated for their effectiveness in terms of the resulting decisions on service users' lives.

3

Anti-oppressive Practice

The values climate

In this chapter we examine the impact of anti-discriminatory and anti-oppressive narratives on the values climate of social work and the implications for assessment. Social work practice has moved away from traditional approaches emphasising a need to diagnose the problems of individual people and their families (largely through psychological knowledge) towards a more emancipatory form of practice which locates those individuals within their social contexts, particularly the structural patterns of society that perpetuate inequalities (for a fuller discussion, see Thompson, 1993, 1997). The traditional values of social work have been accommodated to some extent; for example, unconditional acceptance becomes respect for clients' dignity and strengths, self determination becomes promotion of choice, and non-judgementalism becomes non-discrimination and anti-oppression. However, combining individualism, social collectivity and an understanding of oppression in all its forms involves also accommodating overlapping psychological and social theories, creating a practice tension that is not easily resolved. At the most basic level, psychological theories underpinning different methods of interventions, those which social workers commonly use to 'shape' their assessments, were developed primarily as a means by which individuals could be better understood by 'experts'. Attempting to graft on notions of empowerment to existing theories ignores their in-built Eurocentric bias.

Despite their benevolent intentions, these theories 'essentially reflect the power relationships that exist between us all' (Dalrymple and Burke, 1995, p. 11). These existing power relationships are basically white, male, healthy, employed and Western dominated. McNay (1992) suggests that, while all oppressions are important, gender, race and class are more central to the profit base of our economy and therefore have a greater effect on how lives are lived and dominated (for example, by the exploitative division of labour). Clifford (1994) writes that the material basis of social divisions is a governing factor in understanding real lives, and goes on to suggest that good practice requires the participation of workers whose personal experience of oppression gives them a counter-hegemonic understanding of material as well as cultural and personal differences. By this, some sense of 'fit' is implied between the different levels of anti-oppressive theory – materialist social theory, strategic practice theory and working concepts – which Dalrymple and Burke (1995) maintain should respond to the reality of both service users' lives and social workers' lives. Similarly attempting to reduce the complexities of this practice tension to personal prejudice or structural disadvantage, what Thompson (1998) refers to as psychological and sociological reductionism, can actually increase discrimination; a rigid interpretation of social structural oppression has the capacity to dehumanise social work and result in formulaic interventions (see, for example, Featherstone and Trinder, 1997) as much as a rigid interpretation of psychological knowledge has the capacity to story an individual *as* a problem (see, for example, White, 1995a). We will address these complexities, but will first examine what the various forms of oppression have in common, in particular the abuse of power.

Power

Power is a significant element in every relationship and a main motivating influence. Indeed, all relationships, whether between one individual and another, between one group and another, or between rulers and subjects, can be said to be the result of power. In social work, power may be legitimately used to empower others in anti-oppressive practice or illegitimately used to oppress others in malpractice. Power is also an element in the competitiveness of life and the struggle for resources, employment and education. Social workers, too, can experience a lack of power, and this can help them to understand service users better, but, crucially, the concern for social workers is when power is used to exclude and marginalise: 'we must recognise the power of social workers in terms of knowledge and expertise; access to resources; statutory powers; and influence over individuals, agencies, and so on' (Thompson, 1997, p. 132). In working with marginalised people, and seeking to counteract negative images of self, negative life experiences, blocked opportunities and unrelenting physical and emotional distress, it is essential to take a three-track approach that links the personal with the cultural and structural. Thompson (1993) refers to this as the 'PCS model', P referring to personal/psychological and also to practice and prejudice, and C referring to culture, commonalities, consensus and conformity. S refers to structural aspects, social forces or the socio-political dimension. Thompson describes P as being embedded in C and C in S, yet as all interacting with each other.

It is hopelessly optimistic, however, to think that empowerment can be actualised just by minor tinkering with social workers' preferred theories. Traditional family therapists and psychodynamic counsellors have not readily addressed the complaints of feminists and black people that their theories lack an appreciation of the impact of patriarchal power on women and the impact of racism on black people. Their adaptations have been largely cosmetic and have done little to make social workers more confident of what empowerment, partnership and choice actually consist of (see, for example, Macleod and Saraga, 1988; Cavanagh and Cree, 1996). It is naïve to underestimate the difficulties in operationalising empowerment strategies – powerful people (and powerful theories and methods of intervention) are resistive to yielding power: 'Power concedes nothing without demand ... the limits of tyrants are precise by the endurance of those they oppress' (Douglas, quoted in Dalrymple and Burke, 1995, p. 14). Social workers are not in a position to *give* people power, and their aim to *help reduce* the powerlessness that individuals and groups experience is likely to be limited by other individuals' and groups' investment in power positions *and* in the complex nature of power.

There is an important psychological legacy left by powerlessness that includes lethargy, despair and listlessness – 'learned helplessness' – and, as Freire (1972) called it, a 'culture of silence' in which there is an apparent acceptance of servitude and dependence. The marginalised subscribe to the myth that they get what they deserve, and internalise, and are possessed by, feelings of alienation and worthlessness. For example: 'It is practically impossible for a lesbian, gay or bisexual person who has grown up in British society *not* to have internalized negative messages about their sexuality' (Davies, 1999, p. 55). In a later chapter we will address learned helplessness in more detail, but here we want to stress that approaches that help people come to terms with their situations need to be seriously examined in case they collude with such oppression.

Powerlessness is not necessarily expressed in terms of easily defined oppressed groups; it is much more diverse and complex. Indeed, Foucault questions the relevance of ideas about power as primarily repressive by counterposing the idea of power as productive (see, for example, Sawicki, 1991). Modern developments of power operate in subtle terms through self-regulation. For example, it is difficult to see quite 'who' is oppressing mothers as the psychology underpinning 'good enough' mothering has become internalised. Mothers operate within a 'discourse' that does not need the so-called experts of child-rearing necessarily to be on hand for advice (for a fuller discussion, see Ingleby, 1985).

Similarly, children, a perhaps easily identifiable oppressed group, are not entirely powerless. Foucault considers resistance and power to be interrelated. Marshall (1996) discusses the relevance of the 'discourse' in which children place themselves as necessary for understanding the complexities of their power relationships. Thus, a child at school might be seen to be oppressed in terms of teacher discipline but may be acting in a children's discourse in which the teacher's power discourse is irrelevant. Marshall cites an example of a classroom incident involving young children and a female teacher in which two young boys temporarily positioned the teacher as a subordinate through the use of sexually explicit language. The teacher was unable to reassert control as the dichotomy between adult and child had been redefined as one between male and female, wherein the males are more powerful. The author concludes:

> Thus, through some discourses, children are able to enact strategies that gain power for themselves in relation to adults and can be experienced by adults as powerful. However, in the context of institutional adult authority these [strategies] may produce situations where children are excluded [from school] and can be seen as *powerfully powerless*. (Marshall, 1996, p. 104, emphasis added).

Appreciating that service users can be oppressed but, simultaneously, 'powerfully powerless' helps social workers to understand their own sense of frustration and powerlessness with children in care who truant, abscond or continue with the 'undesirable' behaviour that led them to enter the care system in the first place. These are not simply damaged and powerless children in a simple relationship with a powerful Welfare network, they are active participants in the various facets of their lives, exerting power often outside the linear relationship with the professionals in the Welfare network (see, for example, Barrett, 1997). Similarly, social workers will be familiar with service users who are the most easily identifiable as oppressed – poor, old, downtrodden, disadvantaged families – who exhibit resistance through the only power mechanism available to them, the people Dale *et al.* (1986) refer to as 'passive-resistant'. This form of resistance can be very powerful indeed. Cockburn (1991) suggests that we need to recognise power as multidimensional in that it is spread around, and that almost all of us share in it a little. Similarly, she argues that power is not always negative in that it can mean capacity as well as domination.

The 'isms'

It is clear that some 'isms' are more powerful than others at various times. Measured on a simple scale of 'isms' training, we would suspect social workers in the 1980s to have been more likely to have undergone race awareness training than any other. One reason for this situation could, perhaps, be that black men have much in common with the most easily identifiable powerful group in our society – white men. There are suggestions that masculine solidarity will make blackness the most important issue, deflecting attention from the issue of male power. As two white, male probation officers say, 'There is more that joins men across class and disability, and even race and sexual orientation, than divides them' (Cordery and Whitehead, 1992, p. 29). We return to the commonality of male experience later in this chapter but question here whether it sufficiently addresses the complexities of race and gender.

In the 1990s feminist critiques placed gender more centrally in the anti-oppression debate (see, for example, Mullender and Morley 1994; Fawcett *et al.*, 1996), with practice wisdom incorporating notions that are pro-feminist. Not only is it potentially oppressive to promote any particular 'ism' in that it creates a hierarchy of oppression that elevates one form of discrimination above others, it also ignores the inter-relatedness and complexities of the various 'isms'; most notably, race, gender, class, age, disability, and sexual orientation. More recently mentalism, clientism, and linguistic oppression have also received attention (see, for example, Thompson, 1997).

The inter-relatedness of the 'isms' is evident in our earlier scenario of Mrs Edwards and her family. For example, if we take seriously that to 'separate racism and sexism is to deny the basic truth of black women's existence' (Dalrymple and Burke, 1995, p. 17), how do we seek to understand our hypothetical black woman discussed earlier? And is this complicated by the possibility that the assessing social worker may be black or white, male or female, heterosexual or homosexual, young or old, and thus have different personal experiences of oppression and power *vis-à-vis* not only the potential service user, but also their own institutional authority? Black people, whether male or female, have to negotiate at least three different social contexts: *mainstream* (white) processes, in which they constitute a *minority* (racism), and within that minority context, they also have to negotiate *black cultural* agenda, which can be as diverse as Rastafarianism or Seventh Day Adventism. Their strategies for negotiating these different contexts (like the school children discussed earlier) will not always be displayed in power and oppression terms which social workers would recognise as appropriate to their positions as service users. For example, for black children, Boykim and Toms (1985) argue that 'the mainstream socialisation has to be negotiated *in lieu* of the minority and black cultural agenda'. These agendas clearly conflict with the mainstream one and, for that matter, also *with each other*. Blyth and Milner (1996) show that black boys' positioning of themselves in a racial and masculinist context in school may seem threatening to white male teachers who are concerned with the mainstream disciplinary context. Channer (1995), on the other hand, highlights the importance of religion, the cultural context, as the main issue in Black African Caribbean school achievement, while Hussain (1996) emphasises the importance of religion in transcultural fostering. These are power contexts that are largely ignored in most social work assessments yet are a source of strength for black people to alleviate their oppression in the other two contexts. With adults, race, class and gender inter-relate powerfully in mental health assessments; as we noted earlier, younger, single, black men and older, single, white women are more likely to be constructed as subjects of psychiatric narratives and admitted to hospital (Audini and Lelliott, 2001).

Ageism, particularly, tends to be regarded as an additional category which increases the treatment of old people as non-persons. There is a dehumanisation inherent in old age as 'negative images of and attitudes towards older people, based solely on the characteristics of old age itself, result in discrimination' (Hughes and Mtezuka, 1992, p. 220). Ageism is compounded by the fact that assessing social workers may have some similarity to potential service users in that they are black or white, male or female, heterosexual or homosexual, but they are never old. Although they can remember what it was like to feel the oppression of youth, they can rarely anticipate what it will be like to be old. Perhaps worrying about their own futures, they tend to homogenise older people as automatically ill and deteriorating, inflexible, miserable, unproductive and dependant although older people actually find old age a better experience than anticipated (O'Leary, 1996).

The 'isms' also compete in complex ways, not so much in creating 'deserving' categories of service users, but in constructing people as either/or; victims or perpetrators; cared-for or carers. For example, mothers' needs are often neglected where they are receiving services for a disabled child (Read, 2000), the organisational structuring of social work departments serving to separate 'isms' and create competition. Disability teams rarely have the word 'family' tacked on in the way that children's teams do. The team in which the assessing social worker is located probably influences whether disability and age are prioritised or gender and class. In the latter, the evaluation of gender, through feminist empowerment models, has shifted from highlighting mothers' perceived deficiencies, allowing men to disappear (see, for example, Milner, 1993), to a tendency to construct men as either threatening or useless. This is particularly evident in risk assessments where violence is an issue and there is need to construct one person as a perpetrator. Similarly, Wise (1995) cites an example of a young working-class woman, deserted by her violent husband, impoverished, isolated and unhappy, who deals with her despair by getting drunk and forgetting to come home to her young children. She argues that a feminist empowerment model would ignore the fact that the children are the most vulnerable people in this situation. And a men-as-threatening model underpinning assessments of domestic violence ignores the reality that same-sex violence exists at similar levels to heterosexual violence in intimate relationships (Renzetti, 1992; Leventhal and Lundy, 1999).

However complex, unequal power relations are still at the root of social injustice and have replaced 'libido' as the core force in understanding human relationships. Those who benefit most from any relationship are those with the most power (McNay, 1992), so an assessment of, for example, mothering needs to look at a woman's lack of power and resources, rather than at her personality, or at least at the interaction between these two aspects. And if she is black, black culturalism mediates this through how racism compounds her powerlessness and through membership of community groups that can provide a source of strength and group solidarity. Additionally Thompson (1998) draws our attention to the importance of oppression through the use of language. The most powerful people, those who can enter people into stories about themselves, also create the language used in this process; language is, indeed, man-made (Spender, 1985), reflecting racial and gender divisions. There is also interplay between language and social structure, with language helping to reproduce social values. For example, feminine is a 'marked' category in language where there are pairs of words, such as actor and actress. The word 'actor' functions as neutral term but 'actress' is formally marked as feminine. Close examination of descriptions in case records will usually indicate 'marking' for subjects who are neither male nor white. For example, Denney (1992) shows how the word 'space' has different meanings for black and white subjects of probation reports. For black subjects, space is used to describe physical space, whereas for white subjects it indicates ontological space in which the subject can explore feelings and have space to think. There is also linguistic derogation of women with other pairs of words that do not match, for example, fathering and mothering.

There are also linguistic gaps, such as a dearth of expressions that refer to women's sexual activity in a positive way. For example, women cannot be 'virile', although there are many pejorative words such as 'promiscuous'. The lack of words for many of the activities of women and black people creates silences in which whole areas of experience of people's experiences are ignored (Maynard and Purvis, 1995).

What the various 'isms' have in common is the core value of equal opportunity. Any effective assessment needs to consider the impact of its absence and the absence of equal access to resources. Any fundamental solution to the problems of oppressed groups must include policies that address all elements of oppression.

These policies are difficult to formulate because of the complexities mentioned earlier and because of vested power interests, so social workers need to be aware that their efforts to develop anti-oppressive practice will not necessarily be well supported. For example, Thoburn *et al.* (1995) found that agency policies and procedures were as much a barrier to partnership initiatives in child protection work as were family characteristics. Additionally, assessments need to examine how oppression might be affecting the service user's functioning in the mainstream context. How can we overestimate the sheer grinding stress of experiencing daily injustice for any reason and of feeling devalued because of gender or race? How can we overestimate the psychological effects of being hated, despised, regarded as only fit to service others and discriminated against in housing, education and jobs? The task is enormous but recognising this helps social workers to begin the first steps towards operationalising anti-oppressive practice. Below, we suggest ways in which this can be begun.

Dalrymple and Burke (1995, p. 120) propose that an ethical framework for assessment needs to include the following:

- Assessment should involve those being assessed.
- Openness and honesty should permeate the process.

- Assessment should involve the sharing of values and concerns.
- There should be acknowledgement of the structural context of the process.
- The process should be about questioning the basis of the reasons for proposed action, and all those involved should consider alternative courses of action.
- Assessment should incorporate the different perspectives of the people involved.

Negotiating perceptions

If assessment findings are to be considered valid, to have 'truth', the authors' assumptions and biases must be addressed. Likewise, if an assessment is to show a valid understanding of the subject, it must address the 'differences' gap between writer and subject, their mutual subjectivity, their different backgrounds and experiences of life. Social workers have needs too, and if these are not met they function less well. As Nice (1988) has suggested, social workers are taught and expect, like mothers with their families, to put the needs of others above their own. Recognising their own feelings lays upon them the charge that they are bad social workers. How we function can have an impact on how we see the functioning of others, so any meeting for assessment purposes involves the meeting of two complex subjective worlds.

Social workers also come from the world of the agency, and service users usually have ideas about those agencies that colour how they see social workers and affect the emotional impact they each have on the other. A social worker who over-identifies with agency procedures risks losing sight of the subjectivity and special needs of the user, while a social worker who over-identifies with agency policy risks unfairly rejecting individual need and failing to challenge and improve those policies. On the other hand, a social worker who over-identifies with service users risks failing in responsibility to the agency and in the fair assessment of priorities. To strike a balance between what the service user wants and what intervention the agency considers sufficient for satisfactory functioning requires recognition of our own values, feelings and biases, and the ability to engage in dialogue with the subjective world of service users in an open, reciprocal way (Sainsbury, 1970). For example, Richards (2000) comments that a user-centred approach requires information-getting and provision that is meaningful to an older person and sensitive to their efforts to analyse and manage their situations; these efforts are often revealed in narrative form which can be overlooked in an agency-led assessment.

A conversation, what Freire (1972) refers to as a 'critical dialogue', can be developed in which experiences are shared and differences acknowledged. A shared narrative encourages the development of mutual understanding, deficits in mutual understanding can be acknowledged and a 'moral dialogue' ensue. Jordan (1990) makes the point that where this dialogue is not achieved and service users are perceived as uncooperative, the conclusions reached by assessors are greatly affected. For example, he says that a key factor in whether abused children are accommodated or not is often whether the parents are cooperative, that is, acknowledge the evidence of harm done, accept responsibility for their part in causing it and agree to measures to avoid its reoccurrence, including a programme for monitoring and/or changing their behaviour. This dialogue has been found to go more smoothly where parents conform verbally and agree a plausible explanation in comprehensive risk assessments. It seems more likely that a parent who conforms in this way will form a positive relationship with the assessing social worker, and it is this relationship that appears central to the outcome (Holland, 2000). Thus the outcome of the meeting between social worker and service user is crucially affected by whether their relationship is oppressively adversarial or anti-oppressively cooperative. In making assessments for services, too, there needs to be *negotiation* over issues of fairness, need and availability of resources as understood by both sides. For example, it is important to explore how an old person's need for day care relates not only to the carer's need for a respite break, but also to the availability or otherwise of culturally appropriate services.

Where there is a difference of gender, race or class between social worker and service user, there seems to be a tendency to focus unduly on deficit and/or risk rather than on *strengths* and seeking to establish how people's control over aspects of their lives can be increased. We all, social workers and service users alike, have unmet wants, and if these are ever to be met we must make our story visible and look at the stories of others, to see our situations not as 'no exit' places but as places capable of reform. In this way, we can gain an awareness of where our oppressions are located and of how structural as well as psychological obstacles operate, and have a sense of our ability to be agents of change and locators of resources. This requires the capacity to deal with self-blame, to attribute problems to unfair structures rather than people when that is the case, and to develop necessary supportive networks. Social workers need to identify service users' competencies and to affirm their experiences, so that self-confidence can grow. This requires asking for their stories; listening and taking them seriously helps to build confidence and a sense of being valued. This can be achieved quite simply through offering written assessments for editing by the service user. For example, one 90-year-old woman agreed broadly with the assessment recommendations but asked her assessing social worker to remove the word 'frail' from her description as she had a more robust view of herself. People also need the assertiveness to communicate their wants. Many women, in particular, suppress their own wants, so workers need to take extra care to seek them out. This is even more so with older women and especially where the social worker is male. Men and women often view satisfaction differently (McNay, 1992), and it is therefore often necessary to facilitate mutual listening by such means as circular questioning.

As it is neither possible nor necessarily desirable to provide, for example, every poor black female service user with a poor black female social worker, there will inevitably be large gaps between service users and social workers. This will be even more obvious when religious and cultural differences are considered. However, anti-oppressive practice dictates that workers *acknowledge* and seek to *bridge* these gaps. An openness about one's own culture and values and about one's lack of knowledge of the other person's beliefs is essential at the beginning of any involvement. This is then followed by an invitation to service users to help the social worker see life as they see it.

Social workers ought not to be too proud to ask the service user to help them understand how race or gender factors are affecting their situation. Without such a humble, 'one down' stance, male white social workers, for example, will rightly be seen by women and black service users as coming from another world (see, for example, Jordan, 1989; hooks, 1991, 1993). Written contracts (jointly drafted), advocacy, charters and published value statements also help to engage across the 'gap'. An illustrative example is the Hackney Social Services Department's excellent value statement/charter for social worker assessments (Sinclair *et al.*, 1995, pp. 309–10).

Social workers have been criticised for failing to acknowledge the strengths and coping strategies of minority groups. We suggest that one way in which this can be corrected is by respectfully asking the service users to share their story of struggle and survival in the face of social structural inequity, by asking not only about their wounds, but also about their capacity for self-nurturance, not only about their lack of a sense of entitlement and justice, but also about the strengths derived from their membership of their community group, and also any stresses that that membership might sometimes cause. Sometimes, says Strom-Gottfried (1999), the *absence* of difficulties in a particular area of functioning can constitute a strength. This work involves social workers sharing some similarities and differences in their experiences of both power and oppression. For example, a white female social work student was assessing a black male social work student as part of an assessment exercise. In attempting to bridge the gap in the way outlined, the two students shared experiences of their early lives. To their surprise and delight, they found that they both felt dislocated from large extended families in tightly knit small communities that were collapsing under economic pressures. These communities were located in a white, Lancashire context for the woman and a black African Caribbean context for the man, but they had more commonalities than differences in their experience of oppression.

Bridging the gap is still an unclear area of practice, with agencies tending to stress the need for professional boundaries and workers finding it difficult to be truly empathic (White, 1995b). While personal disclosures that are not necessary for a true engagement with the service user are inappropriate, if there is to be a moral dialogue leading to an appreciation of the other's world view and values, and an understanding of their perceptions and attributions, social workers have to acknowledge at least their lack of cultural sameness and their need to be helped by the other to understand. For example, in understanding an ultra-orthodox Jewish family's threat to 'sit-sheva' for a daughter who plans to marry outside her faith, it would be necessary for most non-Jewish social workers to invite the family to explain their profound distress, which is based on their considering their daughter dead. We are not saying that it is possible to close the enormous gaps of race, gender, class and ethnicity, only that we can acknowledge and reach across them, inviting the other person to reach across to us, and hopefully make real human contact that will be accepting, respectful and mutually empowering.

Black writers (see, for example, hooks, 1993) stress that black people need to tell their story, to set their own frame of reference, to have their values and spirituality appreciated, to be assertive, if they are to ensure continued growth despite centuries of being deliberately crushed (Spence, 1995). Our position as social workers who purport to empower service users demands that we be aware of our own social construction of knowledge and of the influences of our roles and agencies. Social workers' values interact with the very essence of their work in constructing accounts of people's lives and in making judgements on the basis of these accounts. As social workers encourage people to give their own accounts of their lives, they also have to take account of their own lives (Clifford, 1994). They need to be aware of the consequences of their theoretical maps and to seek to move from a 'reproductive' approach towards an 'abductive' one in which collaborative accounts draw more on the concepts and meanings of service users. In their places of work, they also need to own up to their deficits of experiences and knowledge of particular groups, seek to establish community links with groups whose experience and insights are useful to their work, and work towards maximising the range of experience within their staff group. Tamasese and Waldegrave (1996) refer to this as 'just therapy', countering both individual and institutional discrimination through making one's work accountable to subjugated groups by consulting always with local communities or colleagues who have more similarity with the service user. Epston (1998) recommends that the worker is also active in assisting service users develop 'communities of concern' from which they can not only gain confidence and strength but also provide a forum for education.

Similarities and differences

We argue throughout this book for assessing social workers to remain open to the idea that there are multiple interpretations of each person-in-a-situation and to ensure that their assessments are underpinned by the principles of antioppressive practice. This is far from simple, requiring much more than the acquisition of a list of anti-discriminatory tips or how to respond to people who seem 'different' and the development of a 'correct' attitude towards challenging the various 'isms'. As current criticisms of political correctness demonstrate, there is the danger of dogmatism and further stereotyping of service users when dominant narratives are subscribed to whole heartedly; for example:

> I believe there are some times when totalisation is absolutely necessary. It would be self-indulgent and morally unacceptable not to support the anti-racist forces that are attempting to unite black people, and a white person has no right to tell black people how to organise their resistance. However, I believe that solidarity with anti-racism should not be equated with an uncritical and knee-jerk acceptance of ... antidiscriminatory orthodoxy. (Katz, 1996, p. 213)

Such antidiscriminatory orthodoxy was evident in the response of a group of residential staff to the young female residents being targeted by pimps and drug pushers. The home accommodated mainly white young people but was located in a predominantly Asian community. Staff had received anti-racism training and subsequently developed good working relationships with the local community. Although both staff and residents were being seriously harassed by a small group of adults, supported by up to thirty youths, when they refused to allow the adults access to the young women, they felt powerless to do anything about what had become nightly abuse (mooning, banging on doors and windows, bricks being thrown). This was because the 'abusers' were Asian and the (white) staff feared being accused of racism – and undermining their relationships with the local community. This 'knee-jerk acceptance' of antidiscriminatory orthodoxy ignored the fact that there were three groups of people at risk whose needs were not being met: the staff, the young white women targeted, and the young Asian men who were being drawn into criminal activity by the adult pimps and pushers.

Acknowledging the ethnicity of the youths was an important factor in constructing a safety plan; they lived in an area of educational and economic disadvantage, and were additionally disadvantaged by their racial positioning in a shrinking job market. Whilst they should not be pathologised on the grounds of ethnicity, to be colour blind to their racial disadvantage is equally racist (see, for example, Ahmad, 1990). An assessment was undertaken via a group meeting of residents, staff, senior management, local police, and local members of the community, advised by two Asian social workers. This meeting thus brought together all concerned parties, creating a 'community of concern' (Epston, 1998). It became clear that members of the local community already had plans in hand to deal with their identified concerns about youths being drawn into crime through disaffection with their career opportunities. Equally they, too, were worried about the danger of the female residents being drawn into prostitution and drug use and appalled at what the staff and residents were suffering each evening. Enabling minority groups to have their voices heard in this way is much more important than assuming that to intervene would be potentially racist.

In such complex situations involving several people – some oppressors, some oppressed, some service users, some unwilling users and others with no social work involvement – the systems ideas of Pincus and Minahan (1973) can be useful in planning the work, reconsidering values, and co-ordinating efforts. They describe four systems:

1   The *change agent* system, which is made up of workers, colleagues, assistants and so on.
2   The *client* system, which includes those who are willing to engage with the social workers and who expect to benefit.
3   The *target* system, which is made up of those people that the social worker decides to change or recruit in some way – so-called unwilling clients, relatives, other staff, or even the media.
4   The *action* system, which is made up of all those who help with what needs to be done, the social worker and those recruited from the target system.

While the traditional values of social work apply to work with the client system, work with the target system can involve different values. For example, dealing with a powerful, unjust landlord who is exploiting tenants may be characterised by forms of persuasion, such as exposure in the press, that would be inappropriate with others in the system. So we can locate the people in the above scenario into the four systems as shown in Figure 3.1.

Note that the client system is not always the system that most needs to change. Problems in the client system often result from the oppressions of others, including some members of the change agent system. In some situations the social worker may invoke the power of the legal system against abusers of power. One person may be a client in respect of one goal and a target in respect of another. This approach has the advantage

The change agent system	The client system
Home manager, Home staff, Homes adviser, Ethnic advisers, Asian social workers.	Residents and staff (expecting to be rid of harassment and fear), the community, the state and the courts.
The target system	The action system
The abusers and the youths (change their abusive behaviour), some Home staff (to change their approach), some residents (to move them to the client system, to stop drug use), community leaders (to get their support), the youths (to move them to the client system, to address their disadvantage), the police (to get them involved)	Home manager and some staff. [The aim would be to recruit some people from the target system to this system, and then to maintain it as a system until the goal is reached.]

Figure 3.1   Pincus and Minahan's four systems

of encouraging social workers to see that they do not need to work alone; if they build action systems they will empower themselves. In situations of risk, this is particularly important so that the social worker is empowered to take some actions whether a person agrees or not.

To return to individual assessment, even in less obviously complex situations, the person the assessing social worker meets will have been entered into a story by the referrer, and may also have entered themselves into a story, so the various 'isms' can be highlighted or hidden in many and complex ways. Consider, for example, the situations of Karla and Andy which have marked similarities and differences. Both were fifteen years old, the eldest child in a single mother family living in conditions of moderate economic hardship. Both had statements of special educational needs which meant that they were seriously behind their peers academically and found the classroom a constantly humiliating experience. They had both been permanently excluded from school for extreme violence to other pupils at break times. The permanent exclusions followed a series of fixed term exclusions despite remedial teaching (which had resulted in improved reading and writing skills) and attendance on 'anger management' programmes (which had little effect). They both ascribed their fighting to retaliation to racist taunts about which they said the school did nothing; a factor about which they were considerably aggrieved. Karla however was the daughter of a white mother and black father, living in a predominantly white, rural area. The school from which she was excluded contained mostly upper-working-class, white pupils, with a substantial minority of middle-class pupils; the majority of ethnic minority pupils belonging to this group. Andy, on the other hand, was a white child, attending an urban sink school with predominantly Asian pupils. This school had a well developed support system for pupils with special educational needs and an explicit anti-racist policy. Although pupils tended to make marked *progress* at this school it ranked much lower in terms of academic *achievement* than Karla's school.

What would be the 'correct' attitude for the assessing social worker to take in these two instances? Karla's experience of racism might well be more readily sympathised with than Andy's, although racial tensions in his area were high; the area being on the boundaries of a city where National Front involvement had sparked off racial fighting. Should Andy be challenged when he expressed overt racial hatred and should Karla be free from challenging? Were either of them victims or offenders, or both? And was the oppression they subjectively experienced predominantly personal, cultural, or structural – or all three?

Of course neither Karla nor Andy were passive recipients of their secondary socialisation processes. They had actively constructed their own identities. By asking them to elaborate on their initial accounts, it became clear that gender was the more significant element in their different identities. Both reacted to frustration and humiliation at school by 'getting into a temper' both at home and at school, but Karla was not comfortable with an identity of a 'fighting' girl. Racism turned out not to be her major issue (although it had been at her junior school) and she actively wanted to change her behaviour. Andy, on the other hand, coped with humiliation of the classroom (where his masculine identity was a subordinate one) by developing an oppositional masculinity in his social world. He was not only violent at home and school but had also further developed his racist behaviour by entering shops owned by Asian people and instigating fights. His oppositional masculinity also had sexist overtones – he refused to undertake any chores in the home on the grounds that that was 'what women are for', at the same time as taking considerable pride in not hitting women 'that's no fun, they can't fight back'. His mother had difficulty in accommodating his masculine identity as he was now becoming too large and dangerous to his younger siblings for her to construct him as subordinated due to his special educational needs. The day-to-day reality of him being at home all day due to the school exclusion led to her tentatively re-constructing him as 'threatening'. Assessment, therefore, demands a sophisticated analysis of gender; particularly the way in which boys can develop different masculinities simultaneously (Messerschmidt, 2000).

As suggested earlier, there is more that joins men than separates them (Cordery and Whitehead, 1992). Cockburn (1991) maintains that there is a danger in the idea of 'multiple masculinities' in that it deflects attention from the consistency in men's domination of women and children at systemic and organisational levels: '"Troubled" masculinity may be, but male power is defending itself systematically and ferociously' (Cockburn, 1991, p. 216). However, masculinity does not fall from the heavens, but is constructed by masculinising practices, and there is evidence that the way in which men construct 'men-ness' affects masculinities as well as femininities (Connell, 1987). Not all men are dominant; not all dominate. Mackinnon (1987) says that men can be raped, feminised, even 'un-manned': 'they may even be degendered ... For as women differ in their status, so do men in their power' (Mackinnon, cited in Evans, 1995, p. 150). For example, small boys and disabled, old and homosexual men are 'feminised' in that they are not considered 'real men' (see, for example, Marshall, 1981;

Arber and Ginn, 1991; Mac an Ghaill, 1996). The process of construction of black masculinity is more complex and reversed, with black men
being 'over-gendered' and exoticised, and their physicality unduly
emphasised (see, for example, Westwood, 1990, 1996; Denney, 1992).
This construction of men as 'real men' or 'female men' or 'ultra-men'
supports the claim of Sampson *et al.* (1991) that while gender is only one
among many sources of power, it is central. Men have the institutional
power of patriarchy but, at the same time, often experience themselves
as powerless in some contexts. The commonality of oppression experienced by not being a 'real man' would not necessarily reduce the possibility of examining differences (for a fuller discussion, see Segal, 1997).

Hanmer and Statham (1998) set out a feminist approach that looks
at the similarities and differences between female social workers and
female service users. Where two women are involved, the *commonalities* include the shared experiences of life in a male-dominated
society, double workloads (paid and domestic), living with men, often
as subordinates, and caring for dependants. They frequently include
the experience of poverty, connected perhaps with being divorced,
separated, a lone parent or restricted to part-time employment. In
social service departments, many women service users' problems are
clearly caused or aggravated by the men with whom they live. Many
women's resources are over-stretched or inadequate because of
responsibilities for children or other dependants, poor housing, less
access to education, health problems, transport problems and low pay.
In addition, their situation and hardship is often compounded by a lack
of facilities such as day care, nurseries and formal and informal
support networks.

Society places different value on men's and women's behaviour, and
the expectations of caring and service weigh more heavily on women:
women are expected to cope with everything! Self-esteem is greatly
affected by how men perceive women and treat them as inferior. As
Richards (1980) puts it, women suffer from systematic social injustice
because of their sex. However, Evans (1995) holds that women can
possess a superior and more accurate knowing derived from their
experience of subordination, active parenting and nurturing responsibilities. We would argue that this is true also of 'un-manned' men such
as disabled, elderly or homosexual men.

In making assessments, therefore, it may be helpful to ask some of
the following questions of all potentially oppressed service users:

- What expectations do you feel you are not meeting?
- How do you feel you are coping?

- Do you expect too much of yourself?
- Are your burdens such that no one should be expected to do better than you?
- How good do you feel about who you are?
- How appreciated are you by others?
- Could your difficulties be more due to lack of resources than lack of ability?
- What traditional supports are lacking for you in this day and age?
- What particular strengths have helped you to keep going?
- Where could we start building a network of support?

Equally, *diversities* need to be acknowledged. Hanmer and Statham (1988) suggest that how a particular woman's situation and problems differ from one's own should become part of assessment. Differences in status, power, role, lifestyle, race, culture, sexuality, education, work possibilities, access to community resources, degree of stigma and hope are elements of the differentiation of social worker from service user. This also applies to male and female social workers with male service users.

These differences create the gap we were discussing earlier, and a dialogue is required that will result in at least a touching of minds across the divide. In may be, for example, that one woman's experience of living with a man has been abject humiliation, and another's enrichment and growth; the latter needs to learn of the pain of the former, what self-nurturance was possible, and what strengths and strategies enabled survival or escape. In the case of black women, the extended family was historically a source of support, 'combating depression, stress and loneliness and thus reducing the impact of those factors on mental health' (Spence, 1995). The reduction of this support in the lives of many black women in Britain today has a devastating effect on their well-being; they push themselves so hard that they are exposed to excessive stress, and when they do achieve, they still may lack any real sense of entitlement. They often do not feel understood by social workers who must reach across to them, make humble human contact and invite them to 'put us in the picture'. Devore and Schlesinger (1991) make the useful point that while white workers need to be aware of service users' possible fear of racist or prejudiced treatment, black social workers need to avoid the 'stance that says "I've made it, why can't you"' (p. 191), expecting black service users to 'shape up' and not let the side down.

The gap between middle-class, (often) female social workers and white male members of the so-called 'underclass' can be just as wide. We are aware of a recent example of a man who noticed that his mother, aged 90 and suffering from a stroke, was being neglected by the nursing home. He found another home where he felt sure standards were better, but the home in which she was residing called in a social worker because they felt that the resident did not wish to move, despite the fact that she had told her son that she did. The social worker interviewed the mother and agreed she did want to move but failed to confirm this to the other home, who were waiting for this approval before they could receive the resident. In the meantime, due to this delay, the bed at the second home was taken by someone else. The man met with the social worker and her manager to complain, but he felt they were not interested in his problem, denied that his mother wanted to move and would not answer his questions about their earlier acknowledgement that she did so wish. He came away from the meeting having had no sense of engaging with the workers; he said he 'might as well be talking to folk from space; snobs who couldn't give a monkey's curse for my sort; wouldn't listen to me, so I gave 'em hell'.

Ignoring class differences between social workers and service users involves lack of respect. Blair's (1996) study of black pupils excluded from school showed that both pupils and their parents saw class as an important determinant of teachers' treatment of them. What emerged from the study was a 'complex picture of personal and institutional factors which highlighted the relationship between gender, "race", class and age' (Blair, 1996, p. 21).

Practising anti-oppressive assessment

In making assessments, social workers have two main aspects to keep in mind. We have addressed the first, namely how oppression is affecting the service user. The second is how social workers can start being empowering and avoid being oppressive. With regard to the latter, it may be better to ask 'In what ways could I be oppressive if I wanted?' and then think how to avoid doing those things. Do we, for example, assess the strengths of men but the needs of women? What assumptions do we regularly make about minority groups? In deciding who gets what, how are we influenced by the level of respect and gratitude shown by the service user? In the current political climate, are some of the attitudes of the early charity workers returning as we are given the task of rationing ever more limited resources? Do we suffer from what Turnell and Edwards (1999) refer to as the DATA effect (do that already) and become complacent about our antioppressive practice? As Dalrymple and Burke (1995) state, we need to:

- work collaboratively;
- view users as competent;
- help users to see themselves as 'causal agents'; and
- develop people's confidence by affirming their experiences, seeking diverse solutions, since situations are so complex, building and using informal networks, and increasing access to resources and the ability to use them.

At all times, social workers must listen to the stories of people who are oppressed and who are different, retain awareness of the power differences, share similarities and differences, and negotiate in order to learn about service users' perceptions, experiences and resulting psychological consequences, including learned helplessness. We suggest that social workers begin by addressing and seeking to bridge the 'difference gap' by considering the following:

- Has the person been able or invited to tell their story of injustice?
- How can their experiences be validated?
- What awareness do they have of the impact of oppression?
- What beliefs do they have about their capabilities and about the possibility of escape from their plight?
- Do they blame themselves, or blame social inequity?
- How can they be empowered to take action?
- With whom could they collaborate – could a support network be mobilised?
- What resources do they have access to, and what other resources could be located?
- What would improve their sense of control over their life?
- How could they be engaged in a change process?
- How could services be more sensitive to their special needs?
- How could their potential and strength be released, so that they will be able to challenge unfairness and meet their needs?

To return to the metaphor of the climate of social work values, it is important to stress that anti-oppressive practice is not simply about empowering individuals within a linear social worker – service user relationship. There needs to be respect for all the people in each social work situation being assessed, and acknowledgement of their responsibilities towards each other at individual, family, agency and community levels: 'a restored belief in the role of the social worker at the level of *practice* can then provide the basis for a renewal of confidence in social workers' ability to impact on the other levels' (Lymbery, 2001,

p. 382). A useful way of looking at assessment activity is to ask how good are the decisions arising from it. The only way to estimate the effectiveness, or otherwise, of assessment activity is to assess its outcomes for all the people involved. We address this in the next chapter before going on to outline our assessment framework; one which has the potential to balance 'expert' knowledge gained from the research and statutory requirements laid down in government guidance with the 'local' knowledge gleaned from service users.

Summary

- Power, abused, is the main oppression; unequal power is at the root of injustice.
- There are hierarchies of power, related frequently to men and what they have in common.
- Social workers have some power but can also lack power.
- Power concedes nothing until it has to.
- Powerlessness is linked to learned helplessness and is then all the more devastating.
- Oppressed people can have superior knowledge of the human condition.
- The isms are best explored in terms of lack of equal opportunities. They are frequently inter-related and competing.
- Anti-oppressive practice dictates that social workers acknowledge and seek to bridge the gaps between themselves and service users in order to facilitate a negotiating of perceptions in each situation.
- Enabling people to tell the story of their survival is the beginning of empowerment.
- In considering masculinity it is important to note that multiple masculinities and gender identities can exist simultaneously.
- To avoid being oppressive, social workers need to listen to people, validate their experiences and work collaboratively to seek out competence and promote a sense of personal agency.

4

Decision Outcomes and the Assessment Process

User satisfaction

Evaluating service user satisfaction with the decisions arising from what are often lengthy and carefully undertaken assessments is fraught with difficulty because the service user is only one person to whom the social worker is accountable. Davies (1997) suggests that accountability is a complex concept in social work as the worker has to balance service user needs with agency requirements; often underpinned by a legal mandate. This is the source of the tension between risk, needs and resources which bedevils all social work assessments. Additionally this balance also needs to have some sort of match with the assessing social worker's own ideals, or sense of personal duty which brought them into social work in the first place.

That these intertwining threads of accountability affect how a service is agreed and delivered is evident in the research into individual service user satisfaction. The research paints a uniformly depressing picture; from the classic accounts, such as Mayer and Timms (1970), Babuscio (1976) and Packman (1986), to the more recent accounts, such as *Messages from the Research* (DoH, 1995), Sinclair *et al*. (1995) and Morris (1998). And, as we pointed out earlier, it is not always easy to work out who the service user actually is in view of the blurring of roles between carer and cared for. Read (2000), for example, complains that mothers of disabled children are mothers on the margins. Their children's upbringing is professionalised, putting mothers under pressure to do the 'right' thing at the 'right' time despite the professional edicts of the time frequently changing fundamentally within relatively short periods. Evaluation research for knowledge may indicate one change, whilst the construction of different disability models may neglect the carer component. Read argues that successive assessments frequently make contradictory demands on mothers; despite the

Audit Commission's recommendation that the central role of the parent be supported with better information (1994, para 135). Research also shows that one-third of families with a disabled child do not have a key worker (Mukherjee *et al.*, 1991) and it would be interesting to know whether these families felt less or more marginalised.

As we discussed earlier, effectiveness research increasingly measures the outcomes of assessments undertaken to fulfill legal duties; particularly the protection of children from abuse and society from criminal behaviour. Inevitably this means that the service users' broader needs are often lost sight of; for example, despite much government guidance on the need to work in partnership with families and focus on the welfare of the child, little attention is paid to the quality of life provided by the parents for children than the actual abuse incident (DoH, 1995). Similarly Sinclair *et al.* (1995) found that the clarification of assessment processes in government guidance had not resulted in increased satisfaction with care arrangements:

> Although overall the 'Referred' assessments followed procedures which were more systematic, open and participatory, they were no more likely to lead to social work plans which were comprehensive or successfully implemented. Neither did the outcomes for the young people differ according to the nature of the assessment. (Sinclair *et al.*, 1995, p. 20).

Agency requirements also make it more difficult to estimate service user satisfaction, especially as the research tends to focus on individual *projects* rather than individual service *users* as these evaluations, being largely intended to inform planning about community needs (DoH, 1990). In practice assessments have the dual purpose of increasing service users' options *and* limiting the demands made on the service – what Payne (1991, p. 85) refers to as 'professional respectability to cost containment' – so users can find it difficult to express their levels of (dis)satisfaction (see also, Davis *et al.*, 1997).

Complaints systems tend to favour the most angry and/or the most articulate, as does resource provision (Stanley, 1999), thus there is little *meaningful* evaluation of individual service user satisfaction, although user groups – the most frequently consulted service users – do appear to be increasingly dissatisfied with the consultation process (see, for example, Barker, 1994) and the services provided (see, for example, Coombes, 1998; Morris, 1998). The increasingly policitisation of user groups (see, for example, Beresford and Croft, 1993; Campbell and Oliver, 1996) has led to an emphasis on user rights but there is little indication that user needs are any better assessed. This appears largely to arise from the differing influence of evaluations – where the research aims to evaluate for 'knowledge', user group perspectives may well be rationalised within current 'expert' narratives (see, for example, Burton *etal.*, 1989; Dobash *etal.*, 2000). And there is a potential source of (dis)satisfaction from people who would like to be service users but do not receive services; for example young carers (Blyth *etal.*, 1995; Dearden and Baker 1995) and gay people (Davies, 1999; Walsh, 1999).

What is clear from the research is that there are high levels of both service user dissatisfaction and social work burn out and disillusionment at all levels of service delivery. This indicates a possibility that the social worker's accountability to their personal ideals is not being met; perhaps, therefore, a radical rethink of how assessments are undertaken might be welcomed.

Assessment as process or event

Whatever the service user group, it seems generally accepted that assessment is more than a one-off event. For example: 'Assessment was conceived of as both an "event" in the initial phase of early contact between the social worker and the elderly person, and also a "process" whereby there was continual reassessment and monitoring' (Challis and Davies,1986, p. 44).

However, outcomes research shows that this is largely a myth. Social workers almost invariably seek to confirm their original hypotheses (see, for example, Sinclair *etal.*, 1995; Kelly and Milner, 1996b). This poor practice can sustain prejudice and make anti-oppressive practice rather difficult to achieve. Scott's Australian study of hospital and community child protection social workers (1998) provides the most detailed evidence of this tendency. As with Challis *etal.*'s study (1990), the social workers used a framework of assessment that gave salience to a narrower range of factors than that specified in agency guidelines, being influenced most heavily by risk factors. They tended not to consider situational and interpersonal conflicts, although, as discussed earlier, these are the main reasons for elderly people being admitted to residential care in this country. After risk factors, resource limitations had the most influence, with the result that needs factors were largely ignored.

To support a hypothesis developed at the initial assessment conducted within this constricting framework, Scott (1998) found that social workers sought confirming data rather than disconfirming data and that their reasoning was not supported by hypothesis development or exploration. Kelly and Milner (1996b) also found this tendency towards verification of an initial assessment, which meant not only that there was no re-evaluation of the assessment, but also that the social workers' range of options was reduced until they were left with no option but to close a case. They also found that social workers used self-justification to support the initial hypothesis. This most commonly took the form of persisting with the care plan on the grounds that it needed time to work – despite clear evidence that the plan was ineffective.

Sheldon (1995) similarly found that social workers used their interviewing techniques to 'shape' assessments data until they fitted a favourite theoretical model. Equally, he found that after one-off assessment, new information simply built up haphazardly on files, statements purporting to sum up problems and guide further actions being no more than lists of alleged factors loosely thrown together with little information on where they had come from or how they interacted.

While it is easy to sympathise with the resource and risk factors that constrain social work assessments, it is important to recognise that an initial assessment is the most influential determinant in the subsequent management of service user problems. Despite social worker complaints about feelings of powerlessness in the multiagency arena, their assessments provide the frame available to the case conference and influence its decisions. We will discuss this process in more detail later, but here we wish to make the point that there is no evidence that assessment is an on-going process that is improved by the involvement of a formal multiagency group. It is largely an important, single event in which the assessing social worker is the key player: 'Irrespective of whether cases were Referred or not, the district social worker held case responsibility and was therefore the key individual in the progress of the case and the outcomes following the assessment process.' (Sinclair, 1995, pp. 27–8).

Types of assessment

Smale and Tuson (1993) identify three different models of assessment, which appear to be closely linked to the salience given by social workers to risk, resources or needs factors:

1 *The questioning model.* Here, the social worker holds the expertise and follows a format of questions, listening to and *processing* answers. This process reflects the social workers' agenda and

corresponds to the assessment style noted by Sheldon (1995) in which the data are 'shaped' to fit the social workers' theories about the nature of people. These theories are most likely to be psycho-dynamic in nature.

2   *The procedural model.* In this, the social worker fulfils agency function by gathering information to see whether the subject fits the criteria for services. Little judgement is required, and it is likely that checklists will be used.

3   *The exchange model.* All people are viewed as experts on their own problems, with an emphasis on exchanging information. The social workers follow or track what other people are saying rather than interpreting what they think is meant, seek to identify internal resources and potential, and consider how best to help service users mobilise their internal and external resources in order to reach goals defined by them on their terms.

Smale *et al.* (1994) make it plain that they consider the exchange model the desirable one: 'Routine, service-led "assessments" are the antithesis of an empowering approach to assessment and care management' (Smale *et al.*, 1994, p. 68). This, however, is not to say that there are not helpful questions that can deepen understanding, and these questions will flow from some theoretical map, as will be clear in later chapters.

We would suggest that the questioning model is most likely to be used when risk factors provide the main emphasis of the assessment, the procedural model fits assessment subject to resource constraints and the exchange model comes nearest to meeting a needs-led assessment. The questioning and procedural models are often found in combination, while the exchange model embraces the principles outlined in government guidance. It is the only model which has the clear potential to lead to re-evaluation.

Smale *et al.* (1994) provide a daunting list of the skills and values that would be involved in such endeavours. These include: joining with people yet developing a neutral perspective; adopting the central skills of authenticity, empathy and respect; empowering workers and service users so that essential decisions are located with the people who know most about the problems; reinventing practice, being creative; addressing social problems as a failure of a network of people; and testing the fallibility of existing theory and knowledge in each new situation. We hope that this book will provide some practical guidance, some useful tools and a choice of theoretical maps from which to develop more understanding, without causing workers overload and confusion.

There are obvious difficulties that must be addressed if assessing social workers are to balance risks, needs and resources within an exchange model. These three aspects cannot be totally separated – a major need is often the restoration of the person's own problem-solving potential and the mobilisation of his/her inner resources. There can never be a truly neutral perspective, although there can be explicitness. Service users prefer social workers to be explicit even where they do not agree with the perspective. Explicitness aids authenticity, but empathy and respect are more problematic than the social work literature admits. For example, a study of women social workers and women service users found that: 'commonality with service users, beyond the experience of intermittent empathic feelings was regarded as either impossible or deeply problematic' (White, 1995b, p. 150).

It is difficult to show respect when social workers themselves are so little respected by service users and the general public. Neither social workers nor service users are likely to be empowered to the point where they will be entrusted with essential decisions. It is difficult to be creative and reinvent practice when you are subject to criticism much more frequently than praise and when your best efforts are undervalued.

Addressing social problems in terms of a malfunctioning of networks of people is perhaps the most useful starting point for improving social work assessments. Smale and Tuson (1990) consider it naïve to assume that local supportive networks exist 'in nature', and this is perhaps the major difficulty in actualising the values and principles outlined in government guidance. Jordan (1989) refers to effective informal supportive networks as welfare with a small 'w', and it is individuals who lack this sort of welfare who require Welfare with a capital 'W'. The purpose of social work, we propose, is, first, the provision of a formal network of Welfare and, second, the development of an informal network of welfare. This purpose would underpin all assessment work, subsuming the principles of empowerment, participation, cultural sensitivity, multiagency cooperation and value for money. We suggest an overarching framework below.

A framework for assessment

Although we recognise that it is extremely difficult to undertake a thorough assessment in a political climate that emphasises risk assessment at the same time as it limits resources and does not take need seriously, we do not think that social workers should accept these implicit constraints at the first point of assessment. As Chapman and Hough (2001) comment, effectiveness-led practice helps both practitioners and managers target their energies, time and scarce resources, confirms the impact of their work with individuals, and provides greater job satisfaction.

We were struck by how the difficulties and deficiencies of social work assessments mirror early criticisms of social research efforts that attempted to move away from strictly quantitative, 'objective' research in order to achieve a better depth of understanding of human realities by using 'grounded' theory (Glaser and Strauss, 1969). Here, social researchers made no attempt to avoid the 'subjectivity' of the individuals and groups studied, allowing their subjects to tell their own stories, with themes and theories subsequently emerging from the data. This research method has obvious similarities with the exchange model of assessment proposed by Smale *et al.* (1994) in that it is founded on the basis of 'joining with people'.

This type of research suffers from the same problems as social work assessments in that no matter how one tries to allow the theory to flow from the data, researchers do (however unconsciously) hold theories about the nature of people, and there is always the danger that data will be 'shaped' to fit these theories: 'Researchers cannot have "empty heads" in the way that inductivism proposes; nor is it possible that theory is untainted by material experiences in the heads of theoreticians.' (Stanley and Wise, 1991, p. 22). However, this potential problem has been much better addressed by social researchers, and the qualitative methodologies developed have much to offer in the development of improved assessment processes (for an overview, see Robson, 1993).

Social work training devotes a great deal of time to the 'values' considered important in social work practice, but we have found that while students can talk intelligently about values, they find it difficult to demonstrate how they can be held accountable for their actualisation. They seem to think that appropriate action will necessarily flow if they have the 'right' attitude. For example, in our hypothetical scenario, we would expect social workers to be able to understand that Mrs Edwards, as a black woman, experiences double and perhaps conflicting oppression, and feel sympathy for this, but we would doubt that they could explain to her how this would actively affect their assessment. They would probably – and we would suggest fruitlessly – attempt to empathise with her. While empathy is necessary for joining with her, it is not sufficient.

Social researchers are much clearer about how they will be held accountable for their value stance because they will have prepared a statement of intent that is quite clear about relevant ethical issues – what they are, how they influence the research and how the researcher will 'behave' rather than just 'think' or 'feel'. For example, researchers in this field are very much aware of the sensitive nature of their research (Renzetti and Lee, 1993), particularly the fact that they are 'joining with people' who are less powerful than themselves – what Walford (1994) refers to as 'researching down'. Therefore they give careful thought to how they can protect their subjects from harm as a result of their endeavours *before* they begin the data collection phase. Social workers could give more consideration to the possibility that they may do harm as well as good. Their interviewing skills are so well developed that they may elicit disclosures that have little direct bearing on the referral they have received and which could also put service users at risk – particularly where there is potential violence in the family (see, for example, Dobash and Dobash, 1992, on the dangers of couple interviewing in domestic violence). It simply requires the social worker to decide what the boundaries are and clearly state the purpose of the assessment. Sainsbury (1970) maintained that the purpose of making assessments was primarily to represent the individual or family in its struggle for resources, but it should include drawing attention to any form of inequity that may be operating, as well as an understanding of the individual or family dynamics. He added that assessments need to include some consideration of why the situation is described as a problem and how far the agency is responsible for dealing with it. This recognition of the nature of one's agency function is part of every assessment and includes considering whether the user in question is able to use the help that the agency can give.

Additionally, it means thinking about possible interview schedules at an early stage and deciding how free-ranging any interviews can be. The 'open' interview proposed by the exchange model is recognised as particularly problematic in social research (Robson, 1993) and may leave vital areas unexplored. It is most likely that a semi-structured interview format will be the most appropriate one, and social work assessors could do well to consider the careful design of these in social research (see, for example, King, 1994). Focus group research methods are also particularly effective in generating a rich understanding of participants' experiences and beliefs (Morgan, 1998).

In social research, this phase is accompanied by the drawing up of a plan to identify the key informants – the people, the documents and the agencies with the data needed for the assessment. This has the advantage of both broadening the range of data collected and setting limits on its potentially inexhaustible source (Coulshed, 1988). Social researchers also give thought at this stage to how data derived from verbal and written sources will be compared and evaluated (Jones, 1994), and how the data will be checked for authenticity (Forster, 1994). This process could be usefully incorporated into social work assessments to guard against the tendency of social workers to be heavily influenced by the first item of data collection and premature hypothesis development. Subsequent government guidance provides basic checklists to aid this process, but these checklists need to be more systematically used, developed and refined. Obvious gaps in data are rarely evident in written assessments.

Possible explanations will exist at this stage in both social research and social work assessments, but, in the former, they are more likely to be explicit and contain details of how they will be checked. Intuition may be accurate but should be testable. Even where there is only a single explanation, disproof is as important a consideration as proof. This means that when the data collection is complete, not only will themes emerge, but also data that do not 'fit' easily with these explanations will not be discarded. Interpretations can then be extended and evaluated (Jones, 1994), and how the data will be checked for authenticity (Forster, 1994). This process could be usefully incorporated into social work assessments to guard against the tendency of social workers to be heavily influenced by the first item of data collection and premature hypothesis development. Subsequent government guidance provides basic checklists to aid this process, but these checklists need to be more systematically used, developed and refined. Obvious gaps in data are rarely evident in written assessments.

Possible explanations will exist at this stage in both social research and social work assessments, but in the former they are more likely to be explicit and contain details of how they will be checked. Intuition may be accurate but should be testable. Even where there is only a single explanation, disproof is as important a consideration as proof. This means that when the data collection is complete, not only will themes emerge, but also data that do not 'fit' easily with these explanations will not be discarded. Interpretations can then be extended and multiple hypotheses developed. Utilising this approach in assessment activity would enable social workers to cope with the 'cognitive dissonance' that Scott (1998) noted was regularly avoided and fulfil Smale *et al.*'s (1994) exhortations to reinvent practice and be creative in each new situation.

Social researchers are also more careful than social workers in recording and handling data. Huberman and Miles (1994) refer to this as the 'orderliness' of sound qualitative research via good data display. This can take the form of verbatim transcripts, but, rather than remind social workers of their experiences of verbatim recording during training, we suggest that other forms of data display would be equally effective. These include 'memos' (Field and Morse, 1985), flip charts and working diagrams. Memos are particularly useful for storing data that do not seem to 'fit', retaining them for later consideration, while flip chart displays are useful in supervision sessions to ensure that discussion does not centre on one factor to the exclusion of others. Working diagrams such as well-developed genograms and ecomaps are valuable items of data display at this stage of the assessment.

Clear data display aids the next step of social research – the identification of emerging themes. These are noted in the first instance and then 'collapsed' into categories (Burnard, 1991). Only after this process has been carefully undertaken are decisions made about the priority of emergent themes. The social researcher has to demonstrate how interpretation and analysis of data is as free from bias as possible. This is done by what is known as 'reflexivity'.

Reflexivity is a broader and potentially more useful way of checking assumptions than is the usual one-to-one supervision between line manager and practitioner. The role of the line manager is a difficult one as it involves facing both ways within agency structures, and it may not encourage creativity (see, for example, the DoH (1990b) study of enquiry reports). Reflexivity involves checking one's interpretations of the data with people who do not necessarily have a vested interest – colleagues and/or long-arm supervision – and, of course, checking with informants. The aim is not to establish 'truth'; there will be many truths and many realities that require various ways of knowing and being in order to appreciate the full diversity of meanings and understandings that exist. More simply, what is needed is a clear formulation of the situation that 'fits' with a range of other people's perceptions and is 'testable in practice' (Sheldon, 1995, p. 114). The case conference (we explain the problems of group pressures on consensus in detail in a later chapter) is not the most effective forum for good reflexive practice, but acquiring multiagency views separately and then attempting to make sense of the possibly conflicting results will assist in getting more depth to the assessment and a formulation of possible problems and solutions that have broad agreement among key informants.

Reflexivity in a group of colleagues is enhanced if it is carried out in two stages. The first is the *'how to'* stage. This consists of the group listing hypotheses that flow from the heading 'In this situation it is really a question of *HOW TO* . . .'. For example, in assessing a situation in which a seriously abused and neglected child has been thriving well with foster parents for 4 years, but the birth mother wants the child, now 10 years old, to return to her, and the child wants to live with her and her abusive partner, it could be a question of how to:

- collect evidence to oppose the application;
- assess what support the birth mother would need to be able adequately and safely to mother the child;
- find ways of making the birth mother's home safe;
- use the law to remove the dangerous partner;
- find ways of maintaining residence with the foster parents *and* a relationship with the birth mother.

Only when the key worker decides (usually in consultation with a senior colleague) which of these (or other) directions to take does the second stage begin, namely that of *'GO AND* . . .'. This is a second brainstormed list of suggestions or options from which the worker can select, picking out what would be the most immediately useful to *go and* do. This process helps to counter the 'group think' tendency discussed in Chapter 11.

The process of gaining depth of understanding of data begins with looking at the question 'In what ways is the problem a problem, and for whom?' It involves weighing up the situation, tentatively patterning the data, finding theoretical ideas that illuminate and help to interpret the story and make sense of it, then applying some of the theoretical maps to gain analyses, understandings or new accounts, drawing inferences (reasoning from the known to the unknown) and finally considering how to test the interpretations and recommendations. This process may go on after the meeting with the user(s) and it may be necessary to re-interview to check out ideas and share insights. Then there is the consideration of what resources are needed and what resources can be mobilised. This should always include the user's own internal and external resources and what intervention would be needed to mobilise these, so that, ideally, it is not just about meeting need now but meeting it in such a way that the individual's and family's resources are strengthened for coping for the future. Sainsbury (1970) adds that we should always consider whether it is necessary to intervene at all and whether there are any negative consequences from doing or not doing so.

By depth, we do not mean that social workers must know everything about their subject from cradle to grave. A preoccupation with past events has been a positive hindrance in social work assessments – and it runs on the unrealistic assumption that social workers can change people completely. Rather 'depth' means reaching helpful explanations or analyses of what is happening and how things could be improved – being more rigorous and systematic. Thorough exploration of data from a number of sources means not only that social workers will have a wider range of alternatives, thus preventing 'stuckness', but also that we will become clearer about our practice theory. There is nothing wrong with checking whether data fits our existing theory as long as we actually know what it is and can explain it to people, we recognise when the data do *not* fit our theory, and we are prepared to revise and expand our theory and consider other analyses. This does not mean that we have to explain to service users that we are using, say, a social skills training or psychodynamic approach, but it does mean that we should be able to explain to service users what views we hold on how key social roles work and what explanations we have for their malfunctioning, being explicit about our views on the nature of people.

As distinct practice theories are difficult for many social workers clearly to articulate – students usually say that they are 'eclectic' – we will present an explanation of the main ones used in social work practice in subsequent chapters. We will not only outline the theories, but also include the advantages and disadvantages of each theory as an explanation of human behaviour. We do not offer them as prescriptive guides but rather regard them as a series of potentially useful maps to consult once one has identified the territory it is wished to cover.

If a social work assessment is undertaken with the same methodological rigour as sound qualitative research, it will necessarily include: a clear statement of intent, which also demonstrates how one can be held accountable for one's values; a systematic approach to data collection from an identified range of sources, which is carefully checked for authenticity and which identifies gaps in information; the development of more than one hypothesis about the nature of the problems and solutions; and a clear statement on how the final judgement can be tested in terms of demonstrable outcomes. The acid test of the assessment is satisfaction with subsequent decisions and action on the part of service users (empowerment in practice) and service providers. There should also be social workers' own satisfaction at not being 'stuck'. We present below the stages of such an assessment process in a linear model, although some parts of the sequence will overlap as re-evaluations will necessarily emerge during the process of checking the hypotheses.

The stages of assessment

[Note: this long list is not meant to be prescriptive, but only suggestive
of various possible steps in various assessments]

1 *Preparation*
   • Make a list of key informants – people, documents, agencies. Keep
     this on file so that gaps in the information source are clearly visible.
   • Prepare a schedule for collecting data from *all* key informants.
     Adapt agency checklists for this purpose.
   • Decide on an interview schedule. If it is inappropriate to use an
     open interview format, make a list of essential questions to
     which answers are needed. Keep this on file, but give copies
     to the informants where this will be helpful.
   • Prepare a statement of intent that includes purpose, what one is
     able to do, limits and how one will be accountable for one's
     values. Although this may be given verbally to potential service
     users, keep a copy on file.
   • Make a note of early (tentative) explanations.

2 *Data collection*
   • Prepare a contents page for the file, listing the documents and
     where they can be found.
   • Store the data display on file, marking it clearly with details of
     who can have access to it. Store working diagrams, memos, and
     so on in a plastic folder at the back of the file.
   • Check verbal data for authenticity by repeating, summarising,
     and so on. Provide key informants with copies of on-going
     summaries for further checks.
   • Check written data for factual accuracy and mark unsubstan-
     tiated opinion clearly.
   • Consider widening the data sources if the accuracy is doubtful
     or there are obvious gaps.
   • Do not discount any data at this stage but note obvious incon-
     gruities or inconsistencies.

Meyer (1993) has made suggestions for a generic check on what might
be relevant. We present our version of this, which could be adapted for
particular agencies and which could aid more consideration of the
social aspects (Figure 4.1).

	Person	Partner	Family	School/work	Home environment	Community	Society
Historic							
Physical state							
Behavioural							
Cognitive							
Affective							
Relational/ interactive							
Risk							

Figure 4.1   A data collection grid

For example, the community column might reflect a rundown neigh-bourhood, and the society column racism or a media campaign against a particular user group. It is always important that these 'social' columns, and not just the individual or 'psychological' parts of the grid, are considered.

We use the term 'data' simply to signify factual information. Because facts do not always speak for themselves and there is an element of subjective interpretation in most information-gathering, a distinction is sometimes drawn between 'data', which are unprocessed and raw, and 'information', which is interpreted and integrated into other know-ledge. However, we favour data collection with as open a mind as possible, an awareness of biases if possible, and 'weighing' and 'ana-lysis' as separate as possible, allowing for the spiral of theory and data discussed in the next chapter.

3   *Weighing the data*
   • Consider how serious the situation is or how well the client is functioning in the circumstances.
   • Identify persistent themes or patterns emerging from the data and list them.

- Cluster the themes and begin ranking them in order of priority.
- Check priority ranking with the key informants.
- Identify gaps in the data.
- Identify a group of people who will help with reflexivity.
- List the people to be consulted, noting their comments on file.

4 *Analysing the data*
- Identify theoretical perspectives and use them to gain depth of analysis (see Chapters 5–10).
- Develop more then one hypothesis, especially around what the goal of intervention might be.
- Reach useful but tentative explanations for the situation.
- Test the explanations for possible theoretical 'fit' (also what language could have talked them into being).
- Check this with the key informants.
- Run a final check of all the data to guard against the selective use of information.
- Consult with the 'reflexive' group again, if necessary.
- Develop further explanations and list the ways in which they can be tested.

5 *Utilising the analysis*
- What help is needed by the user? By others?
- List the outcomes one hopes to achieve and the consequences one hopes to avoid.
- Clearly explain how these outcomes can be measured.
- Prepare an intervention plan.
- Establish an independent mechanism to monitor outcomes. This could include supervision, multi-agency group or service users.
- Prepare a draft report that lists sources of information, analysis and initial judgement (see Chapter 10, which will also address risk).
- Obtain feedback on the report and revise it, noting any disagreements with one's judgement and the reasons for them.

We have emphasised the need to develop more than one explanation for the data collected because this seems to provide the most effective counter-measure to the problem of 'shaping' the data noted earlier. Sheppard (1995) argues that this is one element in assessment

that justifies the status of assessors as 'professionals', the others being
the development of precision and clarity in the understanding of the
use of concepts and theories, and becoming continually sensitive to
disconfirming information (pp. 187–8). Additionally, a premature framing of the data has the effect of influencing the progress and outcome of
a case regardless of the more usual checks such as supervision and
interagency consultation. We will discuss framing effects in more detail
in a later chapter but present an illustrative example here to show how
developing multiple explanations improves the assessment process. A
probation officer presented the following scenario at her local risk
assessment case conference with a view to deciding whether or not the
service user should be registered as a potentially dangerous offender:

Mr Y, a 44-year-old man, had collected his children for an access
visit and taken them to his club, where he became drunk. He took
the children home early and discovered his wife having a meal with
another man. There was an argument and Mr Y left. After brooding
about the incident, Mr Y drank further and then returned to the family
home, armed with a knife. A fight ensued during which the new man
friend suffered a punctured lung, the wife was cut and bruised, and the
children became very distressed. Mr Y was arrested and bailed. Six
weeks later, immediately after the preliminary divorce hearing, he
once again got drunk and returned to the family home, where he
shouted insults and threw a milk bottle through the window. He was
charged with Section 20 wounding and was sentenced to four years'
imprisonment for the wounding and three months for the criminal
damage.

The probation officer put the following explanations to the risk
assessment meeting:

1   This man constitutes a serious danger of re-offending because:

    • he has a history of offending (housebreaking, stealing, taking
      without owner's consent [TWOC], and drug offences);
    • taking a knife indicated premeditation;
    • the assault had serious consequences;
    • the man cannot accept that his marriage is over;
    • he has little consideration for the effects of his behaviour on the
      children, the 5-year-old having to undergo counselling following
      the fight;
    • his drinking is uncontrolled;
    • he has little to do with his time since he was made redundant;
      and

- his wife reports previous domestic violence following drinking. He denies this or suggests that he must have had 'blackouts' after drinking.

(Sources of information: the offender, his wife and police records.)

2 This man's behaviour was a 'one-off', a typical offence with little likelihood of re-offence because:

- previous convictions were all in his youth, his middle years having been trouble free;
- his barrister recommended plea bargaining for a lesser charge but he insisted on pleading guilty to avoid his wife having to give evidence, thus showing real remorse;
- he now shows concern about the effects of his behaviour on the children and has negotiated with his wife to see them in the presence of relatives to reduce their distress;
- he now accepts that his marriage is over; and
- he has begun anger management and alcohol education programmes in prison, where he is reported to be cooperative.

(Sources of information: the offender and prison staff)

3 This man is likely to re-offend in particular circumstances because:

- it is easy to be remorseful and reformed in prison where there is no access to alcohol;
- he is likely to 'coast' through his sentence;
- he remains angry about his wife's new, much younger man;
- he is unrealistic about how he will avoid arguments in the future;
- there are potential problems over his accommodation on release from prison as housing away from his wife will remove him from sources of support such as relatives and friends, and he resents losing his own home; and
- anger management and alcohol education programmes are untested in real-life situations.

(Sources of information: the prison staff and probation officer.)

No one explanation was decided upon as the most likely 'truth' at the risk assessment meeting, but the ability of the probation officer to propose multiple explanations rather than having to defend a single one meant that the risk assessment meeting members could engage in a helpful discussion. They decided on:

1   What additional data were needed to check possible explanations, for example interviewing the wife away from the new man to check out previous domestic violence, seeking information about the children's emotional well-being, and making arrangements for this to be discussed at a further meeting.
2   What resources would be needed to reduce the potential for re-offending, for example what support relatives could realistically offer this man, what programmes needed to be established to continue and monitor the anger management and alcohol education courses begun in prison, what housing and employment facilities were available in the neighbourhood where the man would live on release from prison and how the marital property could be harmoniously divided.

The main advantage of the probation officer being able to hold more than one explanation meant that she could focus on all three areas of assessment – risk, resources (including the responsibility principle) and needs (including crimogenic needs), the elements identified as important components of assessments leading to effective practice (Chapman and Hough, 2001) – and thus was able to develop a management plan appropriate for all the people involved, which was well resourced, with tangible outcomes and capable of being monitored.

In conclusion, we are arguing unashamedly for the making of high-quality assessment. This entails demanding, thoughtful work rooted in clear theory, and acknowledges useful assessment to be a complex ongoing process. It would be highly understandable if social workers, faced with excessive workloads and many conflicting demands, regarded our framework as unrealistic, but the need in their case is for adequate resources in terms of staff and for supervisory support, rather than for short cuts or shallow work that can so easily backfire or make matters worse.

Before outlining the assessment implications of the various theories informing social workers' understanding of the nature of people, in the following chapter we discuss how those theories can be made more explicit so that an improved decision about what theory will be used can be made.

Summary

- When measured by service user satisfaction, assessment outcomes are largely unsatisfactory.
- Assessment is usually a one-off event with little evidence of re-evaluation.
- Assessing social workers seek to confirm rather than disconfirm their initial hypotheses.
- Assessing social workers often 'shape' data to fit their favourite theoretical models.
- Where risk is a factor, this predominates in assessments to the exclusion of need.
- A social worker's initial assessment is the key determinant to future action and outcomes. Social workers use a questioning, procedural or exchange model of assessment depending upon whether risks, resource allocation or needs are the main factors.
- Social work assessments could be improved if the tenets of sound qualitative research were adopted:

  – a clear statement of intent;
  – accountability of values;
  – a systematic approach to data collection, looking at not only the personal but the social aspects, as exemplified by our grid;
  – the development of multiple and testable hypotheses;
  – decisions that lead to measurable outcomes; and
  – consumer feedback.

- Thorough assessments do not come cheaply; they need to be well resourced.

5

Selecting a Map

We have outlined the issues and the process of making assessments, and we have addressed data collection. Before considering in detail the theoretical maps that guide social workers' analyses of problematic situations, we will first explore the array of social work knowledge with a view to improving how we *weight* data (stage 3 of the process) and then decide which map(s) to select for the purposes of *analysis* (stage 4 of the process).

We aim to provide a way through the thicket of concepts and theories of which social workers become aware in seeking helpful explanations for the nature of people and society, and to locate some signposts. We identify the ideas that will be most useful in making judgments about data and map selection, and address how theoretical maps and data collection are not entirely separate. Additionally, we look at the debate about 'finding the truth'.

The theory thicket

Social workers are introduced to, and familiar with, a wide range of theory from the sociological (see, for an introduction, Haralambos and Holborn, 1990) to the psychological (see, for an introduction, Hayes, 1984). There exists a plethora of research findings concerning specific aspects of people's lives, including psychological research findings relating to such aspects as attachment and loss (Bowlby, 1964, 1982; Rutter, 1981; Murray Parkes, 1986; Howe, 1995), stages of human development (Bee and Mitchell, 1985; Sugarman, 1986), personality development theories (Schaffer, 1990), the hierarchy of human needs (Maslow, 1954), intellectual development (Piaget, 1977) and moral development (Kohlberg, 1968). Sociology offers theoretical insights into social strata, power and oppression (Haralambos and Holborn,

1990), while social psychology looks at, for example, groups and decision-making (Janis and Mann, 1977), and the dynamics of formal organisations (Morgan, 1986). The cycles of development in family life are studied (Carter and McGoldrick, 1980), as are deviance and crime (Walker, 1987), and mental illness (Olsen, 1984). On top of these, there is a knowledge of the law and rights (Brayne and Martin, 1993). So the question readers will probably ask is 'How do all these fit together?'

To answer these questions, we take the reader back to stage 3 of our initial overall framework – weighing the data. It is at this stage in the assessment process that the social worker makes judgments and evaluations on how well service users are doing in their particular circumstances. Are their strengths sufficient or are their limitations too great? Do their capacities and resources seem to be sufficient for coping? How does the difficulty or the particular situation compare with the norm? How much does it deviate from the culturally acceptable, the legal or the affordable? Are the risks acceptable? In other words, is there a problem? The making of these judgments is informed by a background knowledge of all the above theories and is also usually assisted by agency guidelines and procedures (for example, the *Looking After Children* pack: DoH, 1995b), and is underpinned by core social work values and skills, even though these are not often made explicit.

Agency practice will vary according to whether the dominant purpose of the work is the control of deviance, the empowerment of needy and oppressed people, or ensuring people's quality of life (Richards, 1987). However, how any worker uses theory is a matter of great uncertainty, which we hear most commonly expressed via metaphors such as 'once you learn to ride the bicycle, you do it without thinking'. It seems to us that in weighing up the gravity or need of a case, social workers' judgement is informed, and their beliefs bolstered, by the above-mentioned core theory. Most social workers would say this is useful and that they are using more than mere common sense.

The very existence of alternative and often competing theories of human behaviour and human problems does add considerable complexity to the task but we hope in this chapter to provide some assistance in explicit theory selection. It is not, however, the intention of this book to elaborate on these areas of theory. We simply point to them as informing all social work activity and show some key sources where they can be studied. However, they do connect with the maps in that preference for a particular map will lead to more use of, or reliance on, particular aspects of core theory. One theory will fit better than another theory with individual social workers' views of people and difficulties, and with ideas on 'the nature of people' (Aggleton and Chambers, 1986) implicit in any one chosen map.

We wish to emphasise that much of the theory can be used oppressively when social workers use it as if it were *the truth* for particular client situations. Most of it is culturally biased and presented as more 'certain' than it really is. For example, we rightly hesitate to describe any family as normal or abnormal, healthy or unhealthy, although we do need to have some idea of which families need help and which do not (Sainsbury, 1970). Theories help us to develop informed opinions when they increase our understanding of the likely relationships between events in people's lives, the impact of personal history and social background and present needs and behaviours, and when they add to our awareness of the sources of distress, whether external, such as oppression, or internal, such as guilt. They can help us to understand the values implicit in policies, human motivation and the importance to people of their roles in life and their expectations.

The trouble with certainty

We would like to think that theories can usefully help us to consider how some 'solutions' can make matters worse, how outcomes are often so uncertain that it is only at the end of our involvement that they can be verified, how all assessments are essentially tentative and how uncertainty can be a positive.

No assessment should be 'once and for all' – it is a continuing process that is improved as intervention proceeds. It is also revised when work is formally reviewed and needs to be reconsidered when termination is being planned. It remains in focus as effectiveness is evaluated after the work has finished. However it is never to be believed in to the exclusion of other possibilities. Hence we say that rather than seeking to 'prove' hypotheses, we seek to '*improve*' them – and 'proof' will come only when the work is evaluated. Ideally, we need to develop competing hypotheses and look for evidence to disprove them because along with uncertainty comes hope for change, or at least because such an approach would remove the risk of grave inaccuracy. Over-reliance on theory conflicts with what Pozatek (1994, p. 397) calls 'the uncertainty principle' because the very act of observing changes what is being observed. This should prompt us to ask how we can tell that what we see is what was there before we saw it. Without realising this difficulty, workers can disseminate information and 'initiate and maintain a pathologising discourse' (Pozatek, 1994, p. 398) that is oppressive. By way of contrast, the constructionist approach is to work with service users in a way that is respectful of the unique complexity of each person's life and his/her understanding of it. This shift in perspective is necessary to 'account for the unpredictability and randomness that are part of every day life' (Pozatek, 1994, p. 398) in any particular culture. Assessments by professionals all too often get accorded the status of truth and, unchallenged, the resulting beliefs become accepted as true.

This is not only oppressive to service users, but also limits what social workers think can happen. Pozatek (1994) reports seeing many interventions unhelpful to service users that involved a high degree of worker certainty. Understanding people's experience is as important as understanding their behaviour. This requires a collaborative approach to interpreting meaning, an awareness of the power of the prevailing discourse, a willingness to co-construct shared understandings of situations by dialogue with service users, and adopting a stance of uncertainty that pushes us to try harder to grasp a service user experience. Assessments have to be more like qualitative than quantitative studies, and be 'making sense' activities rather than ones clinging to naïve realist epistemologies. Influenced by postmodern perspectives, we believe that no single theory can fully tell the truth and that there is anyway a plurality of truths. Truth can only be interpreted (Parton and Marshall, 1998) and certainty is illusory. We like the expression 'working truths'.

So we take an interpretist view, committed to understanding the *meanings* that service users use to make sense of their lives, meanings that are constructed by the language used in talking about life. Although we do acknowledge the existence of reality that we can 'bump into', we maintain that assessments never fully reproduce it. What we see and hear is evidence or data but we need reflexive checking of our assumptions and our plans for action in coming to an understanding of the meaning of the data. Therefore, while we need to be aware of what is known in the social sciences, and use theory to check our own prejudices as we make the initial judgement in stage 3 of an assessment, we need to welcome uncertainty in work where 'the perturbing agent can only serve to trigger an effect: it is the living being [the service user] who determines the outcome of the interaction' (Maturana and Varela, 1987, cited in Pozatek, 1994, p. 397). What separates the social scientist from the mere technician is the 'capacity to shift from one perspective to another' (Mills, 1970). Parton and Marshall put it well when they say this demands that we can make our minds up about what to do but still remain open-minded. It will be clear to the reader that we are attracted to social constructionism in the way in which we view social and psychological theories; for an introduction to this approach, we recommend Burr (1995) and Parton and O'Byrne (2000).

Map selection

Stage 4 of the assessment framework involves analysis of the data, and this requires an application of one or more of the theoretical maps (derived from methods of intervention) in order to gain a useful depth of understanding that will guide intervention. In our experience, many assessment reports simply describe problems from various subjective perspectives and then give a common-sense summary of the situation, perhaps adding some suggestions for what should be done. When we ask workers how they arrived at their recommendation, they may say that this is what they always do in these cases, or that's the way it is done in the particular agency. The idea of selecting a theory to provide a particular analysis or explanation of how things have become as they are is felt to be only adding to the workers' difficulties and a rather academic exercise in any case, but it is crucial that our theoretical models are made explicit if we aim to practise anti-oppressively. We need to be aware also of the consequences of using a particular map, with its underpinning philosophy, as this may not accord with service user experiences.

There are many 'maps' from which to choose but none of the resulting analytic descriptions can reproduce reality; they can only propose helpful re-understandings:

It is now widely accepted that any statement that postulates meaning is interpretive – that these statements are the outcome of an enquiry that is determined by our maps or analogies or, as Goffman puts it, by 'our interpretive frameworks' (White and Epston, 1990, p. 5).

In considering the factors that influence theory selection in social work practice, it is our impression that *fit* with the original data or type of problem is the greatest influence in theory selection. For example, family therapy ideas 'fit' problems of family relationships, parenting problems 'fit' with notions of skills training, a task-centred approach has particular ways of looking at interpersonal interactions, and behavioural problems 'fit' with the behaviour modification approach. However, substance abuse could 'fit' equally with a behavioural approach or with a cognitive approach such as solution-focused work, and affective disorders such as depression 'fit' with a cognitive analysis of difficulties or psychodynamic interpretations. We need to get 'fit' not only between data and analytic maps but also between our analyses *and those of service users themselves* – except when these are clearly in conflict with the needs or rights of others. The existence of adequate 'fit' between original data and intervention should not, however, be seen as necessarily prescriptive. In assessments of need or risk, notions about capacity for self-care 'fit' well in some situations, such as an older person living alone, but less well in situations such as a parent struggling to manage a child's temper tantrums. At the end of each of the following 'map' chapters, we will suggest some advantages and disadvantages that might be associated with that map and therefore possibly with its use in certain situations.

Perhaps the second greatest influence on assessment is the actual services that are available and the criteria for suitability of these, even when these only lead to fitting people in to the best (least bad) alternative (Wright *et al.*, 1994). The interventions that the worker can personally deliver and the worker's preferred explanation for problems influence theory selection. As the reader will discover, some maps claim to be useful for most situations, and most social workers will feel that they do not need to draw on all five maps.

An alternative way of selecting the most useful map would include the following features. Having engaged with a potential service user and begun to establish trust, thus generating a flow of information or data to which one has listened attentively, one could begin to ask 'Where is the problem/need/solution mainly located, outside the service user, within the service user, or between the user and others?' In other words, is it extrapersonal, intrapersonal or interpersonal? Frequently, a person's need/problem/solution is perceived by the individual or the family as being *both* internal and external (Sainsbury, 1970).

Where the problem or solution is considered to be mainly outside the service user, it is for the most part not the service user who is the main target for change but the social system. Then it may be a matter of advocacy, or a needs and risks assessment and a survey of appropriate resources, or possible systems analysis as a preparation for systemic change.

If it is felt to be inside the person, the assessing social worker needs to ask whether it consists of a habit, in which case behavioural ideas may fit best. If it is a feeling, a psychodynamic approach or a cognitive approach might be considered, while cognitive theory strongly suggests itself for a self-defeating pattern of thinking. If it is most likely to be found between the person and others, task-centred theory, narrative ideas or cognitive theories may help.

Matching theories to types of problem is difficult. This difficulty arises from the fact that more than one theoretical approach may be helpful in any one case and various theories can tackle some problems equally well, depending on the skills of the worker. For example, if a service user is depressed, psychodynamic theory may provide useful insights, but cognitive theory also has its own way of helping with this problem, claiming that feeling is the result of dysfunctional thinking. If the cause of the depression is interpersonal, solution-focused or narrative ideas could be indicated, whereas if the cause is external, tackling oppression and finding resources will be more important. Also, social workers' own preferences and abilities have to be taken into account, as long as they can show that they are effective in achieving service user satisfaction. Some social workers and writers claim that one method of assessment and intervention can suit all situations, an example being de Shazer (1993), who suggests that there are no contraindications for solution-focused work (see Milner, 2001, for a discussion of how solution-focused ideas are applied to a range of social work situations).

Of course, various ways of working may take a longer or shorter time, and since our premise is that assessment is more helpful if it matches the intended intervention, busy workers will favour ideas from brief therapy. We feel that there is little point in doing a thorough Freudian analysis if there is neither the time nor the expertise to carry out the related intervention. Cost will be a further factor to consider. Quickest and cheapest is not necessarily best.

In some situations, the theory will immediately suggest itself because the intervention will be 'ready made'. For example, if the problem is one of bed wetting, most social workers will suggest a reward system such as a star chart or a warning bell, both being based on behaviourist theory. So too is skills training for, perhaps, a man with under-developed fathering skills, and assertion training for those who have not learned to assert their needs appropriately and who may either be too aggressive or too passive. However, we cannot stress too strongly that assessors always need to look at the extrapersonal and the inter-personal before focusing on the intrapersonal because power is an ever-present issue. It is extremely rare in any case for any 'problem' to be entirely intrapersonal.

In practice, the selection of a theoretical framework is usually not a clear-cut matter. Finding the *best fit* will, especially for new social workers, often entail consideration of more than one map and trying them for fit and usefulness. In this process, one would be looking not only at aspects that fit well, but also at aspects that clash or misfit and then weighing up the positives and the negatives. By positives we mean those aspects of theory that shed light on the difficulty and how it might have started and, more importantly, on how it is maintained in existence and what might be helpful in its resolution. By adding together these positives and allowing for any negatives, social workers can compare different approaches for fit and usefulness. There is no reason why the service user should not be included in this process.

The spiral of data, theory and analysis

We now wish to address another aspect that can be confusing to assessing social workers: the overlap between theoretical analysis and data collection. This comes about because the particular theoretical approach that a social worker implicitly holds, or selects, influences the questions asked when reaching for depth of understanding. Furman and Ahola (1992) maintain that it is not the truth of a theory as established by research or some value system that matters but the usefulness of the questions that flow from it. They demonstrate this by using a totally fictitious theory and showing how it can lead to a useful analysis. The social worker begins by saying something like this:

> Come with me on an imaginary interview. In this interview I explain to people that in a dark, damp cave outside of town there lives a gremlin called The Haaja, whose sole purpose in life is to get people to have problems like yours. Any steps to change these problems upset him very much, because his whole life is dedicated to making people suffer these problems, in your case drug taking. Our job is to defeat the Haaja and our first step is to work out what he likes you to do and what he hates to see you doing.

So, in this interview, the theory being used to explain the problem is that such problems are caused by a gremlin called The Haaja. This being the case, the questions naturally include him. They lead to collecting new data that are linked to the theory – data about what the Haaja likes and dislikes. The questions could seek out a list of these likes and dislikes; for example, in a scenario where the service user is a drug user, the Haaja likes the service user to:

- associate with other users;
- not bother about getting a job;

- sleep during the day and 'hang out' at night;
- steal money to feed the habit;
- avoid treatment;
- ignore warning literature;
- squat;
- be anti-police;
- not talk to the family about the drugs.

As the service user completes this list, s/he could be asked if it includes many of the things currently done. Then s/he could be asked to begin a list of dislikes the Haaja may have, such as:

- returning home;
- looking for a job;
- discussing the problem with the family;
- visiting a counselling service;
- sleeping at night;

or anything else the Haaja would really hate, for example:

- reading about drugs; and
- trying to change his/her friends.

And which of these things could you start practising in order to begin to worry the Haaja? Note that the Haaja's likes and dislikes include both *interpersonal* and *extrapersonal* factors. It would not be difficult to include *intrapersonal* factors too.

These questions, driven by this fictitious map, can lead to a helpful analysis that helps the service user to see what might be done to start developing a solution for the difficulty. The service user may begin to see that many of the behaviours now engaged in are ensuring the continuance of the problem, or at least are helping to maintain it, and make its resolution less likely. However, our purpose in presenting this 'theory' is to show how the theory shapes the questioning, which, in turn, leads to sets of data being produced because our very questions construct their own answers: 'New narratives yield new vocabulary, syntax and meaning in our accounts [and] they define what constitute the data of these accounts' (Bruner, 1986, p. 143).

In beginning an assessment, therefore, after having engaged with the service user, it is a matter of collecting initial data by listening to the stories of the potential service users and others. These data will point to a possible preferred theory in the mind of the worker and the resulting questions will provide their own data (service users' answers or information). This will in turn lead to an explanation of this service user's particular situation, the explicit use of more than one theory clearly being an important safeguard against bias. Data collection does not stop dead at the end of a checklist so that inference-making can begin with the use of a theory; rather, these aspects spiral around each other as the theory is drawn on to generate new data of its own. This will be true of any theory that may be selected.

Interventive methods follow from the assessment, which is based on the data, including needs, risks and resources, and on the inferences made. This is not the same as jumping to conclusions too soon and making the data fit one's theory. As we stressed in the previous chapter, social workers should have more than one hypothesis, and both hypotheses and questions are generated by theory. There is always some 'theory' as we cannot empty our heads. Thompson (1995) discusses 'the fallacy of theoryless practice' and shows how complex actions cannot be divorced from thought. He is not just referring to 'book theory' but also to the informal theory that underlies people's explanations of events. It is only when we acknowledge what ideas influence our actions that we are in a position to question them. Without such reflection, we risk becoming dogmatic. In assessment, because social workers ought to know why they are asking particular questions, they need to know and make explicit what 'theory' is driving their questions.

Finding the truth

By now, the reader must be wondering how we can be placing equal value on different theories or even suggesting that a fictitious theory might be useful. Surely the truth about a situation is what counts? We do believe that there is such a thing as truth, certainly in the collection of accurate data or the identification of service users and the resources available to assist with their needs. However, we also believe that there are many, and often conflicting, truths about any one subject's situation, but a true analysis is more difficult. Since an analysis is a making sense of a set of facts and it is possible to construct any number of accounts, we would argue that the most truthful analysis is the one that is the most helpful; the one that leads to the most useful understanding and to an intervention that achieves the service user's goals is the one that has the most truth. For instance, Pocock (1995) gives the example of a difficult child whose behaviour was first explained as 'innate badness', whereas a more helpful explanation for all concerned was that he was angry over his parents' separation. In the current state of the social sciences, it is not possible to prove that any helpful analysis is more or less true than another, and we know of no one who expects that it will ever be possible to reach one analysis universally accepted as the most true. Neither is it likely that we will be able to reach a deeper level of meaning beneath surface appearances that will rule out all other meanings. For constructionism, it is unlikely in social work that there will be one version of events that is true in the sense of making all others false. This can be attacked as leading to a relativism that puts the very premise of constructionism in doubt (Burr, 1995) but its strength is that, if accounts can be said to be neither true nor false, meaning can easily be mobilised in the social world in the interest of particular disadvantaged groups. We know that the powerful are skilled at using discourses ideologically in their own interest.

Positivists felt that experts could acquire the necessary knowledge to explain and correct the world, to make continual progress and to know when they had found the truth of what was 'really' the matter. However, in this age of postmodernism, the subjective meanings of the individuals who are experiencing difficulties are being seen as central, and their 'stories' are being seen as mattering a great deal. Their attributions and explanations are part of the reality and even create that reality. Because there is a scepticism that we can locate 'the truth', what matters is the currently operating created 'truth' of this person and how a thematic map might help us to co-construct with the person a more helpful and empowering account. It is interesting that, later in his life, Freud shifted the emphasis from historical truth to 'narrative truth'. Essentialists feel that truth is something external to the person and something the person can regard objectively, whereas constructionists see it as essentially something that is created by the ideas, thoughts, constructs, beliefs, communications, words and language of the knower. We 'author' our lives, and if they are unsatisfactory we can 're-author' them. Language does not simply represent reality; it makes it.

This approach, that one story is as true as another, can be attacked as an exaggeration. After all, a cat is not a dog. There has to be some fit or correspondence between external reality and what we construe. Except when we are deluded, we can usually tell the difference between fact and fantasy. In our daily lives, we rely on those ideas that are 'object-adequate' (Pocock, 1995, p. 161), that fit with the hard realities which we 'bump into' daily. Some stories are more testable than others, and some stories come to dominate our understanding from time to time. Pocock (1995) takes the view that we can have more confidence in some stories than others, so it becomes a matter of looking for the better story. A most useful theory represents the best story that can be written from a particular perspective to make sense of the uncertainties of life. Indeed, several stories can co-exist, offering different layers of perspective. What we need to locate is the 'pragmatic truth' (Pocock, 1995, p. 160), which will be the most useful in facilitating change in any particular situation as long as the outcome is both ethically sound and useful. It is therefore important to hold to uncertainty, to develop more than one hypothesis and to compare alternative and competing understandings for usefulness.

In another sense, a theory can be seen as a story's *plot*, but we want to keep to the notion of *map* in this book. We hold to the postmodernist view and to the belief that the narrative can create the reality in human difficulties, so substitution of the term 'map' is meant in the narrative sense, as a plot for a story, or as an analogy that makes sense of a situation and gives direction. In social work, the situation is usually a 'stuck' one, where life has become like one episode of a miserable soap opera repeated over and over again. The best map is the one that fits that current situation best and is the most useful in facilitating progress – the most pragmatically 'true' and the most positive and empowering for the service user.

We maintain that social work's search for one cohesive theory is misplaced. Social workers need a selection of practice principles and values, coupled with a range of theoretical models and methods, as a foundation from which they can respond creatively to the infinite range of situations they will meet. This creativity will enable them to mix and match theoretical ideas, test values and techniques, and be eclectic – making deliberate and rigorous selection, and not merely jumbling ideas together – so that their responses to service users will be individualised rather than routine. Rather than being mere functionaries, applying a limited number of options for the resolution of problems, they will be thinking, reflecting, responsive professionals. In the words of Milton Erickson:

> Each person is a unique individual. Hence [work] should be formulated to meet the uniqueness of the individual's needs rather than tailoring the person to fit the Procrustean bed of a hypothetical theory of human behaviour (Erickson, cited in Zeig, 1985, p. 8).

We must avoid being like Blaug's (1995) carpenter who, possessing a hammer, tended to see every problem as a nail. Each theoretical approach has its own usefulness or domain in which it is helpful in some particular way. No one map has been proven to be more effective than another in all situations, nor is it likely that such a map will be found. Many writers (see, for example, Pinsof, 1994) maintain that it is therefore a matter of linking together more than one fitting map to maximise usefulness and reduce deficit. Pocock (1995) supports this pluralist approach, which gives the worker more positions from which to be helpful by selecting 'a highly congruent better fitting set of ideas' (p. 162). A brief example from mediation work we engaged in illustrates how the truth can be altered to increase congruence.

A little girl was having severe tantrums over contact with her mother who, according to the father, had walked out and left them all. This father was distressed and angry, condemning his wife in the child's hearing. He repeatedly said of the child that she was 'disturbed' and 'It will take years to get her back to normal'. The mother was seeking contact with the child, but the child was refusing to cooperate. We worked with the couple, drawing on a divorce mediation map, and the father was able to agree that the child should be told that her mother had not left her; mother and father would be living in two houses in future but they both still loved her and would always be her only parents, and her father now wanted her to see her mother. To the father, we said, 'The child is not disturbed, she is playing a game, the game of being on her father's side and, as soon as she knows that seeing her mother is not disloyalty to her father, she will recover very quickly'. When they were seen a week later, the child was staying with her mother during the agreed times without difficulty. In this case, we had recounted a different plot from that developed by the family, using our knowledge of separating families and of mediation to develop a story that altered the meaning of the components of the problem and helped to bring about change.

Naming the maps

In the following chapters, we will be considering five theoretical approaches, which we have called maps of various kinds. We use the map metaphor derived from Bateson (1977) and subsequently developed by several writers in the family therapy field and by solution-focused writers such as Durrant (1993). This metaphor appeals to us because it helps to deal with the issue of truth.

Suppose one were travelling from a small town in Scotland to a village on the south coast of England. One could buy various maps that might be useful depending on one's mode of transport, one's needs for the journey or how well developed the roads or ways were Assessing a potential service user can feel like entering uncharted (or multiply charted) territory as the worker searches for ways by which to 'arrive' at a 'conclusion'.

Our traveller from Scotland has quite a choice of maps. She could get a motorway map, which would show junctions and service stations. As she passes each of these, she will know how far she has travelled, whether it is in the right direction, and what else she has to do to arrive at her destination. However, she may need a detailed road map to help her find her way when she is not on the motorway. If she wishes to walk, say to raise funds for a charity, she may prefer to take minor roads and footpaths, in which case another kind of map, such as an Ordnance Survey map, showing hills and valleys, might be more helpful to her. Likewise, if she were to travel by boat she would need a map of coastal waters. Perhaps maps also need to be understood by the person being met, or else the service user might not be waiting at the harbour! Maps should ideally have meaning and helpfulness for both parties and be in a language that both use.

Each of these maps could claim to be a map of Britain, and they all are true in what they represent. But none of them is truly Britain; the map is not the territory. On the other hand, if we consider the domain of 'the meaning of experience', we could say the map is the territory – that real meaning is simply that which we construct and narrate. We regard theories of human situations as maps to the understanding of problems, all different, all offering a different construction, yet all potentially useful and equally true. It is crucial that, when faced with the often pressing needs of service users, we avoid taking the 'naïve realist' view and that we are reflexive about the effects of the lenses we use.

Because Freudian ideas relate mainly to getting below the surface of the person and their feelings, we have named Chapter 6 the 'map of the ocean'. On the other hand, behavioural work focuses on observable conduct and on the ups and downs of action, so we have named it the 'Ordnance Survey map' in Chapter 7. In Chapter 8, we have labelled task-centred work as the 'handy tourist map' for several reasons: it is popular with busy workers and offers relatively brief ways of working and an easily accessible guide to assessment that has a wide application. We have used the metaphor 'navigator's map' in Chapter 9 for the solution-focused approach because this is a map specially prepared for locating and getting to a particular goal, as navigator and service user fly towards the constructed solution. Chapter 10 presents the 'forecast map', so called as it deals with oppressive climates and is also future focused; it will address the narrative approach and the notion of 'story' in assessment and intervention. It will be clear that, at least in some instances, one map does not rule out another. Rather, they can complement each other (for example, the maps in Chapters 9 and 10 combine easily), adding a further layer of understanding and providing further indicators towards possible interventions to bring about change.

As we address each of these maps in turn in subsequent chapters, we will offer case examples which we hope will further assist the reader in map selection. We hope in particular to show that several maps can apply in helping in any one situation and to some extent the choice that works best for one worker may be different from that which works best for another. In our view, social workers and service users should be encouraged to experiment and thus eventually devise their own most useful blend of ideas. The really important point is that professionals ought constantly to review their effectiveness and seek out ways of increasing usefulness to users. In this way, their array of maps can evolve over time in an atmosphere of research and evaluation, drawing especially on user feedback, but never claiming to have found the truth. This involves constantly checking for the advantages and limitations of each map, and for ways of making them more useful to the service users by helping to generate really helpful analyses of their difficulties and their solutions.

Summary

- Social workers are informed by a wide range of social science theory in *weighing up* and *making judgements* about human difficulties.
- In developing a deeper *understanding* of difficulties, with a view to deciding on intervention, social workers can draw on a range of theoretical maps, based on the theories from which methods are derived.
- Differing hypotheses result from viewing situations with the aid of these maps. This is healthy since no one map can claim to lead to a single truth and forming alternative understandings safeguards against bias.
- Pragmatic truth, that is that interpretation which is most helpful to both social workers and service users in developing solutions, is the most desirable, provided the work is firmly rooted in the values of respect and anti-oppressive practice.

- Social workers are encouraged to remain reflexive, to consider the consequences of using particular maps and to value service users' own 'theories' about their situation.
- While some maps are rooted in an essentialist approach, we include them as alternatives to be tested for usefulness and for 'fit' rather than to be applied 'correctly' as if they were able accurately to reproduce reality.
- Social workers need more than one map or tool in order to avoid being likened to a carpenter who has only a hammer.
- Having more than one map helps us to retain uncertainty and open-mindedness, which is the beginning of hopefulness.

6

A Map of the Ocean: Psychodynamic Approaches

Social work theory can be said to have emerged in three main 'waves'. The earliest of these was rooted in the ideas of Freud and his successors; it was a medical model and therefore was pathology-based. Subsequent 'waves' have been described as characterised by problem-solving and by solution-building, and we will address them in subsequent 'maps'. Despite its medical origins and its purely psychological theory, the psychodynamic map remains the most used in social work. We have, however, stressed that since external problems become internal and the internal affects the external, looking at nothing other than psychological aspects is as inadequate as looking at nothing other than social aspects; we need to consider both. Also, the ideas in this and the next four chapters all need to be used alongside the 'climatic' ideas outlined in Chapter 3.

In this chapter, we will be considering various ideas associated with the psychoanalytical approach to understanding the nature of people. We are selective in our sources, limiting ourselves to the work of Erikson (1948, 1977), Hollis (1964), Berne (1978) and Bowlby (1982), who have built on and developed Freudian theories in ways which have proved particularly attractive to social work. Our description of the theory will reflect a synthesis of many people's ideas and insights, their terms and their language.

Psychodynamic theory

The Freudian approach (see, for example Freud, 1937) has been labelled 'psychic determinism': viewing our actions as determined by inner forces that develop in early childhood. It places great store on a person's early childhood and on early parental relationships, the past influencing the present. Some Freudians go so far as to say it can even

The mind		The world
Unconscious	Conscious	(Other people and the environment)
The superego The Parent (teaching)		
	The ego The Adult (thinking)	[Reality]
The id The Child (feeling)		

Figure 6.1 Mind and world

be tyrannical in its influence. Therefore this approach can have a feel of digging down deep as an archaeologist would, but more so; it can have a feel of descending into the unconscious as if exploring in a submarine. Our chapter title comes from a comment by Hall (1954, p. 2) that the id is 'oceanic', in that it contains everything and recognises nothing outside of itself; if there is too much rough weather, it can turn nasty. We begin with a simplified diagrammatic presentation of the core ideas in this exploratory map (Figure 6.1). Bear in mind, however, that we are not discussing physical parts of a person but mental constructs that seek to explain people's functioning.

Although the id might not be capable of recognising anything outside itself, Freud certainly did recognise the outside world and its impact on the ego, so we have shown the world of reality on our version of this map and, as we shall show later, a large area of the map will deal with the interaction of the ego with reality.

Freud's earliest distinction was that between the conscious and unconscious mind, considering the latter as the greater part, consciousness being only the tip of the iceberg above the surface. In the 1920s, Freud developed the notions of ego, superego and id. While a large part of the ego, although by no means all of it, can be conscious, the vast majority of the superego and probably all of the id are unconscious. Freud also identified the 'pre-conscious' as that part of the unconscious that we can readily recall, which is just under the surface.

The superego develops through a process of internalisation. The child internalises the values, rules, prohibitions and wishes of the parent and of authority figures, but the process is one that magnifies these rules and records them in the raw, without editing, and they become laden with amplified feelings. So it is not just what a parent says to a child but all the emotion, perhaps terror, that was felt at being blamed, abandoned or hurt in various ways: the small child who breaks a cup can feel that s/he has destroyed everything. Admonitions and rules go straight into memory, carrying the weight of total truth, never to be erased from the tape. The research of Penfield (1952) and the work of Berne (1964) have helped to shape this view of the superego, and Berne (1964) later referred to it as the Parent (using a capital P to indicate that this is an internalised parent) part of the person, the part that tells and teaches. Even though the telling is long lost from consciousness, the recording remains active in the unconscious, shouting loudly.

The superego may be restrictive or permissive (Caplan, 1961). People riddled with guilt can be said to have an over-restrictive superego and people with too little guilt an over-permissive or weak superego. Those with no internal rules, no conscience about hurting others, are labelled sociopaths (commonly called psychopaths). Caplan (1961) talks of the superego as the condemning and prohibiting part of the mind that says 'Do not...', or 'I must not...', and he distinguishes this from the ego–ideal, which says (of a desirable act), 'So as not to let myself down, I ought to do it because that would fit my ideal me'. So, some people's conscience tells them they have to strive for great heights of achievement and set themselves high standards, be thrifty, and so on. On the other hand, too rigid and dominating a superego could create difficulties by way of excessive guilt, leading to neurotic effects such as depression, phobias, obsessions, compulsions, neurotic anxiety and moral anxiety or shame. Reality anxiety (Hall, 1954), however, is seen as an ego reaction to the threat of loss.

The id is that aspect of the person which is primitive, the animal drive: it is the Child (again with a capital C in Berne's terms), full of feelings, capable of rage, operating on instinctual drives and urges, hungry to fill any voids that are felt. Like the superego, according to Harris (1970), the id is also shaped by early recordings of feelings of blame, fear and abandonment. Even those with a happy childhood will record Not OK feelings that can loom larger than all the OK feelings. We can all be said to have a Not OK Child in us. The child who feels unloved may seek to fill a sense of void by theft, sometimes impulsively, as in kleptomania. The id also feels hurt by rejection or oppression.

Berne (1978) distinguishes between two main id drives – *libido*, which is sexual impulse, desire and attraction, and *mortido*, which is the killing instinct, hating, attacking and hitting out violently. He suggests some people are more prone to one than the other, although these are close relatives born of the need to propagate and survive. They explain something of what some people are looking for, so the id is described as being governed by the 'pleasure principle'; the lack of sufficient pleasure leaves it hurting, demanding and wanting irrationally, sometimes leading to a chaotic life of acting out, living for 'kicks' or sending out cries for help, such as the abused person who shoplifts to attract attention to his/her plight, behaving in a way that could be interpreted as asking to be caught.

The third area is the *ego*, the I and Me, the self. Berne labelled this as the Adult (with a capital A) part of the mind, which thinks, decides, plans and relates to the world of *reality*. It is governed by the 'reality principle', exploring and testing, born of curiosity.

The ego is placed between the superego and the id in Figure 6.1 because it acts as a referee between them, struggling to keep a balance between the gratification of needs and impulses and the sacrifice of this gratification to the demands of reality. This is what 'psychodynamic' means – an interaction and tension between (1) the id drives; (2) the superego, with its possibly guilt-ridden prohibitions; and (3) a tension between inner needs and outer realities, in an attempt to keep a balanced ego.

Defences

The ego lives under great pressure from three sides: the id, the superego and real threats in the world. Anna Freud (1936, 1968) itemised various mechanisms of defence used by the ego to help it cope with the instinctual drives of the id and, to a lesser extent, with the condemnations of the superego and the demands of reality: 'the infantile ego experiences the onslaught of instinctual and external stimuli at the same time; if it wishes to preserve its existence it must defend itself on both sides simultaneously' (Anna Freud, 1936, p. 191). She listed denial, repression, reaction formation, intellectualisation, displacement and sublimation as the main defences. Repression gets rid of instinctual derivatives, just as external stimuli are abolished by denial. Reaction formation secures the ego against the return of the repressed impulses, while by fantasies, in which reality is reversed, denial is sustained against attack from outside. The ego uses sublimation to direct instinctual impulses from their sexual goals to higher aims, and reaction formation is the ego further draining itself of the capacity for reversal (p. 190). The existence of neurotic symptoms itself indicates that the ego has been overpowered and some plan of defence has miscarried (p. 193).

Post-Freudians have added to Anna Freud's defences, up to 44 such defences being mentioned in the literature. It has been suggested that there are dual aspects of defences: first, warding off anxiety in relation to unconscious conflict and, second, actively supporting adaptive functions of maturation, growth and mastery of the drives. They list 39 defences, two of which have two subdivisions and one of which has four subdivisions. These include asceticism, clowning, compliance, depersonalisation, eating or drinking, falling ill, identification, ritualization and whistling in the dark. Most people use several of these, at least from time to time, and they can be helpful or not depending on the degree of usage and the particular circumstances. It is important, however, to remember that defences can be helpful or unhelpful, particularly in a crisis when the ego is under great stress. For example, intellectualisation might helpfully involve making lists of tasks or thinking through the traumatic event. On the other hand, defences can be unhelpful when they lead to on-going denial of loss or projection of cause on to others. We sometimes think that projection is the curse of contemporary life in which no one accepts responsibility for anything. Part of the task of assessment in psychodynamic social work is to decide which defences are being used and whether they are a help or a hindrance, and, if the latter, to consider how they can best be confronted.

In translating psychodynamic ideas into social work practice, Coulshed and Orme (1998) write that, in assessing people, we need to see whether the ego can tolerate self-scrutiny without becoming too anxious. In cases in which such scrutiny does not promise for change, we need to ask ourselves what level of support is needed to help the person cope with external pressures. Coulshed and Orme suggest that indications of such lack of promise might be anxiety, dependence, low intellectual capacity and distrust. They warn against 'laying bare' repressed feelings, or offering interpretations to that end, if the ego thereby risks being overwhelmed. An immature, weak ego needs defences to be strengthened, rather than torn down; ego-supporting is to be preferred to ego-modifying in such cases.

Wasserman (1974) points out that it takes a strong ego to be able to mourn, suffer, verbalise anger and even be depressed. So the absence of depression in some situations, while it might appear to be adaptive, might in fact be due to an over-defended ego and therefore be maladaptive. In psychodynamic assessments, social workers look not only at behaviour, but also at the situation and consider the stresses that may be operating, the degree to which the ego is pressed upon and the stresses with which the ego can or cannot cope. So, ego functioning is not only influenced by internal pressures from the superego and the id, but very much also by external stimuli. Social, cultural and economic factors, injustice and oppression, do not remain outside the person: they become internalised. Since practice is often concerned with efforts to influence adaptive capacities, assessments are more likely to be useful if they focus on the interface of the ego with the world: how the ego is learning, controlling and balancing with self-reliance and pride. This will mean that a social worker will not be concerned about intensive psychoanalytic techniques of free association, the recovery of the repressed, or the interpretation of dreams and breaking through resistance. Rather than a blank screen approach, she will offer a relationship, listening and reflecting with the client, joining the resistance (Strean, 1968), so that they can get going with the problem-solving that needs to be done. This does not in every case require the reliving of past traumas.

Ego functions

We would now like to consider the *functions* of ego, another area that can offer useful possibilities for assessment, particularly of the strength of the ego. It is the function of the ego to provide stability, equilibrium and predictability in such a way that, once we get to know someone, we can say that in certain circumstances s/he is liable to react in a certain way that is 'true to character'. This makes for sound relationships. Bowlby (1982) explains this in terms of the child making stable internal representations that will depend upon attachment styles developed in infancy but persisting into adult ways of relating. (Note that the prediction of others' behaviour that makes people feel in control of social situations is explained in different ways in the psychological literature. See, for example, the discussion on attribution theory in Chapter 11). The ego also manages cognitions, perceptions, planning and problem-solving. It makes judgements and decisions, adapts to reality and controls impulses, for example, not hitting out at someone who is being offensive and is bigger than oneself! The ego is responsible for personal growth, coping with stress, using skills and tolerating frustration, loss, pain and sadness. It is the ego that neutralises pressures from the superego and urges from the id. It produces self-assertion, the ability to verbalise feelings rather than act them out, and finally directs our striving, our attempts to achieve and to care. To do all this the ego needs to be flexible, adaptable, resilient, reality based, stable in the face of pressure and tolerant of anxiety and loss.

The ego, therefore, has a massive task to perform, which can make it feel overwhelmed and in need of defences. We all need some defences at times but many clients may particularly need us to strengthen or support their egos, not by breaking through defences with interpretations but by respecting and working with defences, acknowledging the threats they face and discussing the implications and confusion of their ambivalent feelings, or considering their unfinished emotional business, providing support perhaps through a corrective relationship that provides an emotional re-education, so that the client can move on to be an independent coping person.

The term 'coping', however, has particular connotations for feminist writers, who read it to mean putting on a front of coping by splitting off unwanted feelings, getting on with life without a fuss. Women often have no other choice; they dread failing to cope and are likely to suffer serious consequences if they do. For example, women tolerate much domestic violence rather than risk losing their children and put up with accusations that they have failed as mothers to protect their children (Kelly, 1994). Worse still, a black woman is stereotyped as being expected to cope with 'all kinds of hardship and material and emotional deprivation, as though she had no feelings or needs at all' (Lawrence, 1992). Thus we need to consider how reality is structurally more difficult for some people due to the oppressions of society, sexism, racism and other forms of discrimination:

> Following the early work of Richmond, psychosocial casework does promote indirect or environmental interventions as well as direct clinical work, but even today it retains a narrow understanding of what constitutes 'the environment', resulting in social interventions which usually seek little more than to mobilise or modify existing community resources. (Barber, 1991, pp. 16–17)

The terms 'independence' and 'separation', so central in psychodynamic explanations of 'healthy' personality development, have difficult connotations in that, because society is fundamentally patriarchal, women are more likely to have feelings of vulnerability, weakness, helplessness and dependency (Miller, 1973) or, on the other hand, to have learned from their mothers that they must orientate themselves 'towards meeting the needs of others' and 'to be a carer and not to expect to be cared for' (Lawrence, 1992). For an alternative view of ego development, see Mead (1934).

Transactional analysis

Harris (1970), and later Berne (1978), developed the idea of transactional analysis (TA) in order to look at the relationship between any two people, not just parents and their children. They describe the transactions as taking place between the Parent, or the Adult, or the Child of one person and the Parent, or the Adult, or the Child of another. Hayes (2000) states that the main concept in TA is that of ego-states. Jacobs (1999) says that the model describes the related behaviours, thoughts and feelings that are manifested in one's personality and that have both internal and external functions, while Steward and Joines (1999) stress how the interacting states are constantly over-riding each other in positive and negative ways. This is shown diagrammatically in Figure 6.2.

If person A is being irresponsible, sulky or childish, this behaviour is likely to provoke the Parent of person B. This transaction is shown by the line *x*, and *y* is a complementary reaction from B; it is expected and appropriate. Other obviously complementary interactions are Parent–Parent, Adult–Adult and Child–Child. However, if the transactions are crossed, there can be trouble, for example if A's Adult addresses B's Adult but B's response is from B's Parent (telling A off, perhaps), as shown by lines *p* and *q*.

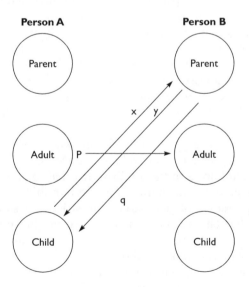

Figure 6.2   Parent–Adult–Child

For Berne (1978), the transaction, 'the unit of social intercourse', is the key unit of study. Transactions will vary, depending, for example, on whether the service user is relating to her social worker, to a partner, to a friend or to her own children. In some situations, she may find that she may need to be helped to practise using her reasonable, reasoning, grown-up Adult more. If practice makes no difference, she may need to be encouraged to get in touch with feelings from the past, which, because they are presently out of consciousness, are dominant in certain circumstances. Events and people in our lives can 'hook' our Parent or our Child, which can appear to 'take over' for a while. Berne further developed notions of 'life scripts', laid down in childhood and often followed later.

Parent–Adult–Child contamination is another interesting idea from Harris (1970). Parent contamination (of the Adult) is when the Adult is holding to unreasonable, taught ideas, such as a strong prejudice against a certain group. This may be accompanied by a 'blocked-off' Child, making it difficult for the person to play or have fun. Child contamination of the Adult is when feelings from the Child are being inappropriately externalised/exhibited in the Adult, for example as delusions. This may be accompanied by a 'blocked-off' Parent, leaving a risk of a weakened conscience, a low sense of guilt or responsibility, and a lack of social control, remorse or embarrassment.

Harris (1970) further expands the Parent–Adult–Child metaphor to describe a manic person as one whose Parent is applauding the Child, and a depressed person as one whose Parent is 'beating on the Child' (p. 105). In both of these, there is Parent–Child contamination, and Harris suggests that such people are probably brought up 'under the shadow of great inconsistency' (p. 105).

It may help here to 'recap' and show an ego gram of a particular service user, Miss O, aged 70, based on the work of Berne (1978) (Figure 6.3).

This can be seen as a graph of the family 'within' Miss O, who had become quite depressed when relatives were 'nasty' towards her because she would not give them a loan. It is based on conversations with her, listening to her memories of her responsibilities as the eldest child, her impressions of her parents as strict and stern, and her assessment of herself as being afraid to have fun but planning little deceptions to help her cope. Her Parent (the capital indicates that this is the internalised version of a real parent) is therefore represented as highly critical and not very nurturing. What nurturing there is tends to be more rescuing than encouraging. Her Child, however, is not very free, being fearful of the critical Parent. It is, however, fairly well

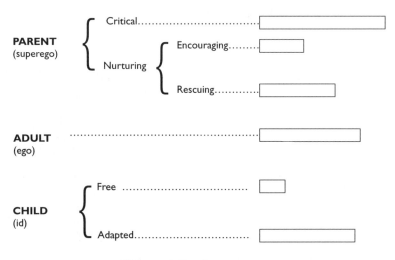

Figure 6.3 An ego gram

adapted, meaning that it has found a good deal of (possibly 'naughty') ways of making do. Meanwhile, her Adult (ego) is reasonably strong, but she still has some growing to do. The critical Parent and the adapted Child are both difficult to manage. Much depends on what level of stress is caused by the world, especially the world of relationships. If this proves to be too bleak and stormy a place, this ego will need quite a lot of support and luck.

Psychodynamic explanations of personality development

Psychodynamic theory sees people as developing in a sequence of stages, each one dependent upon the successful negotiation of the earlier one for its own success. Freud was interested in the early stages of child development, particularly sexual development, while Bowlby (1982) focused more on the social and emotional interactions of this period. Erikson (1948) extended Freud's developmental outline across the life span, including social as well as sexual and emotional influences. Table 6.1 attempts to set out the main concepts.

In psychodynamic social work, this theory suggests that it may be useful to explore whether, and how well, these stages have been negotiated or whether aspects of some stages are still presenting difficulties in the present. It is also important to bear in mind, however, that maturational crises can be compounded by situational crises.

Table 6.1   Stages of human development

AGE	STAGES	
	Freudian	Eriksonian
Birth to 1	Oral (hunger)	Trust vs Mistrust Level of confidence in reality in being able to form attachment, and have needs met
2 to 3	Anal (excretion, muscular control, retention/letting go)	Autonomy vs Shame and Doubt Who is in control of holding and letting go. If parent is over-controlling, child learns shame and doubt
4 to 6	Phallic/Oedipal Male child loves mother; has castration fears Female child loves father; has penis envy; jealous of mother Stage passes as desires are seen to be impossible and child identifies with same sex parent	Initiative vs Guilt Planning to act independently, avoiding if possible guilt about relationships
5 to c. 12	Latency period	Industry vs Inferiority Focus on conscious memory and learning skills, testing others, finding identity
c. 12	Genital – beginning with puberty Young adult Adult Maturity to Old Age	Identity vs Role Confusion Intimacy vs Isolation Seeking satisfactory sexual relationships Generativity vs Stagnation Integrity vs Despair Seeking to accept the past and one's achievements, the mix of good and bad times, and valuing the resulting self

While Freudian personality theory has as many feminist adherents as it has critics (see, for example, Miller, 1973; Barr, 1987; Pearson *et al.*, 1988), Erikson's life span developmental outline has proved more resistive to feminist revision. The criticisms remain acute whether they are specific, such as Gilligan's (1982) analysis of moral development, which suggests that while boys may develop from identity to intimacy, the process is reversed for girls, or more general (Rorbaugh, 1981; O'Hagan and Dillenburger, 1995). This is probably because the entire text is riddled with sexist and racist terms. For example, Erikson (1948) refers to 'the non male form of the female genitalia' and he describes black identity as three different forms of 'nigger' identity. Certainly, social work students love Erikson, but we harbour suspicions that this is because his outline is seductively simple and, all too often, his is the one book to be found on agency shelves when it comes time to write up accounts of practice in theoretical terms.

Bocock (1983) provides a useful discussion on the links between Freudian psychology and the sociology of areas such as deviance, the family, gender and sexuality. As social systems are made up of personality systems, sociologists such as Talcott Parsons have been interested in how one influences the other.

Advantages of a psychodynamic approach to assessment

Whatever criticisms exist of this approach (and there are many, as we will shortly discuss), it remains a useful way of attempting to understand seemingly irrational behaviour. This is pertinent when service users' difficulties appear to reside inside themselves rather than at the interface of the client and structural inequalities. The notion of defence mechanisms can be a useful consideration in the assessment of people who have difficulty expressing their emotions and transactional analysis provides a simple and accessible way of looking at clients' interpersonal relationships. It acknowledges the influence of past events and helps to create a healthy suspicion about surface behaviour.

Insight can empower people to understand what is going on within themselves and between themselves and the outside world. Despite the assumption that psycho-social work is lengthy it is possible to use the approach briefly in the course of assessment. For example, the father of a boy who was not doing well at school was 'in a state', trying to cope with his anger at the teachers while trying to maintain his son's enthusiasm for education. The social worker asked the father whether he had been keen on education when he was at school. He said he had not, and he had a very negative experience of teachers. When it was suggested that perhaps he was still addressing his own past school issues, rather than his son's, this insight helped him to rehearse his meeting with the school so that when it took place he was better able to focus on his son's situation, behaviour and needs in a rational and helpful manner.

Supporters of this model suggest that it is useful for situations in which long-term work with a neurotic person is indicated. Cases of compulsions, hysteria, excessive dependence and people unable to face an emotion (loss, for example) may also fit this approach. One needs to understand the process of transference in order to keep the therapeutic relationship reality focused. Although transference is not strictly a defence, more an example of the past manifesting itself in the present, it is a process that takes place when a person transfers feelings relating to one person, for example a parent, onto the social worker. Thus the social worker needs to consider whether the client is really referring to the social worker or perhaps to some early parental figure.

This approach has also influenced a listening, accepting attitude in social workers that avoids over-directiveness and can be useful in informing the earliest stages of assessment: deciding on the interview format and helping to focus on specific parts of the analysis. All maps lead to a set of questions that can be considered by an assessor, although these are not directly put to the subject. This map suggests the following questions, but rather than developing an interrogation, they ought to be considered as directing a conversation, using the values of exchange and narrative, so that the answers to them emerge:

- Which developmental stage is reflected in the behaviour?
- Is the superego (conscience) overly rigid or overly permissive?
- Is there anxiety? How severe is it? What 'indirect' support might be helpful?
- How dependent or independent is the person?
- Are there signs of ego breakdown?
- What ego defence mechanisms are being employed, or are implicit, in the person's behaviour?
- Which ego defences need supporting or strengthening?
- Or are they strong enough to allow some insight work?
- What threat is the person experiencing? External (social) or internal (psychological) ?
- What ambivalences are present?
- Are there some repetitive themes?
- Have there been past unsatisfactory relationships that need a corrective relationship?
- Which ego coping functions are working or not working for this person?
- What are transactions with others like?
- What 'contamination' is there?
- Does the person know what they should do and yet repeatedly not do it?

- Has the person had a figure with whom they have been able to identify?
- Have I considered the gender difference implications, especially in terms of coping and independence?

Disadvantages of a psychodynamic approach to assessments

As discussed in Chapter 1, psychodynamic theory has had a huge influence on traditional social work practice, but is fundamentally flawed as theory for *social* work because the main focus of concern is the individual, even when social factors have been identified and targeted. This leaves little scope for genuine psychological empowerment (see, for example, Ingleby, 1985; Barber, 1991). As it is based on a pathological, medical model, the social worker is the expert and an exchange model of interviewing is rarely feasible.

Because it is based on middle-class, white, male assumptions about the nature of families, differences and difficulties due to membership of an oppressed group are ignored in any analysis: the 'isms' cannot be included because of the very nature of the theory. Interestingly, Erikson had least to say about his 'adult' stage, despite this being the one where men wield the most power to enter people into stories of their own making which support the status quo; what Hearn (1995b) refers to as virarchy. Thus the theory completely overlooks power differences, being particularly insulting to women. Bowlby (1988), for example, only analyses women's behaviour in his section on domestic violence. Despite this, many feminist writers have managed to accommodate a psychoanalytic point of view (see, for example, Miller 1973). Lesbian, gay and bisexual people, who have perhaps suffered more directly as a result of psychoanalytically inspired mental health interventions, complain more forcibly (Davies, 1999); there is a heterosexist bias in both Freud's genital stage and Erikson's developmental stages (Crain, 1985) that ignores the institutional nature of homophobia. Homosexuality, for example, is explained as a matter of inadequate Oedipal development with weak fathers and dominant mothers in the case of male homosexuality (for an overview, see Kline, 1972), and fear of mutilation via pregnancy in lesbianism (Jones, 1932). By posing the notion that gay people are not 'proper' men and women, the theory effectively ungenders them.

The therapeutic implications of ventilation and reflective discussion in the psychodynamic approach also rest on white, middle-class norms regarding the desirability of self-growth and self-awareness. While this is considered to be appropriate for some ethnic minority groups, such as Jewish and Italian people (Devore and Schlesinger, 1991), it is not considered appropriate in many other cultures. Tinkering with the theory to incorporate ethnic sensibilities is never enough to surmount the hurdle posed by attempting to translate the effects of racism into an individual psychological problem requiring psychotherapy.

The biggest problem for social workers using the psychodynamic map to inform their assessments lies, probably, in childcare work. We do not consider it an overstatement to say that psychodynamic analyses of children's problems have proved at best trite and at worst dangerous. In the former situation, we refer to those superficial assessments that attempt to locate a teenager's abuse by a man as a result of her early attachment experiences with her mother, usually couched in vague terms to do with self-esteem, and resulting in largely ineffective interventions. However, the theory is dangerous in so far as it translates men's sexual desires for children into children's sexual desires for their parents. The issue in child abuse work is not necessarily one of 'unresolved mistrust' for the child in Erikson's terms or 'promiscuity' in Fraiberg's terms (1980) but one of abuse by an adult (O'Hagan and Dillenburger, 1995). And, in making children even partly culpable for their own abuse, the theory implies that their mothers must have been negligent (see, for example, Ward, 1984).

As a theory informing assessment work, it will do little to help social workers meet with men or develop methods for working appropriately with them. However, many of Freud's ideas are common currency (Payne, 1991), and these ideas are not only deeply embedded in social work practice but sometimes involve very strong feelings, resisting criticism.

Outcomes

Most meta-studies of social work outcomes place psychodynamic and psycho-social work as the least effective approaches to practice (see, for example, Thyer's comprehensive review of outcomes, 1998, 2002). Research into this approach is troublesome in any case since the approach places more store on process rather than on results. A recent study by Hilsenroth *et al.*, (2001) showed that, after nine sessions, while 59 per cent of service users felt some improvement in subjective well-being, only 25 per cent showed reliable improvement in symptomatic distress as measured on the GARF (Global Assessment of Relational Functioning) scale. They report that some rapid improvement happens early in the process and is followed by a 'negatively accelerating positive growth curve' – improvement diminishes as the number of sessions increase. It took six months to a year to get 75 per cent improvement. In the early phase, the subjective experience of well-being precipitated reduction of symptoms.

Summary

- The psychodynamic approach offers a considerable analysis of a person's *individual* problems, thus 'blowing up' small pieces of a situation to achieve depth of understanding. This does not necessarily give much direction for planning interventions.
- Ego psychology and transactional analysis ideas are more user friendly for busy social workers than is psychoanalysis *per se*.
- Psychosocial casework promotes 'indirect' interventions, but the environment is usually construed in a narrow way.
- The idea of defence mechanisms contributes to an understanding and assessment of seemingly irrational behaviour.
- Psychodynamic theory has had an enormous influence on social work practice but is fundamentally flawed as a theory for social work as it largely ignores issues of oppression to do with sexuality, gender, race and class.

7

An Ordnance Survey Map: Behavioural Approaches

We now turn to the first of the 'second wave' (problem-based) chapters, where problematic behaviour and thinking is seen as learned. This takes a less essentialist psychological perspective than the psychodynamic approach in that there is less a sense of a 'given' reality within people and more a sense that people learn to be what they are. Therefore they can learn to be different and behavioural disorders can be changed through the application of learning theory principles. Behavioural social work emphasises the assessment process on the grounds that, without a behaviour baseline, intervention can not be judged (Barber, 1991). This involves a detailed examination of specific behaviours to establish how they have been acquired and maintained as habitual ways or paths that people 'walk', day in, day out, step by step, so we describe this map as an Ordnance Survey map.

As with psychodynamic social work, the application of learning theory to social work was initially taken from clinical psychology and then adapted to a wide range of social work situations. We will identify two main strands of learning theory in this chapter: traditional behaviourism, consisting of three types of learning based on the work of Pavlov (1960), Skinner (1958) and Bandura (1969, 1977), and cognitive behaviour modification, consisting of three types based on Beck (1967), Ellis (1962) and Seligman (1992) respectively. The cognitive part of the map looks at how habitual ways of *thinking* can be considered as habitual behaviour, with an emphasis on how unhelpful thinking can be replaced by learning and practising more helpful thinking, and on how these ideas develop useful assessments that can accommodate both quantitative and qualitative aspects of change.

We first consider *respondent* (classical) conditioning, which is mainly based on the work of Ivan Pavlov, a Russian physiologist working in 1911. Any basic text in psychology will tell the story of how Pavlov conditioned dogs to salivate at the sound of a bell by associating the

100

Karen Davies

sound of the bell with the arrival of food. This was described in the language of experimental psychology: the bell being said to be a stimulus (S) and salivation a response (R). This is known as classical conditioning, with a stimulus always preceding a response:

$$S \rightarrow R$$

Responses are not only learned, but can also be unlearned or become extinguished; for example, if food did not follow the stimulus of a bell, Pavlov's dogs ceased to salivate after a while. Probably the most common application in clinical psychology of respondent learning is in dealing with phobias. Here the assessment involves the development of a hierarchy of responses to the feared object before the sufferer is gradually helped to relax and then presented with the item at the bottom of the hierarchy. More greatly feared items are not presented until each step has been successfully achieved. This process is called systematic desensitisation. In other words, the person's reflex responses to the fear such as increased heart rate are gradually removed.

The S–R sequence of learning, however, explains only a narrow range of learning opportunities that involve reflex actions, while *operant* conditioning explains a more extensive form of learning. It has a very wide application in addressing a range of human behaviours in which reflex actions are not necessarily present. This part of the theory also derives from animal experiments. For example, Skinner (1953) demonstrated how pigeons could learn to peck at a set of levers to obtain corn. The reward of food followed their effort, reinforcing the behaviour. In operant conditioning it is the person's actions that operate on the environment; any one act is still labelled a response (R) and the consequence a stimulus (S), even though in operant conditioning responses precede stimuli. The stimulus then elicits a stronger response (R2).

$$R \rightarrow S \rightarrow R2$$

This clumsy use of jargon terms may seem confusing, but as Hudson and Macdonald (1986, p. 28) say:

> do not be exercised over it, simply think of them as different animals, having a familiar meaning in the respondent paradigm (stimulus eliciting response) and an unfamiliar one in the operant paradigm (the association of a behaviour with a consequence).

Operant conditioning is often referred to as the ABC approach. A stands for Antecedents, that cue in the start of the behaviour; B stands for the Behaviour itself; and C stands for the Consequence, which reinforces. Stuart (1974) gives considerable attention to antecedents as a key focus for intervention. He distinguishes between three types of antecedent:

1 *Material and competence antecedents*. These are the tools and skills without which the behaviour cannot occur. For example, a student needs ability, books and other materials.
2 *Instructional antecedents*. These are rules, requests and expectations, not always explicit, set by others. For example, parents often unfairly criticise children for not doing what they were not asked to do, saying they should have known it was expected.
3 *Potentiating antecedents*. These consist of a set-up in which the rewarding impact of the consequence is increased. This can happen in three ways:

 • By restricting the consequence so that it follows only when the desired behaviour has happened. For example, no television viewing until after an assignment has been completed.
 • By providing a sample of the consequence for a person who has never experienced it, for example the excitement of using a computer.
 • By offering a person a choice of consequence from a menu of options, for example going out for a burger, or playing pool.

In assessing problematic behaviour, therefore, it is essential to begin by examining its antecedents and considering how their effect could be either increased or reduced. The behaviour itself (B) must also be mapped out in detail. Sheldon (1982) says that a behavioural assessment takes place independently of the definitions and labels that others place on problems. For example, a behavioural assessment would not state that a person is deluded, but rather it would state precisely what behaviours were involved.

The consequences of behaviour (C) in operant conditioning strengthen or weaken subsequent behaviour. Rewarding consequences, or reinforcers, make it more likely that a behaviour will occur. Positive reinforcers strengthen (reward) behaviour by gaining/giving a wanted/ positive consequence, for example, money; whereas negative reinforcers strengthen (reward) behaviour by removing an unwanted/negative consequence, for example, pain. The unwanted consequence may be present, for example, a twisted arm, in which case the required behaviour enables the subject to escape the pain; or it may be threatened, for example 'You will be grounded unless you behave well from now until 3.00 pm', in which case the subject avoids the unpleasant consequence by behaving well for that period.

Confusion, however, is common here. Because avoiding threatened sanctions is a negative reinforcer, we are apt to think punishment is the same as negative reinforcement. While punishment is usually unwanted or aversive, it does not necessarily remove or reduce behaviour; often it encourages endurance or the avoidance of being observed in the behaviour. This adds to the confusion in that punishment can be said to be either positive (giving unwanted pain) or negative (taking away a want, for example money). Figure 7.1 may help to clarify matters.

There are no absolute examples of positive and negative reinforcers because what is perceived by one person as negative or bad may be considered by another as desirable, and vice versa. Something unpleasant or painful would probably be considered negative by most people but others may enjoy it or see it as a proof of macho strength, for example. Thus the terms positive and negative (like good and bad) must always be seen as *perceived by the service user*.

A vital part of a behavioural assessment, therefore, is establishing what is or is not rewarding for the particular service user: 'It is a good general rule that the "customer knows best"' (Sheldon, 1982, p. 113). When making behavioural assessments, social workers can expect to find both positive and negative reinforcements operating with unwanted behaviour being reinforced. They may be part of this learning process. For example, the social worker who rushes round to the foster

REWARD (that is wanted/liked)		An AVERSIVE consequence (that is not liked)	
STRENGTHENS the behaviour that precedes it.		WEAKENS the behaviour that precedes it.	
This REINFORCEMENT can be:		This PUNISHMENT can be:	
POSITIVE or NEGATIVE		POSITIVE or NEGATIVE	
Gaining a positive e.g. Sweets	Avoiding or ending a negative e.g. not getting caught, or pain stops.	Getting a negative e.g pain or a shout	Losing a positive e.g money fines
Behaviour is also weakened by the absence of reinforcers			

Figure 7.1   Reinforcement and punishment

home each time a child exhibits unwanted behaviour and never visits at times when the behaviour is acceptable may be unconsciously reinforcing unwanted behaviour.

Reinforcement is more effective the nearer in time it is to the behaviour and when it is consistent, although there are different schedules of reinforcement; for example, continuous or intermittent. Intermittent reinforcements have a more lasting effect on behaviour. Schedules of intermittent reinforcement may be 'fixed ratio', like pay for piece work, or 'fixed interval', like a weekly wage. There are also variable ratios in which the number of performances of the behaviour is varied before the reward is given, and variable intervals where the time between rewards is varied. These variable schedules provide the most lasting effects on behaviour.

The third type of traditional behaviourism is based on Bandura's (1977) social learning theory, or vicarious learning (modelling). Very briefly, the theory says that we learn by observing and imitating others. These models give advance information about the likely consequences of behaviour and social learning theorists claim that this is a more efficient way of learning than is classical or operant conditioning. Here learning is further facilitated if the observer sees the model's behaviour being rewarded, if the model is reasonably like the observer (which aids identification), if the model is popular or of high status, for example a professional sports person or a television personality (the 'wannabee' syndrome), and if the observer can practise the behaviour immediately and gain reinforcement.

In using the traditional part of this Ordnance Survey map, assessment begins after a 'get to know you' phase, with a detailed description of the target behaviour(s) or required behaviour(s) in precise terms. This requires the direct observation of current behaviour, either by the social worker, the service user or a third party, who counts the frequency of certain behaviours in certain circumstances, listing antecedents, behaviours and consequences. A log may be useful here, for example that suggested by Schwartz and Goldiamond (1975) (Figure 7.2).

The behaviour modification approach promotes several techniques that are useful for reducing unwanted behaviour and strengthening wanted behaviour. Social workers may wish to check through a list of these ideas and consider which might be the most effective for the removal of a particular problem. In general, operant techniques are appropriate for operant behaviour problems and respondent techniques for respondent problems (Fisher and Goceros, 1975).

Persistence with behaviour despite distressing consequences suggests that such behaviour might be the result of limited choice

Time	Activity	Where	Who was there	What you wanted	What happened
7.00					
8.00					
9.00					
10.00					
11.00					
and so on until bedtime					

Figure 7.2   Record of behaviour

alternatives, given the history and circumstances of the person involved. The task is therefore to help construct new ways of producing positive consequences that might be accompanied by less distress.

A traditional behavioural assessment would attempt to establish a baseline of behaviour using points in the following sequence:

- Decide on the goals with the client in strict behavioural terms, that is those which are not only clear to the client but also capable of measurement.
- Where, when and how often is the new behaviour required?
- How would the service user measure success?
- What will other people notice about the behaviour when this happens? This could be at home, at work or at leisure.
- How will this differ from what is happening *now*?
- What areas of life will be changed for the better?
- Has there been any condition under which the problem was not a problem?

Next set a *baseline* for the current behaviours (wanted and/or unwanted), showing how often they occur, hourly or daily, over a period of a week or two. Then decide whether the problem is one of an excess of unwanted behaviour or the lack of wanted behaviour, using the following questions:

- What behaviours are in excess and what behaviours deficient?
- What behaviours need to be increased or decreased?

- What behaviours are occurring in the wrong place and at the wrong time?
- If it is a matter of removing unwanted behaviour, how is it being maintained or reinforced?
- Is the consequence one of positive reinforcement or negative reinforcement?
- Can these reinforcers be removed?
- What alternative behaviour could be put in its place? This needs to be carefully considered because behavioural change techniques have been shown to have more power in strengthening than weakening responses, so 'no deceleration technique should ever be used unless alternative behaviours are positively reinforced' (Stuart, 1974, p. 411).
- What are the antecedents or cues
  - material/competency?
  - instructional antecedents?
  - potentiating antecedents?
- If the behaviour is acquired by modelling, can contact with the model be discontinued?

If it is a matter of needing to develop wanted behaviour, ascertain:

- what new behaviour could be desirable;
- what antecedents are missing and need to be put in place;
- what is considered by the client to be rewarding;
- what reinforcers are available or could be gained;
- because reinforcers need to be administered immediately and consistently, who would be available to do this; and
- whether the new behaviour could be acquired by modelling; and if so, is an appropriate model available?

If it is a matter of strengthening current behaviour, check out:

- What are the antecedents?
- What are the consequences?
- How can more rewarding consequences be achieved and by whom?
- What schedule or reinforcement would be most efficient?

The answers to these questions should be used to build up a baseline. Your data display would look something like this:

CASE EXAMPLE

A student has a problem with doing college assignments on time.
Goal: Wants to get next essay finished on time.

- This requires a considerable amount of reading and note-taking.
- If he read a chapter an evening and made notes on it, he could be better prepared.
- This could be done in the bedroom, away from distractions.
- A daily log of chapters read could be kept.
- This will be better than wasting time watching television.
- Change is needed now because of college deadlines.
- Unless dealt with, the problem will continue until the course is passed.

The student's difficulty could be seen as an excess of unwanted behaviour (watching TV) or as a deficit of wanted behaviour (study). Because it is easier to strengthen weak behaviour, he decides to look for ways to strengthen studying and he decides the bedroom is the best location.

The consequences (in the longer term) of more effective studying are passing the course and avoiding the embarrassment of failing. Since negative reinforcement is more powerful, the student asks his

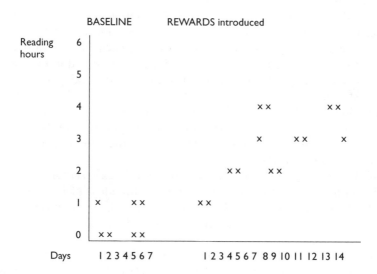

Figure 7.3   Behavioural baseline

partner to remind him of this consequence. There is also something (a certain crunchy chocolate confection) that he finds very rewarding, so his partner acquires some of this and shares it when a chapter has been read. The rewards of watching TV cannot easily be removed, this is a further reason for concentrating on rewarding the study behaviour. However, modelling can be assisted if the partner also reads instead of watching TV at study time. The emphasis, in the short term, is on the pleasant consequences of having the chocolate following a period of study. The student knows that this work will avoid dreaded failure in the long term.

Cognitive–behavioural theory

The cognitive dimension to behavioural approaches looks at thoughts as if they were behaviours where unhelpful habits may be learned. It also suggests that behaviour is mediated through thought processes just as much as through a series of responses to stimuli. As Cigno (1998) explains, the focus is therefore on current causes, here and now, on the basis that people are not just responding to stimuli, but also interpreting and construing them in various ways that maintain problematic behaviours and states such as depression; for example, through self-blaming. This is particularly relevant to social work, which seeks to individualise service user behaviour but does not always find this easy; insight does not necessarily change behaviour, nor does traditional behaviour modification always prove effective. Indeed, although the latter seems scientific, logical and accessible, each human situation contains so many variables that even Skinner commented in his novel *Walden Two* that predicting behaviour is rather like making a weather forecast. On the other hand, as the term implies, the cognitive dimension considers 'how behaviour is guided by the perceptions and analysis of what we see' and how 'irrational thoughts or disturbances in perception lead us to process our view of the world incorrectly' (Sheldon, 1995, pp. 184–5).

Within this cognitive model, there are numerous variations, but we will confine ourselves in this brief outline to the ideas of Ellis (1962), Beck and Tomkin (1989), and Seligman (1992). The work of Beck and Ellis has been further developed by Burns (1992) and Dryden and Yankma (1993).

A cognitive approach had been implicit in the ego psychology of the 1940s, but both Ellis (1962) and Beck (1967) redefined emotions as clearly cognitive in essence, Ellis (1962) describing them as a strongly evaluative kind of thinking resulting from what he termed self-talk, internalised sentences and self-verbalisation (Ellis had built his ideas partly on the work of Adler who had parted company with Freud on cognitive issues) – all aspects that could be un-learned. Emotion, in this approach, 'is a feeling a person experiences after estimating what an event *means* to him' (Werner, 1970, p. 254), inferring that people must be confronted with the disparities between their perception and reality, and offered alternatives to inaccurate perception, the discrepancies between stated goals and actual behaviour being addressed. Behaviour is shaped neither by unconscious inner drives nor by externally conditioned habits but by a third force, cognition, the self-determination of the individual who *uses* both internal forces and the external environment. 'Action is not completed unless conscious thought processes support it' (Werner, 1970, p. 252).

Werner saw choosing goals, evaluating events and self, and solving problems as the three conscious cognitive processes intimately associated with personality development. For Werner, change in these three elements listed above results in changes in personality. For example, a person whose personality is characterised by withdrawn behaviour is not necessarily seen as fixated at one stage of development. Instead, this is seen as probably due to frequent failure to attain desired goals, and a 'personality change' can be effected if that person experiences success in goal achievement. In assessment work this leads to asking questions about perceptions of goals, of expectations, of self and of difficulties (in general about one's private logic).

In the case of the student mentioned earlier, these questions led to the discovery that, while his goals were constructive and realistic, there was a possible opponent in that the children did not understand or agree with them; the family atmosphere was rather indulgent but also reasonably competitive. A private logic of 'Do I really have to be so hard on myself?' operated, and there were early recollections of being sent to the bedroom as a punishment, so there is quite a mix of emotions and perceptions, the clarification of which was helpful both as an understanding of the difficulty and as providing signposts towards change.

Ellis (1962) was primarily interested in anxiety and depression states and how these were caused or maintained by thoughts. He developed an ABC alternative to that of operant conditioning. For Ellis, A is the Activating event, such as loss of employment; B is the Beliefs one has about that event, such as 'My whole life is ruined'; and, C is the emotional Consequence, mostly for Ellis, 'I'm depressed'. He suggests that cognitive processes, rather than simple reinforcements, influence behaviour, with people usually blaming the Activating event for the Consequential emotion. Ellis seeks to break this A–C connection and show the service user that the emotion follows from the Beliefs (B) about the event rather than from the event itself (A). This explains why different people react differently to the same event. Ellis would say that A–C thinking is a distortion and needs to be replaced by B–C thinking.

Ellis (1962) also outlined a whole set of cognitive distortions, the most common being that people oppress themselves by believing they *must* do, or have, or achieve, certain things. He coined the words 'musterbation' to challenge this process in the application of cognitive therapy and 'awfulising', the process whereby merely unpleasant or uncomfortable experiences are described as worse than 100 per cent bad. For example, when the bus is late, some people will refer to this as disgusting. Burns (1992) added to this list of damaging cognitive distortions:

- *All or nothing thinking*: what is short of perfect is a total failure.
- *Over-generalisation*: a single failure is a never-ending pattern of failure.
- *Mental filter*: selecting and dwelling only on the negatives.
- *Disqualifying positives*: rejecting them as not counting.
- *Jumping to conclusions*: making negative judgments on little evidence and also mindreading that ascribes negative rather than positive intent.
- *Magnification/minimisation*: exaggerating one's faults or another's strengths, or shrinking one's own strengths (also known as reversed binocular vision).
- *Emotional reasoning*: 'I feel it, so it must be true'.
- *'Should' statements*: by which one whips and punishes oneself before one can be expected to do something. Additionally, 'should' statements directed at others lead to anger and frustration.
- *Labelling/mislabelling*: 'I am a loser', 'He is a dirty rat'.
- *Personalisation*: seeing oneself as the cause of negative events.

In cognitive therapy, Ellis (1962) takes a prescriptive approach, strongly debating with, confronting and challenging people to correct their distortions and replace them with more rational reasoning. Such rational reasoning is supported by (behavioural) rewards in the first instance until the service user achieves the self-rewarding effect of attaining an agreed goal. Beck and Tomkin (1989) have a more gentle style that leads people to reconsider their beliefs and is, perhaps, more

	Situation	Emotion	Automatic thought	Relational response	Outcome
Date					
Time					

Figure 7.4   Response record

rigorous in the assessment stage of therapy. They developed a system of identifying negative automatic thoughts, for example, 'I can't make real friends', 'I'm stupid', 'I always say the wrong thing', 'Everyone knows how disorganised I am', 'I'm no good'. Burns suggests the keeping of a daily log to identify the details of both the behaviour and the accompanying cognitive processes which might look something like Figure 7.4.

An automatic thought will usually be a form of self-criticism, whereas a rational response will be a self-defence or a rebuttal of an automatic thought. For example, parents experiencing problems with their children may catch themselves thinking 'Where did I go wrong', while a more rational response might be 'I am not a bad parent; I do try; I cannot control all that goes on in my children's lives'. Keeping an assessment record such as that shown above becomes the therapy in that the service user comes to appreciate the improved emotional and relational outcomes of more rational responses. Burns (1992) provides a selection of checklists and self-evaluation instruments that a service user completes. These facilitate data collection and diagnostic analysis because they include many of the assessment questions a social worker needs to consider.

Cognitive approaches have their own specialised therapeutic off-shoots, such as the Institute for Rational–Emotive Therapy, which suggests that service users list irrational beliefs, then dispute them, before putting 'effective rational beliefs' in their place (see, for example, Dryden and Mytton, 1999). An example of an irrational belief is: 'I can't stand it when he...' or 'I can't stand it when I do not have the drug', an effective rational alternative being 'It's unpleasant and uncomfortable, but I can stand it'. Equally, the irrational belief 'I cannot be happy unless I have someone to love me' could be replaced by a rational response such as 'As an independent person I can love myself, so I can always be loved, and this will make me more attractive to others'. Yapko (1988) suggests some further examples of distorted thinking that may lead to depression: 'It's me'; 'It will always be this way and it affects everything I do'; 'It can only be this way'; 'Life always has been bad, therefore it will always be bad'; 'The whole thing is ruined'. This approach leads to the following questions during the assessment phase:

- What cognitive distortions can be heard in the client's story?
- What automatic thoughts enter the mind when things are not right?
- How is the person putting him/herself down?
- How can these irrational beliefs be disputed?
- How can rational beliefs be developed?

Learned helplessness

Cognitive theorists are also interested in the concept of learned helplessness (Seligman, 1992). This is a state that results from repeated exposure to unpleasant events that are beyond the control of the individual so that whatever a person does has no predictable effect one way or another. An example of this is a woman who sometimes gets battered when she does something and sometimes gets battered when she does not do the same thing. This information about the lack of connection between effort and outcome grows into an expectation or belief that responding to one's situation is futile, that all future efforts will fail in the same way and that it will always be so. For example, a social worker arrived at a home to find a woman being beaten violently by her husband. She hurried the woman and her four children into her car but was amazed at the woman's behaviour. This woman had become so accustomed to the futility of any action on her part during violent episodes that she sat perfectly still in the car, apparently calm, while her husband beat the car with a spade. This learned helplessness continues even after some good outcomes; good days are attributed to luck or to the efforts of others and only serve to prove one's own helplessness. There are some similarities with the hostage syndrome, in which victims of kidnapping become attached to their captors and blame themselves for the trouble, although the main features of learned helplessness are lack of energy, negative mood, self-condemnation and withdrawal.

As these features are similar to those of depression, Sheldon (1995) maintains that depressive and anxious people attribute success to good luck or the task being easy, while attributing failure to lack of effort or poor ability, adding that irresponsible people do the opposite. This means that even when action could be taken, a person who has learned helplessness is unlikely to try anything and it is important not to label this as 'unmotivated' or 'lazy'. Barber (1991) describes this as a psychology of powerlessness, which explains the passivity of many recipients of social work services – single mothers on income support, disabled persons dependent on others, victims of child abuse and domestic violence.

Learned helplessness highlights the need for social workers to combine psychological and sociological factors – not only to attend to external resources but also to mobilise internal resources, considering the dispositional factors within each person. Additionally it may be more immediately helpful and empowering for the service user in the short term if accessible dispositional factors are changed while situational factors are addressed as part of a long-term strategy. It is important to bear in mind that attributions are not just the product of an individual's mind but are also influenced by culture. When internal attributions are addressed, the service user may then be empowered to make more appropriate external attributions. In assessing learned helplessness, Barber (1991) suggests using the following questions:

- How long have things been bad?
- What efforts have you made to change things?
- How much success have you had?
- How many good times have you had compared with bad times?
- What do you put your good times down to?
- What do you put your bad times down to?
- If attributed to internal causes, do you put it down to effort or ability? (Effort is easily improved.)
- If attributed to external causes, do you put it down to luck or task difficulty? (Real luck is totally outside our control but, since there is an element of one making one's luck by planning and effort, some so-called luck can be self-made).

Advantages of a behavioural approach to assessments

Behavioural approaches have considerable appeal for social workers because they offer a systematic, scientific approach that makes it possible to structure the work: 'The objective is spelt out clearly, the method pre-defined, and the end product always measurable' (Davies, 1981, p. 54). The initial stages of assessment are given prominence in this approach and the production of behaviour baselines aids data display.

Additionally, a strict behavioural approach has the advantage of going some way towards meeting the values of social work in that client participation is encouraged, labelling discouraged and accountability made evident. Sheldon (1982) argues that a behavioural assessment has the advantage over other approaches of not 'squeezing out' the client's story or shaping the evidence to fit a favourite theory, so this careful attention to detail is particularly useful in 'blowing up' aspects of client situations so that all variables can be explored. When the ideas about learned helplessness are taken on board, this has the potential to bridge the gap between psychological and sociological explanations of behaviour and maintain the focus on social as well as individual factors. O'Hagan and Dillenburger (1995) maintain that a functional behavioural approach offers a new, thorough, non-abusive approach to child-care work.

Disadvantages of a behavioural approach to assessments

Despite the claims of behavioural social workers that the approach is value-free and client friendly, it remains in practice largely psychologically reductionist. Although the cognitive-behavioural approach can improve people's responses to inequality, it is no substitute for addressing social problems. In residential work, for example, usually it is only the immediate environment of the service user that is examined; even with behavioural groupwork, it tends to yield little more in the way of solutions than the establishment of token economy regimes. Whatever the value of these, they do not take into account the realities of, for example, children's experiences in residential care where homes are understaffed, underfunded and, in some cases, abusive.

Also, the approach is not as value-free as it claims. For example, Ellis's (1962) rational therapy is really all about appropriate white, masculine assertiveness. It would be difficult to challenge many women's 'irrational' beliefs as they may well be embedded in the 'rational' context of patriarchal relations. Renzetti (1992), for example, suggests that many lesbian women remain in violent relationships because of 'learned optimism'.

The scientific nature of traditional behavioural assessment rests on modernist assumptions about certainty and, in practice, assessments need to include the cognitive aspects. Even then, there often appears to be a tendency to go for a rushed solution after a limited assessment; see, for example, the modified and limited use of social skills training in groupwork. We are left with the same basic criticism we made of psychodynamic approaches: it is usually easier to bend the theory so that the assessment suggests an intervention that changes how an individual accommodates their lot rather than actually looking at whether that 'lot' should be changed. This is, of course, the perennial problem of social work, as it always seems easier to change an individual than challenge the status quo.

In conclusion the traditional behavioural approach can be used on its own, as can the cognitive dimension. Added together, however, they provide a more powerful analysis of a wide range of troubled situations, examining what precedes and follows behaviour environmentally, and also what thoughts and resultant feelings precede, accompany and follow from the behaviour, giving clear indications of which interventions are most likely to be helpful.

Outcomes

Research into the outcomes of behavioural social work (Sheldon, 1995) suggests that a combination of traditional behavioural approaches and cognitive approaches produces better results, and the cognitive dimension is being increasingly applied to a wider range of problems. Vennard, Sugg and Hedderman (1997) found that the use of cognitive-behavioural work was more effective than psycho-social approaches for reducing anti-social behaviour in both adults and juvenile offenders, and Buchanan (1999) found it the single most effective (problem-focused) approach for children with emotional behavioural problems. Concerning work with children, Sutton (2000, p. 4) concludes that 'there is abundant evidence that when practitioners develop a warm, empathic and respectful therapeutic alliance with family members and can help them to employ principles and concepts drawn from cognitive-behavioural theory, they have been able to help thousands of children with a variety of problems.' However, even though other studies found that cognitive-behavioural work produces the most positive outcomes, the meta-analysis of Gorey, Thyer and Pawluck (1998) did not find evidence to support this and it probably has not been compared with constructionist approaches.

Summary

- Behavioural approaches offer a detailed and thorough method for the analysis of problems, suggesting useful techniques to aid assessment.

- These approaches are most effective in developing strategies to strengthen behaviour.
- Despite the advantage of rigour in the assessment of behavioural problems, this approach is little used by social workers.
- Cognitive behavioural approaches, in that they emphasise the role of thought processes in behaviour, offer a more acceptable approach to assessment and intervention for many social workers, as they help them to understand the emotional component of behaviour difficulties.
- The emphasis on learned helplessness gives behavioural approaches the potential to deal with anti-oppressive practice issues, and Barber's questions can be useful in analysing helplessness and in starting empowerment and increasing self confidence.

8

The Handy Tourist Map: The Task-centred Approach

The map presented in this chapter is also from the 'second wave' of social work theory. It, too, is problem focused, having much in common with the cognitive element in the previous map, but it moves further both towards social constructionism and towards acknowledging and dealing with external social factors in human difficulties.

This chapter addresses the task-centred approach to social work assessment and intervention – probably the most used approach of the past 20 years after psycho-social casework. This theoretical map differs from those in preceding chapters in that, while it is implicitly behaviourist and cognitivist, it did not originate in clinical psychology but is based instead on research into social work practice and written specifically for social workers. We refer to it as a handy tourist map because it involves no elaborate or complex theory, its principles could fit on a folded card, and social workers use many of its elements, perhaps without naming them, as a guide to where they need to get to in much of their work.

Task-centred theory

The task-centred approach arose from disenchantment in the 1960s with the existing open-ended and long-term ways of working. William J. Reid's dissertation at Chicago University in 1963 was the first statement of the ideas, which were subsequently developed by Reid and Shyne (1969), Reid and Epstein (1972), Reid (1978) and Epstein (1988). The main British publication is that of Doel and Marsh

(1992). Most recent texts on social work interventions include the task-centred approach (see, for example, Coulshed and Orme, 1998).

There are certain assumptions underlying this approach, many of them drawn from the (cognitive) philosophical writings of Goldman (1970) and from the crisis intervention ideas of Parad (1965). Briefly these are:

- The usual and best way to get what you want is to take action.
- Action is guided by beliefs about the world and self, and these are the basis for plans of action.
- Many psychosocial problems reflect only a temporary breakdown in coping.
- Time limits help to motivate service users, before the edge of discomfort becomes blunted with time.
- One positive problem-solving experience improves one's ability to cope with the next difficulty.
- 'Normal life consists of one damn thing after another' (Dorothy Sawyer's character Lord Peter Whimsey). Difficulties are mostly normal; they become problems only when they become 'the same damn thing over and over' (O'Hanlon, 1995) as a person becomes stuck.
- We are what we do, and feelings flow from behaviour.
- Feelings can be viewed as beliefs about wants.

From wants to goals

Problems are defined by Reid (1978) as unmet or unsatisfied wants as perceived by the service user. These perceptions may often be unclear but, more importantly, an unmet want is often attributed to the potential service user by someone else. For example, person A may say 'My partner B has a drink problem – he needs to control his drinking'. This is the attribution of a problem by person A (the 'referrer') to person B. A is seeking help for B, so A's want/problem is really 'I have a problem with my drinking partner'. That is the only 'acknowledged' problem so far. B has not acknowledged any want; he is not an 'applicant', and it is mainly service users who are applicants in some way that concern us in the detailed use of this map.

Of course, in statutory agencies especially, many of the people we work with are 'referrals' rather than 'applicants'. They are the unwilling people whom courts, child protection panels, schools, parents and families refer to us. These people may say they have no unmet want with which they wish us to help. In these situations, task-centred work does not move forward unless, and until, some want is acknowledged, even if it is only 'I want you off my back'. Unwilling 'referrals' can be engaged by exploring how it is that others see them as having problems or as being problems, how the situation is affecting them, whether there is something they would like to see changed, and whether there is something they could do that would free them from interference in their lives. When they acknowledge some such want they become 'applicants'. In this approach, therefore, the first step in assessment is to establish whether this person has any want, that is 'Is there anything you want to change?' 'Do you want my help in achieving it?' Some people see themselves as confirmed failures in life and may not believe that any help will make a difference. They may need to consider the questions 'If effective help was available, what would you like it to tackle?' and 'Are any of the attributed problems real problems for you in any way?'

This approach takes nothing for granted and asks the most basic and obvious questions, respecting potential service users' states, seeking to start where they are and looking at life through their perception of it. Epstein (1988) describes this phase as the 'Start up', in which the worker establishes whether there are acknowledged wants in the mind of those referred for help.

The next step focuses on *wants*, to firm up *goals*, assessing whether they are specific and achievable and, if so, in how much time, particularly how short a time. This consideration of time-limited work is seen as crucial for motivation and clearly fits well with the current requirement that assessments should include the costing of interventions. Many potential service users will have more than one want; these are prioritised at the assessment stage and usually no more than three are targeted. Once agreed, these (three) problems become the basis of the goals of the work. Where, when and with whom these problems arise is explored, as are the consequences of behaviours, the meaning the problem has for the person and for significant others, and also the social context.

Three considerations arise in clarifying *goals* at this point:

- What needs to be done or changed?
- What constraints make this difficult?
- What tasks will be required of the service user and/or the worker, mainly the service user, in order to begin to improve matters?
- How long will it take? Discussing and agreeing time limits appears to greatly heighten motivation. We suggest that when in doubt about length, err on the brevity side.

NAME	What I want from them	My chances of getting it	What they want from me	Their chances of getting it from me
Dad				
Mum				
Kate				
Paul				

Figure 8.1   Want Sheet

We also recommend the Want Sheet (Figure 8.1) designed by Masson and O'Byrne (1984), which is particularly useful where two or more people are involved, as in family conflicts. Instruments such as these help people to clarify wants or, often more importantly, to express wants. The vagueness arising from an inability to explain, clarify and express wants is often a further problem compounding the original problems.

Clarification at the assessment stage is in itself also a major part of helping. Since the aim is to help or 'coach' service users in taking action to deal with the problem themselves, the service user, rather than the social worker, being the main agent of change in this approach, clarity and agreement are vital at this point. Each member of a family or group can be asked to complete a Want Sheet and then share it with each other, giving them an opportunity to challenge misconceptions about each other's expectations within the group. Such exchanges can give valuable information about the potential of the group for sorting out its problems through its own action. The approach therefore is essentially an empowering one with the social worker serving/servicing the user(s).

The meeting of a want is equivalent to reaching a goal. Every social work text will stress the need for clearly defined realistic goals that are salient to the service user; however, there may be a tendency among some social workers to busy themselves with tasks and miss out on the work of identifying goals, which in turn makes evaluation difficult. The task-centred approach sees the clarification of wants/goals as a crucial step in the assessment and helping processes.

Problem classification

The next step in problem analysis is that of classification. This is particularly useful if, as is often the case, there is more than one problem. Reid (1978) classifies problems into eight types:

1 *Interpersonal conflict*: interactions with others are presenting difficulties; 'We don't get along'. The problem is in a relationship be it marital, parental, school or work conflict.
2 *Dissatisfaction with social relationships*: 'I am not assertive; I get picked on'. The problem here is more general, within the individual rather than between them and others.
3 *Problems with formal organisations*, such as housing, schools, hospitals and state benefits systems.
4 *Difficulty in role performance*, such as parent, spouse, worker or student.
5 *Problems with decisions*.
6 *Reactive emotional distress*, such as depression or anxiety resulting from a situation.
7 *Inadequate resources*, such as of money, food, work or housing.
8 *Others*, not included in the above, such as behavioural problems associated with addictive or compulsive patterns, substance abuse, crime and gambling.

In the assessment stage of task-centred work, it is also important to seek out how various problems are *interconnected*. This can arise in two ways. First, actual problems in different categories can be interconnected, such as drinking, unemployment and lack of money. Having identified these connections, the potential service user together with the social worker can consider which would be the most useful to tackle first as, in dealing with that problem, other problems may take care of themselves. The second way in which interconnectedness can arise is in the problems of different people, for example two parents where the problem of one is maintaining the problem of the other in each of their cases. We find that service users find it helpful to be given a scale, setting out the eight types in a way such that they can write in the problems and score them at the beginning of work and again at the end (Figure 8.2).

Next, there is an analysis of the *cause(s)* of the problem. This is where there is a major shift of thinking from earlier approaches to social work. In this approach there is no question of seeking out the original cause of a problem. Even where a prior event, for example

Problem	NIL	LOW	SOME	A LOT	SERIOUS
Interpersonal (Add some detail)					
Social relations					
Formal organisations					
Roles					
Decisions					
Emotional distress					
Resources					
Others					

Figure 8.2   Problem scale

a loss, is recognised as starting the problem, it is what the service user is making of that loss here and now that matters. The event cannot be changed, but the person can be helped to grieve, to accept the reality and to plan a new life without the lost person or status. Of problems, it is said that they simply happen. Rather than searching for complex 'original' causes, social workers look for *obstacles* that are contributing to *maintaining* the problem in existence by preventing its resolution. It is those *'causes' of the problem continuing to be* that really matter. The removal of these obstacles will allow the change to happen. The focus, therefore, is mainly on the here and now, with perhaps some attention to the recent past, because irrespective of the original cause that started the problem off, the cause that counts is the cause that is 'blocking' the resolution of the problem in the present. These are current things that the service user and worker can do something about – we can do nothing about changing history. It is important in this approach not to interpret service users' behaviour and explanations in terms of irrational behaviour, resistance or defence mechanisms. Doel and Marsh (1992) refer to this as 'shooting the reflective parrot' that sits on the shoulders of many social workers trained in essentially psychosocial approaches.

In a task-centred assessment, 'cause' equals *obstacle* preventing the problem from being moved. There are four main obstacles:

1 *The social system*. This could be the family, extended family, community, formal or informal networks, or society at large (as in the case of many oppressions). Here the task-centred approach is clearly saying that the cause of problems can be outside the individual. Where that is the case, to see it anywhere else would be unjustly to pathologise the service user. However, obstacles are frequently complex and can include both internal and external elements.

2 *Beliefs or constructs* about the world, life, self and the problem. Beliefs can be factual or evaluative, and their accuracy or consistency can be challenged.

3 *Emotions*, which are translated into beliefs about wants. For example 'What I want is lost or unobtainable' = depression; 'What I want is wrong' = guilt. Moving feelings to an explicit cognitive level makes them easier to deal with, since the underlying beliefs can be disputed. For example, a person feeling guilty about being sexually abused can be helped to see that it was not they who initiated the behaviour.

4 *Attempted solutions*, or actions being taken, that are making matters worse. There are three main types of attempted solution that can become obstacles:
   - Seeking utopian goals, or aiming too high, such as wanting children to be 'angels'.
   - Trying too hard to do what can only be spontaneous, for example trying to get to sleep or trying to get a stepchild to love you.
   - Seeking to change attitudes when the service user could settle for behaviour, or wanting someone to want something they do not want. Examples of these attempted solutions include challenging children for stomping up stairs because they do not think they should have to go to bed so early, or complaining that a child is not enthusiastic about going to school. In both cases not settling for the behaviour concerning going to bed and to school will turn a minor difficulty into a problem. If the 'attitude' were simply ignored, there would be a better chance that it would go away. Tasks can be designed to undo these unhelpful attempted solutions.

This assessment process in a task-centred approach checks out which of the main obstacles might be operating in any given situation – the social system, beliefs, emotions or attempted solutions, namely utopian-ism, trying too hard or changing attitudes. By this point, some analysis and ideas about what might be helpful in working towards the goal will be developing, and a working agreement begins to be formulated as the assessment proceeds to the next stage.

Task selection

The next step is task selection, working out with the potential service user which tasks could be attempted to bring about change. A wide range of tasks is usually developed and these are discussed, the social worker and potential service user collaboratively assessing which would be the most useful, which are within the potential service user's reper-toire and, if they are not immediately capable of being done, how much help, coaching and rehearsal the potential service user would need in order to be able to do them. If outside resources are needed, the assessment needs to consider what are they and who should get them.

In this step of the assessment process, decisions are made jointly with the potential service user, discussing the task options available and considering:

- the potential benefits of each;
- the work involved in carrying them out;
- any factors that may make a task difficult;
- what practice, rehearsal or guidance may be needed;
- the overall plan for carrying out the task;
- and how and when progress will be reviewed.

It is only at this stage, having made the above preliminary assess-ment, that tasks can be selected or set. The following are some of the options available in selecting tasks:

1 *Exploratory tasks.* These further examine the problem or challenge factual beliefs. A parent may say, 'My son is always disobedient', so the task could be to count up the occasions when he obeys or disobeys over the next week and set out to catch him being obedi-ent as much as possible, or at least once.
2 *Interventive tasks.* These are used to make a change or move towards solving the difficulty or meeting the want, such as parents going out together more. Attempting such intervention by way of experiment provides valuable evidence for the assessment.

3   Tasks can be *simple* (one action) or *complex* (several actions or parts). However, simple tasks are preferred in this approach.

4   *Single* (done by one individual) *or reciprocal tasks* (someone does something and another person reciprocates).

5   *Physical or mental tasks*. It is recommended that mental tasks be made as physical as possible, for example by making lists of one's ideas or observations.

6   *Incremental tasks*, beginning with small steps and then increasing in difficulty as the client gains in confidence and skill.

7   *Pretend tasks*, such as pretending that something has changed, for example a depression having lifted, noting the difference or seeing if someone else notices anything different.

8   *Reversal tasks*. These entail doing the opposite of what the service user has been doing to tackle the problem. These are especially recommended where the attempted solution is the main cause of the problem being stuck.

9   *Paradoxical tasks*. These may be considered where straightforward tasks have failed and where they can be preceded by a positive reframe of the problem. These ask the service user to not change or to make the problem worse, and, unlike any of the above tasks which are negotiated with the service user and which hope for compliance, these are not negotiated or discussed. The hope is for refusal, the intention here being that the service user will recoil from the injunction and thereby change.

Whichever tasks are chosen, they work better when a brief *time limit* is set. Reid (1992) found that goals and tasks without time limits were less effective; he suggests that when longer work is required it be broken down into short periods for task-work towards specific goals.

Task review

When reviewed, tasks provide useful information not only about the problem, but also about the most helpful way of addressing it, about the motivation and capacity of the service user and about the likely time and effort that will be required. The final step, therefore, is task review. If the tasks are carried out and some progress is found, the assessment is well on its way to completion; we already know what needs to be done – it is only a matter of estimating how long it will take to complete. If, however, the tasks are not done, or they have made no difference, we know that further analyses and changes are required. If the tasks are completed but ineffective, this is valuable information that will increase the likelihood that more effective tasks can, and will, be designed. So the step of task selection is retaken. If, however, the agreed tasks have not been carried out, a further set of issues need to be considered:

1 Has the service user a clear understanding of the task and its relevance?
2 Has the service user any adverse beliefs, such as thinking that the task has little value or that doing it will be frightening? Has s/he the necessary self-confidence to perform the tasks?
3 Does the service user have the necessary skill to perform the task completely and consistently? If not, how can this be acquired?
4 Does the service user have the necessary concrete resources to carry out the task? These may be money, accommodation or the support of friends.
5 Are there reinforcements necessary to encourage the service user in the persistent carrying out of the tasks? If so, from whom could they come?
6 Are the social worker's attitudes affecting the service user's performance? Does the service user's forgetfulness or anxiety annoy the social worker, or does his/her behaviours or attitudes make the social worker feel contemptuous in any way?

The task review will not only seek to discover any reasons for tasks not being carried out but will also include supportive discussion, especially of any beliefs and anxieties that may be impeding progress. This is followed by the planning of more appropriate tasks or rehearsal for their performance.

In summary, the following assessment questions arise from this map.

The service user
• Is this case a matter of a referral or an application?
• Is the service user's want attributed or acknowledged?
• What change is wanted by others, and is that a problem for the service user?
• What does the service user want to do about it?
• Does the service user want help to do that?
• What are the applicant's own wants?

Type of problem
• How can the problem(s) be classified?
• Is there any interconnectedness between problems?

Type of goal
- Is the want/goal specific?
- Is the goal achievable?
- What constraints make change difficult?
- What needs to change?
- How long will it take to reach the goal?
- Where, when, how often and with whom does the problem arise?
- What meaning does the problem have for the service user and others?

Analysis of 'cause'
- How is the problem maintained: by beliefs, emotions, the social system or attempted solutions?
- What are service user's beliefs about the situation and about the want?
- If the 'cause' is an attempted solution, is it seeking utopian goals, trying too hard or seeking attitudinal change?

Task selection
- What tasks will be required to make the necessary change?
- Will the service user be able to carry them out?
- What help or rehearsal will be needed to prepare for task implementation?
- What other resources will be needed?

On first reading, these questions may seem to be too obvious and simplistic but that is really their strength. It is all too easy to make assumptions and end up putting words into the mouths of service users; it is good practice to take nothing for granted and to ask all the 'fundamental' questions possible. Even where the nature of the problem is clear and specific, we still need to learn from service users how best to help them proceed in small steps towards their goals. Encouragement over small achievements and seeing them as a cause for optimism are vital elements in the 'coaching' process.

CASE EXAMPLE

A social services department received a complaint from neighbours that they could hear shouting, and what seemed like a child being hit coming from the K family's house.

The visiting social worker explained who she was and the purpose of the visit, making use of good engagement skills to gain access to the home despite some early hostility and fearfulness on the part of the Ks. The couple had been together for three years and there were two children, Sarah aged twelve and Jason aged three. Sarah was Mrs K's child from an earlier relationship, and Mrs K had lived alone with Sarah for several years. She had a low-paid, part-time job and struggled to pay her way, accumulating £4500 in debts. Mr K had not been aware of the debts until about 18 months previously when a court letter arrived. He had felt very angry and had started to drink more than usual, often on his own. He also had back trouble and had been unemployed for the past six months, which was getting him down. Mrs K also said she felt a bit depressed and that everything seemed to be falling apart. They agreed that there had been loud arguments; he was angry over the debts and she would respond that his drinking and attitude was making things worse. Over the past 18 months, they seemed to talk only when they rowed; he had hit her once (a 'slap on the face') and he had lost his patience with Sarah. They both said he had not hit Sarah but he had frightened her and made her cry. At one point, he had briefly left the family, returning for Jason's sake.

Given these data, the worker was able to establish that Mrs K wanted to be less depressed and more able to deal with the debts (her two main acknowledged wants), and she felt that Mr K should help her more in the home instead of just shouting about things. Mr K wanted his wife to be honest over the debts and to be more firm in dealing with Sarah (two 'attributed' problems), but he did acknowledge that he needed to watch his temper in order to avoid hitting anyone in the family. Both Mr and Mrs K, however, expressed feelings of hopelessness about the future in that debt, unemployment and health problems were seriously frustrating and heightening the risk of abuse and family break-up. This led to a vague acknowledgement that they needed some help or guidance of some sort. At this stage of the assessment, they could be said to have a mixture of attributed and acknowledged problems, some vague goals and many constraints. The social worker next showed them a 'problem scale' and, talking them through it, asked them to enter their problems and use ticks to show how serious they considered the issues to be. With some encouragement and advice, they produced the sheet shown in Figure 8.3.

This exercise helps to set out the situation in a non-blaming way so that, for example, Mr K was able to accept that drinking was at least a minor problem. The completion of the scale led to some discussion on the *interconnectedness* of the problems. Did the fighting make the

Problem	NIL	LOW	SOME	A LOT	SERIOUS
Interpersonal *Aggressive arguments*				X	
Social relations *Few friends*					X
Formal organisations *Courts*		X			
Roles *Budgeting*				X	
Decisions	X				
Emotional distress *Feeling depressed*			X		
Resources *Debts, no job*			X		
Others *Drinking* *Backache*		X		X	

Figure 8.3   Mr and Mrs K's completed problem sheet

depression worse? Did this affect their ability to tackle the debts better? Did the drinking make the rows and the debts worse, or were they causing it? Where would the most effective starting point be? At this point, they were not ready yet to face up to the problems of their relationship, their inability to talk things out or their lack of social life. They were, however, more clear that something needed to be done, and they were willing to have the worker see them again to plan some action together. Before leaving, the worker left two copies of the Want Sheet with them and suggested the *task* of completing their sheets separately and privately, then sharing them for discussion one evening when the children were in bed. A second visit was arranged for a week later.

As she departed, the worker began to consider what obstacles might be blocking this couple from satisfactory functioning:

1 *Beliefs*. As she had listened to their accounts, she had a sense that they believed they were each being blamed by the other, that they were caught for ever in growing debt and that they had lost any real hope of financial coping or of happiness. Mr K seemed to think that his back was permanently damaged, but he had not continued with medical check-ups. The social worker could gently discuss and question these beliefs with the family.

2 *Emotions*. The belief in the loss of prospects could explain the depression. Mrs K was also isolated in that there was little communication with Mr K, so she might have been feeling unloved and alone. This depression and sense of isolation could be addressed by examining the underlying beliefs.

3 *The social system*. Reduced welfare benefits and a shortage of employment were affecting the family, as was the lack of nursery school places in the area. It may be possible to act as advocate concerning these issues.

4 *Attempted solutions*. How had they gone about the debt issue? Was Mr K's drinking an attempted solution? There was no evidence of utopian thinking in the session. It would be useful to check what efforts, if any, Mr K had made to respond to his wife's depression. Attempts like 'cheer up' tend to make the other person feel worse! These questions could be explored at the next meeting and tasks could be negotiated to help counter any such attempted solutions.

In the next session, the social worker planned to use these questions to obtain a more in-depth assessment of their situation and review the task with them. By the end of the second meeting, the couple were clearly saying they wanted help in improving their relationship in terms of talking with each other and their children. Using incremental steps, Mr K decided he would visit his doctor about his back and both parents would attend for debt counselling. Additionally, they agreed to spend fifteen minutes talking, at least two nights a week, without the television on and when the children were in bed. This constitutes three simple tasks that would be monitored over four more sessions with the social worker, who by now was well placed to write a report on this family and the likely prospects of their being able to care safely for their children. The review element of the task-centred approach would provide further assessment should the tasks not be done or should they fail to bring about the service users' desired changes.

Advantages of a task-centred approach to assessments

Reid (1978) suggests that this approach is suitable for any specific, acknowledged psychosocial problem that is capable, with some help, of resolution by the service user's own action. It can serve 'as a basic approach for the majority of clients served by social workers' (p. 98). Used in full, as the sole method, its range is narrower than if it is used along with other approaches. For example, as well as engaging in tasks, victims of trauma and people in grief may need to talk at length to an understanding listener who can facilitate their self-expression. Given some creativity in developing appropriate tasks, this approach is suitable, therefore, for most potential service users who are capable of rational discussion, perhaps with the exception of those with existential problems, seeking for meaning and identity. These need time for a lengthy, 'searching and free-ranging self examination' (*ibid*., p. 99).

Various texts criticising the relevance of Eurocentric approaches to social work with black service users and their families (see, for example, Logan *et al.*, 1990; Devore and Schlesinger, 1991) find task-centred approaches less problematic than those in the maps described earlier. Logan *et al.*, (1990) maintain that this is because the task-centred approach acknowledges the person-environment interaction and the place or impact of the social system on the personal. It also respects the beliefs, values and perceptions of the service users and listens to their definitions of their problems and their concerns. In this approach, 'the problem' is always 'the problem as defined by the service user'.

This approach also encourages service users to select the problem they want to work on and engages them in task selection and review. Logan *et al.*, (1990) found that minority ethnic groups preferred this level of personal responsibility, as well as the action orientation of the task-centred approach. They add, however, that white workers need to concentrate on keeping a 'strength focus', assuming the existence of community and cultural strengths and seeking to locate them. The task review is clearly vital for checking cultural appropriateness and whether different world views are being overlooked. Issues such as language differences also need to be addressed. Staying with specifics reassures members of some minority ethnic groups who may feel threatened when a lack of specificity by social workers suggests that they are attempting to take over the person's whole life. Last, it clearly helps to develop service users' confidence in social workers if the latter show themselves willing to carry out their share of tasks, especially if they show themselves to be assertive brokers of services, actively helping to remove environmental barriers, locating information and conferring with other agencies and with those the service user considers relevant, such as community leaders. And, just as they review the efforts of the service user, social workers ought to review their own performance of tasks, what they have and have not done, and the reasons why. This accountability is assisted by the clear data display developed in the assessment process. In this way, the approach can be seen to be truly collaborative, empowering and taking into account the social dimension.

It will be clear that because this approach prefers to assess *during* intervention rather than before it, time and care must be spent in carrying out a useful assessment. However, because tasks will have been tried out, much more realistic practical information will be available. In a period of three weeks or so, a considerable number of trials/ experimental tasks can be completed, provided these are started at the end of the first meeting without waiting to plan the perfect action. In this way, service users have an opportunity to demonstrate their capacities as well as their needs and, together with the worker, gain a useful understanding of what is maintaining the problematic situation and what might be a helpful way of dealing with it. It is also our experience that this collaborative style, with its focus on actions rather than feelings, sets the scene for the mutual bridging of difference gaps in an unthreatening way. The tasks are set to attack the problem and they, and not the person as such, are the focus.

Disadvantages of a task-centred approach to assessments

In our view, there are few disadvantages of this approach if it is used rigorously, although its capacity for empowerment perhaps needs to be more explicit. In the case example above, the child is not directly empowered or involved; children should be heard and their views taken into account. Some social workers, believing the approach to be value-free and intrinsically non-oppressive, take this as read and make no further efforts to address issues of empowerment and anti-oppressive practice. The coaching role of the worker could be open to abuse, perhaps encouraging an overworked social worker to be overly directive. Like all other approaches, it needs to be accompanied by the values of anti-oppressive practice set out in Chapter 3. Additionally, the emphasis on simple tasks may give rise to concrete solutions that can obscure the advocacy role mentioned earlier.

Although, in theory, the approach should be ideal for group and community work, there are few examples of this happening. It may be that, like other approaches, it lends itself most easily to individual and family problems.

Outcomes

After years of research Reid and Epstein (1972) published several results showing a high degree of progress within limited time scales; for example, in a study of social work with children in their last year at school, 80 per cent of the children reported that their overall situation had changed for the better; 20 per cent reporting no change. However when independent assessors studied the files they reported evidence of improvement in only 21 per cent of cases, although in the opinion of other people involved with the children ('collaterals'), there was improvement in 60 per cent of the cases. Reid and Epstein provide example of work with families, where 72 per cent reported improvement in the main problem and 56 per cent said the problem was either better or no longer present; 45 per cent felt a lot better.

Similar results were obtained in Britain by Goldberg *et al*. (1985) in a study of the method's use in various settings. Of the clients who completed the series of sessions, most reported that they were pleased with the approach and that their problems had reduced. Sadly, perhaps due to the brevity of their training, workers decided that because there was no agreement about the target problem at the problem clarification stage the approach was unsuitable for one-third to a half of cases and there was no improvement for those out of touch with reality and those who lived life as a series of 'cliff-hanging' crises. They did not report what other approach was more useful for these service users.

Gorey, Thyer and Pawluck (1998) suggest that where the target for change involved a social dimension (such as some element of the environment or of a social structure) the task-centred approach did better than the cognitive-behavioural approach.

Summary

- The task-centred approach includes some behavioural ideas but it is mainly a cognitive approach.
- In the main, it views difficulties as temporary breakdowns in coping.

- It defines problems as unmet wants.
- It sees the 'causes' of problems as those *obstacles* that prevent resolution, that is in the four obstacles that maintain problems, namely beliefs, emotions, attempted solutions and the social system.
- Once obstacles are removed, people can work towards their wants mainly by their own efforts.
- It offers a unique problem classification and problem clarification process.
- Goals are reached by taking action, by performing tasks.
- Coaching in task selection and task preparation is central to the helping process.
- Time limits and task reviews aid motivation and promote optimism and empowerment.
- A sound assessment is best made after task analysis and task experimentation. The more time there is for this, the better.

9

The Navigator's Map: Solution-focused Approaches

This chapter presents the first of two theoretical maps which belong to the 'third wave' of social work theory. Unlike the approaches outlined in the previous three chapters it eschews pathology and problems. A solution-focused approach has some features in common with a task-centred approach in that it is largely a cognitive approach and frequently leads to tasks to be carried out by the service user. However, the focus is quite different. While task-centred approaches focus on understanding *problems* and seeking ways of removing or at least alleviating them, solution-focused work focuses on understanding *solutions*, maintaining that it is not necessary to understand a problem in order to understand its solution. Any link between the problem and the solution may be nominal. This approach begins at the end (the solution) and works back from there, rather like a navigator plotting a sea journey, pinpointing the destination first and then drawing a line back to the present position.

Solution-focused theory

This approach originates mainly from work developed at the Milwaukee Centre for Brief Therapy by Steve de Shazer and his colleagues. In a succession of publications over the past seventeen years, de Shazer (1985, 1988, 1991, 1994) set out the solution-focused approach, which can be described as postmodern and constructionist. His philosophy is largely based on the psychotherapeutic ideas of Milton Erickson (1959) and on the theories of language and meaning of Derrida (1973) and Wittgenstein (1980). This philosophy is set out more fully in Parton and O'Byrne (2000) and Milner and O'Byrne (2002). At its simplest its practitioners hold an unwavering belief in the capacity of service users to discover their own, workable solutions to their problems.

Examining in great detail 'what worked', de Shazer's team perfected a set of economical techniques that form the foundation of the approach. Many of the techniques will be familiar to social workers adopting different approaches but solution-focused workers use them to explore service users' futures, not to understand past events. Analysts have found that social constructionism best explains *how* these techniques are successful, so we can say the theory grew *out of* effective practice; the key to the renewed confidence in social work to impact on other levels of practice to which Lymbery (2000) refers. We can say the practice itself is atheoretical in that it uses the 'local knowledge' of service users (which is theoretically limitless) rather than depending on 'professional knowledge'. Thus it embraces one half of the evidence-based practice development, effectiveness, remaining cautious about the evidence-based practice which makes generalisations about the nature of people. It is deeply sceptical about the ability of the 'grand' modernist theories and explanations to deliver truth, holding to a plurality of truths, including those contained in the 'local' theories of service users. Therefore it avoids any form of diagnostic labelling and sees professional categorisation of people as disempowering. For example, the Finnish psychiatrists, Furman and Ahola (1992), reframe 'depression' as 'latent joy' and 'borderline personality disorder' as 'a search for a new direction in life'.

Instead it takes a *not knowing* stance towards people's problems, preferring to remain *curious* about people's stories and views, about their strengths and potential, about occasions when the problem was less, and about how that happened – curious about the seeds of solution. Rather than seeking to understand (based on some grand theory), it merely seeks more *helpful* 'misunderstandings'. There is a preoccupation with *difference*, with what was different when things were better and what needs to be different for them to be better again. It utilises each problem-free aspect of the person and engages in *problem-free talk*, engaging the person, rather than the problem. Indeed it sees the problem as outside the person, or perhaps as Thompson (1995) says, the person is *in* the problem. The person is not the problem, the *problem* is the problem. The social worker joins the person *against* the problem and thereby gets a different story. Therefore this approach seeks not to be pathology-based and thus its assessments are not based on identifying deficits. This is particularly so in the assessment of dangerousness, solution-focused workers finding it easier to assess safety, which is measurable, than risk, which resists quantification; in other words, it is easier to assess the presence or start of something – safety – than it is to assess the absence or cessation of something – risk.

This solution-focused approach seeks to find the seeds of solution in a service user's current repertoire, seeking those occasions or *exceptions*, however small or rare, when the problem is less acute in order to identify when and how that person is doing or thinking something different that alleviates the problem. This involves listening carefully to, and then *utilising*, what the person brings to the encounter, focusing on problem-free moments, constructing an envisaged future when the problem is no longer there, and getting a very detailed description from the service user of what will be different then and whether any of that is already beginning to happen. In partnership, both the service user and the social worker build a picture of a possible future without the problem. Talk (language) is seen as powerful enough to construct life; talk of life with the problem constructs a problem-laden life; talk of life without the problem constructs a problem-free life. Talking in detail of what will be happening, what people will be saying, what effect this will have on relationships, and so on, provides the *experience* of a glimpse of that life; that life then becomes a possibility and the person experiences a sense of personal agency in setting out to construct it. The new story can even include a changed or different self, especially an accountable self. Assessments that fix people's identities, conflating the person and the problem, are avoided as new possibilities become visible. From this assessment process, messages and tasks emerge for the service user to consider between sessions.

This approach thus has a view of assessment different from most others. Rather than assuming that information about a problem will help to find its solution, the assumption is that we can understand a solution without necessarily knowing a great deal about the problem. Searching for an understanding of a problem usually leads to a laundry list of deficits or negatives, whereas this approach says that what is needed is a list of positive strengths and *exceptions* to the problem. Lists of deficits often risk overwhelming both the service user and the social worker, engendering hopelessness and a tendency on the part of the social worker to use such expressions as 'unmotivated', 'resistant' or 'not ready to change'. In solution-focused assessments, 'resistance' is regarded as an inability on the part of the worker to recognise the service user's 'unique way of cooperating' and an indication that more careful listening needs to happen. For example, Iveson (1990) says that when people repeatedly shout about their complaints, or complain in other ways we find difficult to hear, they are invariably people who are not being heard. To hear them we must accept their language as rational and meaningful, even when it appears irrational, unreasonable or perverse. The solution-focused approach 'can be summed up as helping an unrecognised difference become a difference that makes a difference' (de Shazer, 1988).

As Durrant (1993) puts it, psychological assessment tends to assume that qualities are measurable entities, that there are 'normative' criteria for determining healthy functioning and that we need to identify deficit and fault before planning intervention. He contrasts this with the solution-focused approach, which assumes that the meaning of behaviour and emotion is relative and constructed, that psychological and emotional characteristics are partly a product of the observer's assessment and interpretation, that intervention need not be directly related to the problem, and that social workers should build on strengths rather than attempt to repair deficits. This approach therefore develops an apparently 'atheoretical, non-normative, client determined view' (Berg and Miller, 1992, p. 5) of difficulties in which change is regarded as constant and inevitable. As a result, it makes sense to find what bits of positive change are happening and to use them to develop a solution. If social workers do not look carefully for what the service user is doing when the problem is not happening, or is not perceived to be a problem, these exceptions will go unnoticed. The most striking example of this is the 'pre-session change' question. Because de Shazer's team believe that change is constant, that no problem, mood or behaviour happens all the time or to the same degree, new service users are asked what has changed since the appointment was arranged. The team found that a considerable proportion of people reported some change. By then asking 'How did you do that?' they quickly got a solution-focused assessment under way.

The exceptions can be very small indeed, as the following example shows. Helen's aftercare worker put a lot of effort into preparing her for independent living after many years in a children's home, but found, two years on, that Helen was depressed, tearful, unable to leave her flat unaccompanied, spending most of the day watching television or telephoning her worker and relatives with long tales of her misery, developing an eating disorder, on poor terms with her natural father and brother, and making heavy demands on the worker's time. Intensive psychodynamic-based work helping Helen to come to terms with the effects of her abusive past on her current functioning and behaviourally-based work on her fears of going out alone failed to effect any improvement. Taking a solution-focused approach, the worker discovered that Helen was free from sad and intrusive thoughts when she watched television programmes about the archaeology of

Roman Britain. Helen became animated when discussing her one interest and talked about her preferred future as an archaeologist. Rather than dismissing this as Utopian thinking, the social worker built on this exception. Helen began to read books about Roman history and then had to get on better terms with her father and brother as she wanted a lift to visit local museums to further her interest. She bought a book on Roman cookery during one such visit and tried out some of the recipes at home, thus developing a solution to her eating problems. Her 'depression' lifted considerably and three months later she applied for, and was accepted on, a distance-learning module of a university degree in Roman archaeology. She applied for a grant to pay for her studies, approached a charity for assistance with buying a computer, and paid off her debts so that she could change her telephone system to enable her to access the internet for her studies. In order to complete her module, she will have to attend a residential study weekend at a Roman site so she will soon have to find her solution to her inability to leave the flat alone. Her aftercare worker is feeling better too, as the work has become much more interesting for her.

Assumptions

The assumptions that underlie solution-focused thinking could be expressed as follows:

- Problems do not necessarily reflect a deficiency.
- The future is more significant than the past; an understanding of what will be happening when the problem is ended avoids the need to understand the cause of the problem.
- The explanation for events is they just happen; blame for what has happened is avoided but responsibility for what happens in the future is encouraged.
- Change is constant and inevitable – there are always exceptions.
- Meanings and changes are constructed by talk.
- Staying on the surface of the words is important in hearing what the service user is saying – looking beneath the surface is looking at one's own theory and thus finding what the worker expects to be there.
- Unless there is a goal that is salient to the service user there will only be confusion and drift – for a yacht without a destination port, no wind is a good wind.
- As long as the goal is legal and morally acceptable, no limits are put on service user aspirations for a joyous future.

Techniques

The main techniques are simple questions, the 'miracle question', scaled questions, coping questions and 'pessimistic' questions.

The *'miracle question'* is helpful in developing goals with people who are not sure what their goals are or who find it difficult to believe in a better future:

> Suppose to-night, while you are asleep, a miracle happened and the problems you have to-day are gone in a flash, but because you were asleep you don't know this has happened. What would be the first difference you would notice in the morning?

This is followed by gentle prompts about new behaviours, new attitudes and new relationships, followed by 'Is any little bit of this happening already, sometimes?' So the miracle question helps to get a picture of the future without the problem and the follow-up searches out small exceptions to the problem. When these are found the key question then is 'How did you do that?' This is not only a compliment but it presupposes personal agency and builds up possibilities of repeating what they are able to do at least once. With some small exceptions, a minimum of motivation and a little imagination, when we use constructive questions the possibilities are boundless and the potential service user can get ready for change without analysing the problem – the subject can 'describe what they want without having to concern themselves with the problem and without traditional assumptions that the solution has to be connected with understanding or eliminating the problem' (de Shazer, 1994, p. 273).

Scaled questions are used in a particular way in this approach. These questions can be directed at service users' estimations of the severity of their difficulty, at their level of confidence about reaching their goal or at their willingness to work hard to make progress. A scaled question is usually put like this: 'Suppose we had a scale of 0 to 10, with 0 being the "pits" and 10 being "there is no problem", where would you put yourself on that scale?' This scale is set up 'in such a way that all numbers are on the solution side' (de Shazer, 1994, p. 104), but it is impossible to be sure about what any number really means, even for the service user. They and we know that 5 is better than 4 and less good than 6, so answers provide a way of grading progress – or its lack – for both social worker and service user. But, more importantly, scaled questions and their answers help to make concrete what is not concrete, making it easy to describe what is hard to describe.

Numbers get their meaning from the scale to which they belong; they are content free in so far as only the subject has any idea what they mean. But when we ask 'How will life be different when you move from 5 to 6?' and 'What will important people in your life notice that is different?', these future-orientated questions help the service user to begin constructing progressive change. Scaled questions also make it much easier for a service user to talk about behaviour which either embarrasses them or reminds them of failure and censure. For example, fourteen-year-old Jade had been told at every school exclusion meeting that her aggressive behaviour was unacceptable, to which she reacted in a sullen manner, but she could describe her efforts to control her temper through scaling:

> I've only got to four or five (she had hoped to get to six during the summer holidays) and I'm worried it'll go down to one or two when I start back at school. But it's better than it was. I was minus five at middle school!

In discussing a problem such as depression, scaled questions help us to get away from the idea that one is either depressed or not, as if depression had an 'on–off' switch. Suppose a worker asked, 'So if 0 is how depressed you were when you asked for help and 10 is when you will be unaware of any depressing feelings, where are you now?', any reply above 0 would indicate that the depression was less bothersome now and that things are already moving towards the goal (de Shazer, 1994).

Kral (1989) produced an assessment device, the 'solution identification scale' (S-Id), to aid this process (see Parton and O'Byrne, 2000). Referrers are asked to score 39 different strengths as not at all, just a little, pretty much and very much, examples of strengths being such details as 'sleeps OK', 'is happy', 'is considerate', 'tells the truth' and 'shows honesty'. While this helps to focus attention on strengths, and allows weaknesses to be acknowledged, it also ensures that progress is not ignored, thus providing a better chance that the location of steps towards solutions can be found. It has the added advantage that it can be completed by potential service users as well as referrers, giving tangible evidence of a partnership approach. Kral also suggests four basic questions at the initial assessment stage:

1 To estimate self-concept, he asks 'Think about the best person you could be and give that person 100 points. Now tell me how many points you would give yourself these days'. Most people without

serious problems give themselves between 70 and 85. If a service user says, for example, 60, this would influence the second question.

2   'On a scale of 1 to 10, how much are you satisfied with your score of 60?' If highly satisfied, the person is not considered likely to be a good 'customer' (a term that will be explained shortly).

3   'When you move from 60 to 70, what will be different that will tell you that things have changed?' or 'Have you been at 70 before and if so what was happening then?' or 'What is the highest you have ever been and what was going on then?' Although these variations of the same question ask nothing about the problem, they open the door to finding exceptions, in which will lie the seeds of solutions. They also clarify for the service user what change is within his/her control.

4   'What are the chances, on a scale of 1 to 10, that you could do that again?' This question hints that the person should make such a change, thus helping to estimate commitment and pave the way for a task assignment.

Clearly, these questions have nothing to do with why the problem is happening. They are about goals, where people are positioned in their situations and what the service user is doing that is different when there is less of a problem or no problem. They are about 'putting difference to work' (de Shazer, 1991): the questions explore what is different when the problem is not happening.

A distinction can be made between problems and unhappy situations. 'Problems' relate to patterns of behaviour, attitudes, beliefs and moods; 'unhappy situations' relate to losses (for example, loss of work, of a person, or a resource) and to environmental events (for example, the weather). While there are solutions to problems, many unhappy situations have to be coped with. In their case, *coping questions* are important, such as, *How do you manage to get by? Are there times when you can cope better? What helps?*

Meeting agency requirements and service user needs

de Shazer acknowledges that social workers have several roles to play, mainly those of social controller, mobiliser of external resources and therapist. He stresses that, although social workers will be in one role or another at different times during their involvement with a service user, social workers rarely clarify this either to themselves or to the service user. He suggests that, in order to remind themselves and service users, social workers should ideally have two rooms or at least two chairs and move from one to the other as the work changes. The work carried out in the first chair is related to social control – work with unwilling people; it may involve data collection, completing agency assessment schedules. However, meeting the needs of the agency at the same time as the needs of the service user is also made easier through a recognition that social work referrals fall into three categories, requiring different sorts of questions to accommodate the goals of the agency, the family and any individual service user. de Shazer identifies service users as customers, complainants or visitors.

A *customer* is a person who acknowledges the need to make some personal change and who wants to be helped. In these instances the work is usually straightforward, falling into the needs-led assessment format. The second category, a *complainant* is rather more complex, involving as it does a person who wants the social worker to change someone else but does not wish him/herself to change. The complainant often has a vested interest in the problem being located in the complained-about person so they are given an observation task to help them join forces with the complained-about person against the problem. Asking complainants to do more observation, but with exceptions noted also, builds on their strengths – they are good at observing – and provides an opportunity for them to become customers. For example school teachers of disruptive pupils will have many complaints about a potential service user, and these concerns should be listened to and taken seriously if one is to engage the teacher in a way that will be helpful. We can, however, change the information we collect by asking teachers to help in the development of a solution by listing, in detail, those times when the pupil is or was doing *better* in class. Examples of times might include 'When she sits with a certain person' or 'When she is reminded to write down her homework'. How social workers and service users 'see' situations is crucial in a solution-focused approach. Once we 'see' a pupil as 'troublesome', we see only trouble, so we need to consider in what ways s/he is not troublesome, and we also need to consider what difference it will make when the pupil sees him/herself differently and is not seen to be troublesome. This involves an explicit awareness that we and referrers can suffer from 'delusions of certainty' and 'a hardening of the assumptions' (O'Hanlon, 1989, personal communication) in the sense that people tend to see what they believe or expect. Similarly, parents who complain about their children's behaviour are carefully listened to, but they are encouraged to identify exceptions/strengths by asking them what makes them proud of their child.

A *'visitor'* is a person who is neither a customer nor a complainant but is visited by, or visits, the social worker because there is no choice; for example, where contact is mandated by statute, a parent or another person in authority. In the case of visitors, it is essential to clarify, as one does with 'referrals' in a task-centred approach, that while the social worker may have a controlling role, s/he is also willing to be helpful should the potential service user agree. This help could relate to getting rid of the statutory order, usually by developing those behaviours for which the order was intended. Scaled questions with wide boundaries are useful here to enable the visitor to take some responsibility for their behaviour without being totally condemned. For example, 'if 0 is Rosemary West and 100 is Mother Theresa, where on this scale would you put your mothering?' or 'if 0 is a teetotaller and 100 is drunk in the gutter everyday, where would you rate your drinking?' As no person is going to say either 0 or 100 in this example, *wherever* they locate themselves admits of some need to change or develop. Similarly where service users and social workers disagree about the possible levels of risk, a safety scaling question can be asked. For example, Geoff's partner left him after a series of physical assaults. This behaviour, combined with a childhood history of sexually abusing his sister meant that the social worker considered him too high a risk to be permitted contact with his eight-month-old son. His estimation of the risk he posed was considerably lower on the grounds that he had come to terms with his own experiences of sexual abuse and undertaken a sex offenders' course. He was asked what *he* would be doing differently that would convince a judge that his son would be safe with him. Safety approaches to child protection work are described in more detail in Chapter 11.

We now offer two flow diagrams (Figures 9.1 and 9.2) to show the process of a solution-focused assessment; the first in the initial meeting with a service user and the second in subsequent meetings. In this process, the boxed questions are central not only to assessment, but also to intervention. Like a task-centred approach, there is not really an assessment that precedes intervention as the two processes intertwine.

With 'customers' for whom a situation is vague, a 'formula' (or standard) first session (F1) task is given, asking service users to list all those things that are happening in their life that they want to continue to happen. By listing what does *not* need to change, this exercise helps the clarification of appropriate goals. Sometimes people are so overwhelmed by their problems that they say they want to change everything and, here, it is useful to ask them to 'take a step in a direction that will be good for them'. This helps them take a step

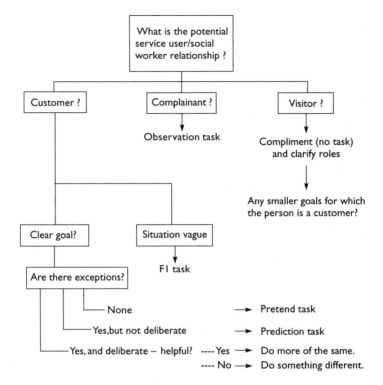

Figure 9.1   Solution-focused work – session I

towards taking responsibility for their futures and, thus, a step away from victimhood.

When a service user is unable to recall an exception, a pretend task is suggested, for example pretending to be not depressed one half of the week and noticing what is different or what other people see is different. This helps to develop and identify possible exceptions that make a difference to the problem.

Where exceptions are spontaneous or the result of other people's efforts, that is, not deliberate on the service user's part or seen as outside their control, service users can be asked to predict when spontaneous exceptions are going to happen. For example, a service user who compulsively steals could be asked to predict days when the urge to steal will or will not come. It has been found that service users can improve their ability to predict this correctly with practice and, of course, when they can get a high proportion of predictions correct, the question is 'Are the exceptions really spontaneous, or do you have some control?'

An alternative flow diagram has been developed (Wilgosh *et al.*, 1993) for second and subsequent sessions (Figure 9.2).

This diagram shows how progress, or the lack of it, is assessed in this approach and how changes, or the lack of them, are responded to. Where something is better, this is explored in detail, using the EARS process:

- Eliciting from the service user what exactly the changes are;
- Amplifying these changes by asking the service user what difference the changes made, who noticed the changes, what they saw that was different, and so on;
- Reinforcing the change by complimenting the service user; and
- Starting again, discussing any further changes that are reported by the service user and how s/he can 'do more of the same'.

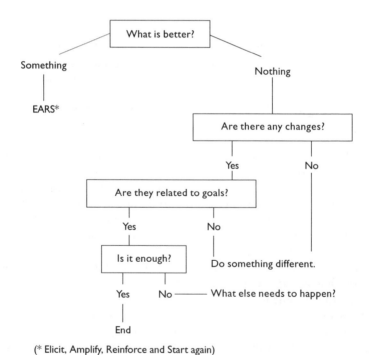

(* Elicit, Amplify, Reinforce and Start again)

Figure 9.2   Solution-focused work – session 2

Key features/considerations

1 *What does the person want?* What 'project' are they willing to engage in with us? By approaching them in a non-blaming, respectful way, highlighting strengths via compliments and what they do that is useful, most people will work towards what would be better for them (getting rid of a problem).
2 *What can the person do?* This is to be found in the exceptions and in the part of the goal that is already happening.
3 *What else needs to happen to get to the goal?* To make life safe enough? To remove someone's concern? Make coping better?

Solution-focused reports, then, address the following points:

• State the difficulty without analysis; state the service user's ideas about it and their rating of severity. Include your rating or that of other reports if necessary.
• What is okay – strengths and abilities?
• Is it a 'problem' or an 'unhappy situation'? If the latter, how is it being coped with on a scale of 0 to 10 (service user's rating, with perhaps your comment).
• Is the person a visitor, complainant or customer?
• What do they want? Clear picture of the goal? Or of what they think others (for example, parents) want of them. Their view and your view of what is needed (or needs to happen).
• What can they do (related to the want)? Is it spontaneous or deliberate? Is it helpful or not?
• What else needs to happen (be done)? (Their view and that of significant others).
• Their level of motivation? (after some work on solution construction).
• Their level of confidence in their ability, their chance of being able to do what is required?
• Risk? The balance between signs of safety and signs of danger.

Not all agencies understand the underlying assumptions or appreciate this new type of assessment. If the agency has a set format, we suggest you fit the information into it as far as possible. Where this is not possible, do a solution-focused assessment as well, for your own use, ensuring that the service user's focus and capacity for self-agency gets sufficient attention. Sometimes one worker can do the agency-required assessment and the worker who takes on the intervention does a solution-focused assessment as they work with the service user on solution-focused lines where the assessment becomes part of the solution (see Parton and O'Byrne, 2000, and Milner and O'Byrne, 2002). An example of how solution-focused feedback notes for service users can be written in a format which is appropriate for agencies where records are open is given below:

> Jack, 33 years old, referred himself to a domestic violence programme following a serious assault on his partner. He is facing a charge of GBH and is the subject of a court order barring him from approaching the family home. His eldest daughter, who witnessed the assault, does not wish to see him but he has regular contact with the two younger children (he looks after them at weekends while his partner is working). The 'hand over' of the children takes place at the garden gate and he has brief conversations with his partner at these times. The following notes describe the first session, much of which was taken up with listening to his 'side' of the story. Note that his words are used, rather than being 'translated' into social work language, and *what* he does (the very few exceptions) are separated from how he *does* these. His strengths are vague but potentially foundations for solutions. The format is designed to increase the possibility of progress, so as to give change a chance before an assessment is finalised.

PROBLEM

> Jack has a problem with his temper. Temper works on him in different ways; like when he is hurt by his partner's, and her sister's, comments; when his brother winds him up; when people threaten him in pubs. All these situations are made worse by him not being able to argue. He would prefer an easier life and to get back with his wife.

EXCEPTIONS/PROGRESS

> 1 Jack used to be a heavy drinker but now he only drinks two or more cans a night. He still sleeps all right.
> 2 He is concerned about his brother's drinking and tries to advise him on this.
> 3 Since he split up from his partner, he has done a lot of thinking about his behaviour and is beginning to take responsibility for his actions (even though he feels very provoked, he knows it is not right to hit women).
> 4 Before, he used to do stuff and think afterwards but now he thinks what it will do to people.

5 Jack has as much consideration as he has temper. He is thoughtful with his partner and does things to please her. He has always helped in the home and been a caring father to the children.
6 He resisted a wind-up when he met his sister-in-law in a night club last week.
7 He felt like hitting his brother last week but he didn't do this.

THOUGHTS ON SOLUTIONS

1 Jack did stop drinking by realising that it is no good, changing to a less strong drink, and cutting down.
2 Even though Jack has a problem with his temper, he can still act respectfully in many situations. He appreciates that his wife has a right to be upset, respects her opinion, trusts her, can be honest, realises that he has no right to use violence to get his own way, challenges attitudes that support violence, and can resist taking drugs. He is also beginning to listen to his partner without interrupting, remember that it is all right to *feel* anger but not *do* anger, ask for what he wants politely, and has plans to promote a violence-free relationship.
3 His plans to promote a violence-free relationship include: waiting for her to calm down when she's upset and going back to his flat when he feels put down. If he notices angry words starting he has a plan to prevent them. He can do this with his partner, his flat mate, and his brother but he hasn't started using any of them in other social situations yet (like the pub). This will be hard because he has been taught to hit back.
4 Although Jack can walk away from wind-ups and not hit, this is difficult for him because he doesn't want people to think he is an easy touch. Sometimes he has to fight to keep his reputation. Violence has advantages for Jack as well as disadvantages. We will have to think how to keep the former but lose the latter.

HOMEWORK

1 More of the same when he talks to his wife as this is working.
2 Jack could give some thought to how he can help his brother cut down his drinking in a different way (giving him advice or hitting him isn't working at the moment).
3 He might like to think what he needs to do differently so that his oldest girl will want to see him again.

AFTERTHOUGHTS

I   [Project worker's name] did wonder how often Jack has to fight to keep his reputation? Is it more or less than it used to be? Also, she forgot to ask him what an easier life will look like. Will it be about getting his own way? About making the people in his life happy and safe? Or a bit of both? Maybe Jack can explain this a bit more next time.

Advantages of a solution-focused approach to assessments

Solution-focused approaches have a very wide application, their main advantage being the emphasis on listening to the service user's story and focusing on exceptions, which is both anti-oppressive and empowering, seeking solutions within the user's life rather than in the worker's head. It is an economical way of working and is not only the least intrusive approach but also the most painless in that it takes the easiest route to finding solutions; Jack, for example, was violence-free and reunited with his family after six sessions, despite the very slow start. Additionally, the way in which service users' situations are framed to emphasise gains reduces risk in practice and increases creativity.

Disadvantages of a solution-focused approach to assessments

We find it difficult to think of any major disadvantages, although some older people who are very muddled in their thinking are not usually able to answer scaled questions. The approach is intrinsically anti-oppressive because of its central emphasis on empowerment, respectful uncertainty and minimum intervention, but feminists have argued that the emphasis on competence and strengths tends to overlook gender and power differences (Dermer *et al.*, 1998). Gender differences are discussed by several solution-focused writer/practitioners (see, for example, Letham, 1994; Berg and Reuss, 1998; Dolan, 1998; and Milner, 2001); the main implication is that tracking the service user's language does runs the risk of ignoring the reality that much language is constructed by men and does not always allow for a full understanding of women's experience.

Because the approach involves a complete change of emphasis from those traditionally used by social workers there is a danger that the technique might be too hastily applied or used inappropriately or uncritically, neglecting the philosophical basis. It is essential for social workers hoping to employ the approach to get into the habit of reframing situations and listening carefully to service users. Although the approach creates a good flow to the work, it still requires careful analysis. Using it well is not as easy as it sounds. The notion of understanding a solution without understanding the problem could be misread for finding a solution before knowing anything about a problem. If this latter reading were taken out of context, it could result in muddled work in which people are not sure what they are doing or why they are doing it. Properly understood, however, solution-focused theory is not saying this. The problem is not ignored but it is not necessarily deconstructed in the traditional way. However, courts and agencies, long accustomed to traditional assessments based on theories of pathology, will take some time to get used to this way of thinking.

Outcomes

Solution-focused approaches have been evaluated more extensively than problem-based approaches; there are over thirty outcome studies that demonstrate the effectiveness of this approach, a selection of which are listed in Parton and O'Byrne (2000) and Milner and O'Byrne (2002). These studies show that the effects are not only as good or better than any other known method, but they are as long-lasting. An interesting aspect of these studies is that they show no difference according to client group, ethnicity, age or gender. The approach has been shown to work equally well with anorexia, violence, drug abuse and mental health problems, regardless of learning ability. In one of de Shazer's studies (1991), when clients were followed up again 18 months after completion, their reported success rate was up from 80.4 per cent to 84 per cent after an average of 4.6 sessions. In another study, the success rate at six months was 80 per cent, at 12 months, 81.5 per cent; at 18 months – 86 per cent. It seems that when people realise that they have personal agency and can change their lives, they go on making things better. These studies were based on service users' evaluations of whether they had reached their goal.

Summary

- There are three types of service user: visitors, complainants and customers. Assessing which type each service user belongs to and to treating them accordingly enables the social worker to recognise multiple and/or competing goals.

- de Shazer holds that problems simply happen and that it is not necessary to understand the problem in order to develop the solution; solutions can be constructed without deconstructing problems. Listening to service users needs to change. Social workers do not need to know about cause or pathology; they need to listen for strengths, possibilities and the seeds of solutions.

- The person is not the problem; the problem is the problem, thus the approach avoids pathologising service users.

- The seeds of, or clues to, solutions are in the exceptions to the problem. There are always exceptions; if the person cannot believe this, s/he can be helped to see exceptions by pretend tasks and 'problem-free' talk.

- There is a strong future focus. Talking about 'life after the problem' constructs a future without the problem.

- The approach offers three 'rules': if it ain't broke don't fix it, if something works do more of it, and if something doesn't work do something different.

- Searching for difference is valuable; that is, what is the person doing that is different when the problem is less of a problem?

- The approach makes us clearer about empowerment by mobilising service users' resources and responsibilities.

- Risk assessment shifts to building signs of safety.

- Intervention does not wait until the assessment is complete – they work together, at least in the early stages.

- The approach builds personal agency and responsibility.

10

A Forecast Map: Narrative Approaches

This chapter presents the second of the theoretical maps belonging to the 'third wave' of social practice; like the previous chapter it is more interested in service users' futures than pasts, in potential rather than pathology. As the term 'narrative' implies, the approach provides options for the telling and retelling of service users' stories of their lives (developing alternative stories) but the term has been developed further than the storytelling involved in psychodynamic or cognitive behavioural approaches. Narrative approaches share the solution-focused notion that there are no fixed truths but, additionally, emphasise that some 'truths' have more weight than others. Hence the intention of narrative assessments to take into consideration the 'climate' of social work, addressing power issues explicitly through the deconstruction of dominant cultural stories which have the capacity to marginalise and oppress service users. Building on the service user's own metaphors, it develops a 'forecast' that adds in all those 'sunny spells' that are often edited out when problem stories are told or written, without ignoring the 'highs' / 'lows' of oppression by powerful narratives.

A narrative approach challenges people's beliefs that a problem speaks their identity; a totalising effect which conflates the person with the problem. In seeking to separate the person and the problem, thereby developing a sense of incongruity between the two, this approach opens up new possibilities for responsibility taking and accountability. Traditional psychotherapeutic concepts are reconstructed in narrative approaches: interpretation is how service users can make meaning of their lives rather than be entered into stories by others. Resistance is the way in which they can resist the influence of the problem on their lives.

Narrative theory

The approach was developed mainly in Australasia by White (1988, 1993, 1995, 1996; White and Epston, 1990; and Epston, 1998). It is

153

more political and social than other approaches, being based on the sociology of the postmodernist Foucault (1972, 1973, 1980, 1988) and the sociolinguist Halliday (1978) concerning the oppressive effects of dominant narratives on people's understanding of the validity of their ways of living. White (1995) argues that there isn't a single story of life which is free of ambiguity and contradiction and that can handle all the contingencies of life. These ambiguities, contradictions and contingencies stretch our meaning-making resources, especially when there are dominant cultural stories about particular sorts of behaviour. These stories tend to concentrate on identifying the behaviours seen as desirable by the most powerful groups of people, thus people whose behaviour does not conform to this become storied as deficient in some way. White refers to this as being entered into a story, a story which people come to believe about themselves:

> these stories or narratives form the matrix of concepts and beliefs by which we understand our lives, and the world in which our lives take place; and there is a continuing interaction between the stories we tell ourselves about our lives, the ways we live our lives, and the future stories we then tell. (Payne, 2000, p. 20).

Whereas solution-focused assessments search for exceptions to problems and, therefore, concentrate on problem-free talk, in narrative assessments the problem is first deconstructed. This takes the form of searching for *unique outcomes* – times when the service user actively resisted the influence of the problem, a contradiction to the dominant story, or plot in Epston's terms (1998, p. 11). Deconstructing the problem is done by reflecting with service users how they came to be recruited into a *problem-saturated story*. This includes discussing that story in a way that separates the problem from the person, developing a sense of alienation between the person and the problem. This *externalising* conversation is helped by giving the problem a name of its own and by asking questions that establish the influence of the problem on the person, and their influence on it. This can be seen as discussing the *person's relationship with the problem*. The service user, having been invited to explore the effects of the problem; for example, 'it causes arguments' or 'it means I might lose my kids', is then asked if that is something they want in their lives or not (an evaluation of the problem or their relationship with it). If they do not want it, they are asked to justify that evaluation by explaining, for example, reasons for not wanting it, and what it that says about them as people. In this way they make a decision to start reclaiming their life from the influence of the problem and this clearly makes for a promising assessment.

White (1996) states very clearly that while the alternative narrative offered may be seen as part of radical constructionism he does not accept that 'anything goes' simply by giving it a new name. Because narrative is constitutive of people's lives, shaping and structuring them, we must be accountable to those we seek or assess or help. Not all stories are equally good in their effects. And not only do service users enter themselves into stories but so do social workers; consider, for example, stories about natural mother love that led to charges of over-optimism in child protection assessments. Payne (2000) discusses the implications for social workers of deconstructing their own stories. While he acknowledges that racism and patriarchy are cultural beliefs rejected by most social workers, he reminds us of the need for constant vigilance against the more subtle manifestations of these stories; for example, the way sexism may be demonstrated through verbal tone and the dominance of conversations. This is particularly problematic for male social workers as they live in a culture in which such attitudes are embedded; for example, a man attending our domestic violence programme told us that his male probation officer cut across his telling of his marital difficulties by challenging the service user's use of the term 'bird' to describe his partner: 'listen to you! Bird!' No doubt the probation officer believed that he was challenging the service user's sexism but, at the same time, he was demonstrating his own capacity for it. Jenkins (1996) refers to this as the danger of acting from a position of self-righteousness and moral superiority. In narrative assessments, therefore, critical self-monitoring and regular checking out with other people is essential (as we discussed more fully in Chapter 3).

Jenkins argues that there is only a fine line between responsible assessment and intervention, and therapeutic abuse: 'I work hard at establishing a context for a client to own his own "discoveries" and do not see myself as the architect of his new thinking and behaviour. Yet, all the same time, I am acting strategically and intervening towards this end. Is this really self-enhancement?' (1996, p. 129). He advises being mindful at all times of the risk of insensitively pursuing our own agendas at the expense of service user experience, and this is particularly complicated where social workers are impelled by agency-led assessment requirements. Payne (2000) also addresses the ethics of externalisation, concluding that the process is transparent as the service user can hear exactly what the worker is saying. Nevertheless, in deconstructing and reconstructing stories, social workers need to be aware that the choice of questions asked is influential on the way the assessment is focused and differences in values, beliefs and meanings between the service user and social worker require explicit attention (Milner, 2001).

Strand (1997) suggests that externalising the problem and its internalised narrative in an attempt to unmask the relationship between self and hidden political realities requires advanced conceptual understanding, whereas a solution-focused approach only demands a rethink of the definition of one concept – the problem – without concern for its effects on self-definition. This, he thinks, makes narrative approaches unsuitable for people of limited intellectual ability. We have not found this to be the case. Indeed, the similarities between narrative and solution-focused approaches in terms of their theoretical base, particularly the relevance of social constructionism, means that the approaches can be combined in assessments.

For a helpful account of this approach we recommend Gilligan and Price (1993) which presents the de Shazer and the White approaches as different, and opposing in some ways, giving a particularly clear analysis of the White approach. O'Hanlon (see, for example, O'Hanlon and Beadle, 1994) has also combined the American and Australasian approaches in a creative fashion which stresses the importance of language. In his view, language can easily make difficulties sound, and become, fixed. His aim is to reconnect people's sense of possibility and hope when things seem unchangeable. He is concerned about the danger of 'iatrogenic inquiry' whereby problems are caused, or worsened, by an assessment or attempted intervention. He stresses the importance of avoiding negative assessments 'that discourage, invalidate, show disrespect or close down possibilities for change' (O'Hanlon and Beadle, 1994, p. 10) and maintains that, since service users are experts in their own lives, we need to check our work with them as we might with another professional. Included in this approach is Milton Erickson's principle of *utilisation*, considering carefully how a social worker can identify and use fully the strengths, exceptions, or unique outcomes that the service user brings to the assessment. Like White, O'Hanlon holds service users accountable for behaviour that impacts on others but this is about accepting responsibility for future behaviour, not blaming, looking for bad intention or suggesting that service users are bad people. People are presumed to be resourceful enough to deal with changing; the social work task is to connect them with their, often unrecognised, resources and join with them in locating these and any other resources they may need, whether external, personal, interpersonal or spiritual – in a word, possibilities. Milner (2001) offers a combined approach which specifically addresses gender differences in both assessment and intervention in social work in the UK. Jacob (2001) demonstrates how the approaches can be combined in work with people with eating difficulties.

The techniques

Narrative approaches to assessment tend to be more fluid and wide-ranging than solution focused ones. The service users' alternative stories are developed via the techniques of *externalising the problem, externalising internalised narratives* which support dominant stories or plots about the problem, *thickening the counterplot* to strengthen the alternative story, and the provision of *narrative feedback*. As all these techniques reveal and increase unique outcomes, they are not necessarily used sequentially, there being much more overlap than there is in the more structured format of a solution-focused assessment.

Central to *externalising* is how people have come to believe that they are the problem; separating the two via externalising conversations is an effective way of identifying unique outcomes (White, 1990, p. 95). These unique outcomes include not only when the service user actively resisted the influence of the problem, but also ways in which they subverted it, endured it, or delayed its effects. In order to encourage a service user to have a different relationship with both the problem and the narrative that supports it, early on in the assessment the problem is spoken of as an external enemy oppressing the person. This aids the non-pathologising of the service user; it is the problem that is the problem. Externalising conversations help the service user to stand back from the problem and recover a sense of self-agency as they separate themselves from their own subjugation and begin to resist the influences that recruited them or that invited the problem into their lives.

To aid separation of person and problem it helps to give the problem a name as soon as possible, using the service user's own narrative metaphors. Often the service user can suggest a richly descriptive name for the problem; for example, we have experienced 'temper' named as Total Upset, Fiery Red Bomb, Black Cloud, and Raging Bull. Equally common is a more anonymous naming, such as 'It'. In naming the problem, service users then find it easier to describe the influence of the problem on their lives. For example, Zaffir was so crippled with anxiety following an unprovoked assault on the street that he was unable to go to school. The assessing social worker's initial name for the problem was thus 'anxious non-school attendance' or 'school phobia'. Zaffir talked at length about his anxieties about the possibility of a further assault but, once he had named these anxieties as Sad Fear, he was able to recognise the influence of Sad Fear on all aspects of his life. It was making him tearful, stopping him eating or keeping himself smart, and ruining his hopes of getting an education. He did not want to keep Sad Fear in his life and the one unique outcome he could identify was when he had 'talked back' to a voice in his head that told him to be 'more scared'. Through this externalising conversation he was able to extend his unique outcomes by telling the voice to go away if it couldn't come up with something new to say or swear at it in Punjabi. Thus there was no need to assess possible depths of anxiety or label him as a problem.

Externalising conversations are particularly useful in the assessment of service users who hear voices. Instead of assessing for the possible presence of auditory hallucinations or delusions, the social worker interrogates 'voices' as unhelpful beliefs which can be resisted or subverted. For example, Jacob (2001, p. 70) provides a set of cartoons depicting 'Monster Bashing Methods' for thoughts and beliefs underpinning eating difficulties. White (1995) suggests that it is helpful to question the purposes and motives of the 'voices'; for example, 'are these voices *for* you having an opinion or are they *against* you? These voices throw you into confusion, whose interests are best served by this confusion? What is it like for the voices to have to listen to your thoughts for a change?' And, later, 'what is it like for them to know that you are developing a disrespect and mistrust of them?' Thus a narrative approach is very different from traditional approaches to the assessment of mental health states.

Less specific questions which not only elicit unique outcomes but also aid goal setting include:

- How did the problem seduce you into thinking that way, or going along with it?
- What influences led to your enslavement by the problem?
- What prevented you from resisting it? What were the restraints?
- Does it really suit you to be dominated by it?
- What effect or influence does the problem have on your life, or on those close to you, on your relationships, self image?
- What effect do you have on the life of the problem?
- Given a choice between life with the problem and life free of the problem, which would you choose?
- (When the problem has been named), tell me about the times you made Anxiety wait. How long has Temper been making your life miserable? Tell me about a time you didn't fall for the story Anorexia has been telling you?
- (When there are unique outcomes), what are the implications for the sort of person you are when you refuse to cooperate with the problem's invitations?
- What does it say about your ability to undermine the problem?

Note that these last two questions are reflecting on the qualities of the person rather than on their actions. White refers to this as adding to the *landscape of consciousness/identity*, enriching a possible alternative story through a *language of action*. The language is the language of resistance and liberation and it is used to understand how the service user submitted to the problem's ways and how these ways are not liberating, or ideally suited to the service user's preferred way of living. This involves looking back at the past to some extent, before going on to becoming future- and solution-focused, but it is not a blaming look at the past or a search for deficits. It is empowering in that it develops a sense of the service user being intrinsically okay, as *not being* the problem, but as being oppressed by it and sometimes colluding with it. Thus the explanation that is developed is not one that seeks the cause of the problem in the person but one that seeks to understand how this, basically okay, person became ensnared by the problem's invitations.

Frequently part of that enslavement is caused by societal attitudes, such as attitudes that suggest that the consumption of alcohol is socially necessary or that women should be the main carers in families. More accurately, people are *restrained* in these ways from resisting the problem or from taking responsibility in various ways. A narrative style, storying the separate lives of the person and the problem, encourages a sense of ownership of one's life; a sense that the service user and social worker can co-author a future story, breaking away from the performance of the past unhelpful story and thus experiencing the capacity to create change. New narratives yield a new vocabulary and construct a new meaning, new possibilities and new self-agency. White (1996) has found that more service users than expected are able to re-author their lives and we cannot assess their capabilities to do so until we afford them the opportunities created by narrative promptings.

Externalising conversations thus aid the development of alternative stories and encourage the service user to take action against the problem. They emphasise context, deconstruct the objectification of people, and challenge dominant stories through which 'disorders' and 'pathologies' are constructed; what Epston refers to as 'spy-chiatric gaze' (1998, p. 127). Externalising conversations invite people to take up a position toward the problem and consider whether they want to continue living with it. In the case of violent or other oppressive behaviour on the part of a service user, accountability is not minimised; instead the beliefs and attitudes supporting the violence are externalised, *externalising the internalised story*, enabling other ways of responding to situations to be discovered. Here the work of Jenkins (1990, 1996) is particularly useful. He suggests that much male violence is supported by dominant stories about 'being a man' in which the need to 'be someone' is exaggerated and extreme. He invites men to take responsibility for their behaviour by asking questions which externalise this internalised story, the 'blueprint' of his marriage. The man is invited to externalise patriarchal restraints and consider their influence in his life and the extent to which he has slavishly and blindly followed a set of oppressive and unhelpful beliefs:

- If a man takes this recipe on board, what sort of marriage is he going to be building?
- Is he going to want his wife to be her own person with her own ideas or his person with his ideas?
- Is she more likely to respect him more if he tries to get her to be his person or if he allows her to be her own person?
- If she was just doing what she is told, would she be more likely to give love out of desire or out of duty? (Jenkins, 1990, p. 82).

Stephen, for example, explained his hitting his wife as a result of frustration with her unfair treatment of their three-year-old child. An argument would start between the adults when he came home tired from work and his wife would vent her frustration on the child. Stephen was extremely critical of her mothering, about which he had a clear set of beliefs – a dominant story about nurturing motherhood under all circumstances. When asked about his blueprint for being a husband and father, he said that it varied, depending on what he had seen on television. Sometimes he saw himself as a 'lad' and sometimes as a caring parent. As stories about how to be a father are not well developed in our society, he had only internalised the mothering half of his family story, supported by a dominant cultural story that said it was okay for men to tell women what to do.

It matters little what sort of blueprint people develop for living in their marriages as long as this story works equally well for both partners. Narrative questioning does not aim to push a particular story or suggest that a person is thinking distortedly; it aims only to assist a person to tell a different story if they discovered that 'habitual, significantly limiting discourses, derived from...history and from "assumed truths" in contemporary society, no longer made sense' (Payne, 2000, p. 59). Externalising the internalised story also differs from the insight-giving of psychodynamic approaches in that ways of interacting with others are not revealed as maladaptive attachment patterns. This is only another (psychological) story; one that has become embedded in contemporary stories about commitment and 'being there' for friends. We find that many young woman have internalised this story and then struggle with friendships which do not meet their expectations. They tell us that they think there is something wrong with themselves but, rather than assess them for deficencies in intimacy, we ask them questions about their story of friendship:

- What is the most important thing you get from your friends? Support when you are troubled? Having a laugh? Someone to go out with?
- Can all your friends do all these things?
- Can a person expect the same level of commitment from all their friends?
- Which friends are you closest to?
- What is the difference between your supportive and unsupportive friends?
- Are some of your friends emotionally supportive and others social friends?
- Perhaps there are different sorts of friends: silver, gold and platinum?

Similarly with women service users, and many social workers, we question stories about the all-nurturing nature of mothering:

- Who comes first in your family? Second? Third? (and so on)
- Does it feel comfortable always to be at the bottom?
- How can you put yourself a little higher without being selfish?
- Are your expectations of your mothering reasonable? Attainable?
- How much responsibility can a mother take for her family's behaviour?

Another totalising and restricting story we frequently interrogate is the story of 'low self esteem', one which is popular with both social workers and service users. Despite being affected at birth with mild cerebral palsy and then being sexually abused by a close relative, and subsequently rejected by her family, Susie managed to live independently as long as she had intensive support. Every time she appeared to be coping well and that support was reduced, she reverted to cutting her arms. A reassessment then focused on externalising the internalised story which told her she could not function without intensive support. She had entered herself into several contradictory stories;

her story of sexual abuse told her that she was worthless, her story of support provided her with feelings of self esteem but that she needed to work through her experiences of sexual abuse, and her disability story told her that she was a worthless cripple. Cutting herself was her form of resistance to feelings of worthlessness so the disability story was interrogated, questions focusing on 'where she belonged' – using her words. This enabled her to develop an alternative story of her life; one in which she would mix with other adults who had the capacity to make her feel good about herself.

The initial assessment is then checked out with the service user in two ways; by *evaluating the interview* and *the provision of written narrative feedback*. The former consists of simply asking the service user at the end of the interview if the session had been what they expected, whether or not it had been helpful, and whether they felt understood. The solution-focused question 'what would I have been doing differently if I had been more helpful?' is a useful one here. For example, Geoff said that he was quite satisfied because his previous experiences of social work intervention and specialist counselling during his period in care meant that he realised it would take a long time for him to come to terms with the pain of his previous experiences of sexual abuse. As he was being assessed for his dangerousness towards women (he had hit his partner several times) and his child (he had sexually abused his sister), his psychological story was not only unhelpful in that it provided him with an excuse for his behaviour, it also maintained him as a victim of circumstances, thus limiting his ability and willingness to take responsibility for his behaviour. Externalising this internalised story was, therefore, an essential element of a narrative assessment in Geoff's situation where time was particularly short in view of his child's needs.

It may be worth mentioning here that in child protection work this approach turns Finkelhor's theory upside-down (Trepper and Barrett, 1986). For Finkelhor, abuse happens when a perpetrator breaks through the 'blocks' of internal inhibitors, external inhibitors and child resistance. Therefore it is suggested that work needs to *strengthen* these blocks in order to prevent further abuse. The perpetrator has some deficit that makes an abuse of power possible and that makes stronger blocks necessary (deficits may be such as to limit responsibility). In the narrative approach however, the perpetrator is presumed to have started life 'okay' but his/her capacity for caring became *inhibited* by various factors that *restrained* caring and *invited* inappropriate self indulgence. The person is not 'damaged' and is held fully responsible for accepting the invitation. Therefore the worker's task is to *weaken* these invitations and restraints, to undermine them and to expose their lies, excuses, methods and thus their influence, so that caring is no longer inhibited and signs of safety can be built up.

Written *narrative feedback* differs from the more usual formal social work assessments which distance the social worker from the service user when the former becomes the expert author of the latter's life. White and Epston (1990) argue that such an author has a 'library of terms and descriptions that have been invented by and considered the property of this particular domain of knowledge' (p. 188). This 'expert' knowledge, combined with the invisibility of the author, creates the impression of possessing an objective and detached point of view that does not actually exist; it bolsters a view of the social worker as benevolent expert, with the moral assumptions implicit in their specialised narrative hidden by their construction of the subject. Permitting the service user to read such an assessment report does not allow them the scope to do more than disagree with factual errors; the meaning-making (interpretation) being the social worker's.

Narrative approaches challenge this view of recording by providing the service user with written feedback which uses their own words and explanations: what Epston (1998) considers to be the work of a con-scientious scribe: 'who faithfully notes down the proceedings for posterity and makes available a client's history, capturing on paper the particular thoughts and understandings with which they make sense of their lives'. (p. 96). This provides a check on the social worker's accuracy of perceptions, reduces power imbalances between the worker and service user, and encourages co-authorship. Epston writes long letters which include the metaphors people use to tell their stories and any unique outcomes, commenting on these as a means of expanding the externalising conversation. Letters need to be adapted to the reading and concentration levels of service users; for example, children with learning needs may need a pictorial record of any unique outcomes, whilst a card briefly summarising recent events is more appropriate for elderly people with memory difficulties (for a fuller discussion, see Milner, 2001). Letters are also unsuitable for most agency records, particularly where the assessment is risk-focused. We find that the format of written feedback described in the previous chapter is appropriate for both solution-focused and narrative approaches, as well as for agency records; see the following example of the copy of the agency notes sent to Geoff after the first assessment session. Here an 'afterthoughts' section was used to introduce an externalisation of Geoff's underdeveloped fathering story. This encouraged him to return for the second session in a cooperative frame of mind, anxious to discuss his proposed safety plan, and talk about how he could put his child's needs before his own needs for his partner to return to him:

Problem

Geoff does not feel good about himself at all. On a 'liking himself' scale he is somewhere near the bottom. This is partly because he has had a horrible life (being abused, getting put in care, not being allowed to go home where there are children, getting into drugs and other offending); at the moment it is mostly because Sharon has left him and taken Dean with her. Sharon has been having affairs and when she wouldn't talk about it, Geoff got frustrated and hit her pretty badly.

His wildest dream is to be living in a happy family with Sharon but it is not likely that she will come back. He would like to have contact with Dean.

Unique outcomes

1   Geoff is a truthful person who can face up to what has gone wrong in his life and take responsibility for it.
2   He managed to stop taking drugs after he met Sharon.
3   He has survived being sexually abused as a little kid and he doesn't abuse kids.
4   He can remember one time when he felt good about something he had done. This was when he was in prison and his cell mate was upset. He calmed him down and helped him talk it through. His cell mate wrote and thanked Geoff for his help.

Thoughts on solutions

1   Geoff shows he takes responsibility by the way he filled in the 'overcoming violence' chart. He didn't try to make out that he is better than he is and was very honest about hitting Sharon, not listening to her, putting her down, checking up on her, and stuff like that.
2   He survived being sexually abused by owning up to it, having counselling, and volunteering to go on a sex offenders' course. He feels that his experiences have made him more aware of it and less likely to harm a child.
3   Geoff knows that when he is helping other people, he feels better about himself.

Homework

1   Geoff will write to Sharon, through social services, and ask her to fill in the 'overcoming violence' chart for him so that he can see if her ideas about his behaviour are the same as his – or different.
2   He will do one small thing each day to help other people and see if this makes him feel better about himself.
3   He will work out a safety plan which will convince the judge that Dean would be completely safe if he is allowed contact.

Afterthoughts

[name of assessing worker] did think afterwards that she should have asked Geoff more about what he would be doing when he is in a happy family. Would he be working? Looking after Dean? Helping around the house? Doing the garden? Perhaps he could tell her more about his ideas for being a good family man next time they meet?

Note that, as in solution-focused approaches, tasks are set, although these often include invitations to continue externalising by asking the service user, for example, to think about their life as a video. They are asked whether they are the lead actor, director, script writer, and so on, and then asked to visualise the final scene, which depicts a satisfying life, before developing scenes to be 'shot' which develop a new plot. This is part of subsequent work where assessment and intervention overlap; what narrative workers call *thickening the counterplot*. Although 'thin' descriptions of life (that edit out unique outcomes in the old plot) often arise from a person having been subject to 'expert' diagnoses and commentaries and 'thick' descriptions are elicited by examining the service user's actuality and complexity of life (for a fuller discussion, see Payne, 2000, pp. 33–4), a problem-saturated story has mass and considerable evidence to support its momentum:

Problematic stories have an advantage. They've been around for a while. Their plot is thick [thick with deficits; thin on strengths]. Like a snowball, they have packed together certain incidents and episodes in the family's life, finally freezing them into a solid mass. The once innocent snowball becomes a force with which everyone has to reckon. These problem-saturated stories can become very pervasive. The trouble is that their effects are negative and discouraging. (Freeman *et al.*, 1997, pp. 94–5; our parentheses added)

Thus the alternative story, the counterplot, needs strengthening. Juxtaposing the plot and counterplot thins the plot and thickens the counterplot, and this is done in assessment by specific questioning:

- What kind of alternative story would be required if the service user/ family/social worker were to tell another version at odds with the problem's story?
- How might the service user/family/social worker look and act in an alternative story different from the way the problem's story told them to look and act?
- How might the anomalies, irregularities and strangenesses that lie outside the predictive reach of the problem's story be considered meaningful events in the life of the service user and powerful antidotes to the problem?

An additional way to thicken the counterplot when there is no-one in the service user's life to tell the new story to, is to use narrative metaphors which emerge in externalising conversations. These can be more complex than the simple 'naming' of the problem; for example, Pete had no particular name for his problem with temper and frustration, although he knew that these were worse when he had been drinking heavily. Paradoxically his unique outcomes occurred when he was responsible for controlling temper and frustration fuelled by drink in others; when he worked as a nightclub bouncer and as a barman he could 'see things from the other side' and be different. 'Turning to the other side' emerged as a metaphor which strengthened his counterplot, enabling him to incorporate this more fully into his life. For example, he literally turned over in bed when he wanted to switch from sad thoughts about all the losses he had incurred as a result of his temper outbursts to a 'happy side' when he wanted to explore the possibilities for his future life.

Also aiding thickening of the counterplot is asking the service user's permission to broadcast the news. This could take the form of developing 'communities of concern' as discussed earlier, but the main intention is to thicken the emerging alternative story by asking the service user what advice they would give to people with similar problems to their own. Thus they have to explain how they overcame the problem, and how they spotted its sneaky ways of setting up the service user for slip back.

Advantages of narrative approaches to assessment

A central dilemma for social workers for many years has been how to manage the tensions between care and control, individual and social needs, risks and safety. Narrative approaches to assessment manage this perhaps more fully than any of the other approaches, enabling the assessing social worker to incorporate her understanding of oppression most fully. The approach clarifies partnership without neglecting responsibility-taking and, by highlighting service users' local knowledge, has the capacity to produce individual assessments which have real meaning for service users.

Additionally, the approach has a wide range of applications. The type of problem does not limit its use; it is effective with service users of limited intellectual capacity, including elderly people who are muddled in their thinking, people with learning needs, and those who might be storied by others as having major mental illnesses. Like solution-focused approaches, it can be used with individuals, families and groups. These groups include support groups for people with 'anorexia' or 'schizophrenia', community groups of aboriginal people tackling problems of diabetes that are partly the result of poverty, and groups of AIDs workers in villages in Malawi. In larger group work, externalising conversations have been shown to lead to an exposé of the problem that empowers the taking of community and political action (see various reports in the Dulwich Centre Newsletter, Adelaide, South Australia).

Disadvantages of narrative approaches to assessment

We find it difficult to think of any major disadvantages but this may be because we have a strong personal preference for 'third wave' approaches to social work, and caution the reader not to be carried away by our enthusiasm; we are aware that we must not push out our agenda. The main disadvantage for social workers trained and experienced in other approaches is the very real difficulty of deconstructing their own stories; for example, they would need to question cautious notions about 'setting up the service user to fail' because narrative approaches are based on a premise that the service user is 'set up to succeed'. Thus they have to be prepared not only to make their 'stories' explicit, but also to abandon cherished theories about the nature of people. Some social workers also find it more difficult to start an assessment using this approach in view of its fluid nature and the assessment process can take longer than the more structured solution-focused approach, thus it is in some way more intrusive. Also the emphasis on using the service users' own language does run the risk of colluding with male metaphors of control; the notion of resistance readily lending itself to 'fighting talk'. Thus linguistic oppression must always be guarded against.

Outcomes

Research into narrative approaches is in its infancy, yet Gorey, Thyer and Pawluck (1998) found that where there is a 'mutual client–worker strategizing' to change an external target 'the prevalence of moderate to large interventive effects may be fivefold greater' compared with cognitive–behavioural approaches. They found that when the problem is defined as transcending the individual, 'that is the problem does not reside "under the person's skin"' the work is 'very effective' (p. 274). They add that practice based on oppression theories has 'possible greater effectiveness' compared with traditional problem-solving approaches, for example in work with survivors of abuse. We are also aware of the work of Fisher, Himble and Hanna (1998) in studying the externalisation of problems in work with compulsive adolescents. They made the problem 'the enemy' and found that eleven of fifteen participants who provided follow-up data showed significant improvement following a seven week programme.

Summary

- The narrative approach believes people are multi-storied and endeavours to make the service user the privileged author of their life.
- It encourages multiple perspectives and acts to deconstruct stories of 'expert' knowledge.
- Deconstructing problems in a liberating narrative is helpful and promotes the separation of the person from the problem.
- It encourages a perception that change is always possible.
- It encourages many possible futures through the co-construction of alternative stories.
- Written language as feedback helps people to reflect on how to break free from difficulties.

11

Making and Finalising the Judgement

Having looked in some detail at the theoretical maps that can be used to guide social workers towards helpful analyses, we turn in this chapter to the issues around finalising an assessment in a report.

Problems of trying to keep an open mind

We suspect that social workers would find it preferable to use the exchange model of interviewing recommended by Smale and Tuson (1993) as the main route to assessment if potential service users all entered into the assessment process voluntarily. As is evident by the wide range of terms in the literature describing recipients of different social work interventions, the assessing social worker rarely meets with an individual on a truly voluntary, partnership basis. In a discussion on ethical issues, Wise (1995), however, makes the distinction based on power differentials. While she finds it appropriate to use the term 'service user' for the recipients of social work interventions voluntarily entered into, she retains the term 'client' for those who have social work imposed upon them because the social worker has a mandated responsibility to protect vulnerable members of society. In either situation, social work intervention involves unequal power relations because the social worker can do something to people against their will which they cannot do to social workers, or because social workers have something people want and can decide whether or not to give it to them. Inevitably, this means that decisions are made involving some sort of judgement.

Social workers are regularly exhorted to retain an open mind about their judgements. Indeed, judgmentalism has become a dirty word in social practice to such an extent that we sometimes find practitioners tolerating harmful circumstances for some family members in their

169

efforts to avoid appearing judgmental of other family members –
usually the older ones. For example, rather than be seen to impose
'middle-class' standards of housekeeping on working-class families,
some social workers we have met seem to feel they must sit in considerable discomfort in filthy homes. We worry that such workers do little
about the children of such homes who attend school smelling of urine-
soaked beds. There is a very important distinction, however, between
'making a judgement' and 'being judgmental'. Social workers are
required to face the challenge and responsibility of the former in
order to be helpful; they need to avoid the prejudice, closed-mind-
edness and blaming implicit in the latter. The avoidance of making a
moral judgement remains in itself a moral judgement; as Davis and
Ellis (1995) say, social workers are, at the very least, responsible for
accommodating the complexity and individuality of people's living
situations within the confines of bureaucratic decision-making.

Social workers have to assess needs, evaluate risks and allocate
resources in a way that is as equitable as possible for a wide range of
people in various situations. Inevitably, the rights and entitlements of
some people will be restricted. We suggest that coping with this
difficult balancing act cannot be facilitated by attempting to avoid
making judgements, assuming that holding the 'right' values will
make it any easier, or attempting to promote partnership where it
patently does not exist. Keeping an open mind is particularly problematic because all people are liable to be biased in all their assessments of
each other. Good will and well-meant activity are no guarantee of
impartiality. Social psychology suggests that we are all 'cognitive
misers' in that we do not use fresh eyes each time we assess another
person because we simply lack the time that this would involve. So we
use quick and 'dirty' cognitive processes to move information speedily
through our system of organised social knowledge (Forsyth, 1986).
And we make mistakes. This chapter outlines some of the more
common decision-making distortions.

Individual decision distortions

Selective attention

Although we all probably pride ourselves on our objectivity, research
shows that we commonly weight some evidence from our assessments
more heavily than others. Traits that have extreme value carry more

weight than traits with moderate value. For example, child protection case conference minutes often contain positive statements about a father's intelligence and ability to impose order on a disorganised household (traits with extreme value), while failing to comment on traits that may have a negative impact on the children, leading to judgements such as 'He is the better parent of the two' (Kelly, 2000). Also, the value we ascribe to various traits is influenced by factors such as race. For example, Denney (1992) argues that black physicality has more extreme value than white physicality in probation reports on male offenders. Similarly, social workers are more likely to give more weight to mothering behaviours than fathering behaviours as the former are more detailed and prescribed (Milner, 1996), particularly when the information is negative, because we have a tendency to give more weight to negative and less to positive information. This is particularly evident in the emphasis on *problem* identification in much of social work knowledge.

There are also two other effects of selective attention: vivid, distinctive or unexpected data are perceptually more salient, and primacy effects overwhelm recency effects, giving truth to the old adage about the need to make a good first impression. The subjects of social work assessments are most likely to encourage these effects, the reason for their referral being usually one which is distinctive. As they will initially be seen when they are at their 'worst' (an overload of negative information), they will then present the assessor with an initial impression that is difficult to dislodge. Turnell and Edwards (1999) argue that talking about the 'five percent' of problematic behaviour which brings families to the attention of child protection services ignores the 'ninety five percent' of ordinary family competence, with such an assessment focus reducing whole people to problems, undermining hope, respect and co-operation. Social workers have traditionally attempted to overcome this bias by developing a sort of optimism (for an overview, see Corby, 1993), although this tendency can be counteracted more easily in certain interventions. For example, the 'assessment through intervention' style of the tourist map and the navigator's map help to address the issue since the social worker waits to see what change is possible.

Stereotyping

Data collection risks being simplified by stereotyping that permits the classification of people into ready-made compartments so that responses are prepared for particular persons. Unfortunately, there can be some truth in stereotypes – indeed, people give strong signals by the way in which they present themselves, indicating the categories to which they consider themselves to belong.

The danger is that information on which categorisation is made may be faulty because of the selective attention errors mentioned above, or because differences from a stereotype that indicate a person's uniqueness may be ignored. For example, a social worker with a stereotype of Asian families concerning the importance of family networks assessed an Asian woman as depressed due to social isolation because she had no links with her extended family. This completely ignored the fact that she had made a conscious decision to move away from her family, whom she saw as the cause of her problems in the first place.

Primacy effects work on stereotyping in a peculiar manner. If the first impression is a good impression – which will be weighted heavily for both salience and primacy effects – a halo effect can sometimes operate in which a person's very positive characteristics colour one's perception of their various other characteristics. This is quite different from picking out positives as well as negatives in assessment work and can have grave consequences. For example, positive stereotyping about the strengths of black mothers meant that Tyra Henry's grandmother was assumed to be sufficiently competent to safeguard Tyra's welfare despite severe financial, emotional and material privation (London Borough of Lambeth, 1985). Another inherent danger in stereotyping is that it tends to produce negative as well as positive self-fulfilling prophecies about people. Putting people into erroneous categories tends to perpetuate myths about them, as has been amply demonstrated by research into social class, race and gender effects on educational achievement. The results of research into social work attitudes shows that social workers are, like everyone else, susceptible to stereotyping effects, with concomitant self-fulfilling prophecies. Davis and Ellis (1995) found that when social workers were responsible for allocating scarce resources, they labelled people who appeared knowledgeable about their entitlements as 'demanding' and those who tried to exercise choice or challenge workers' judgements as 'fussy' or 'manipulative'.

Two studies using vignettes in which the only significant difference between different children was race also reveal unconscious stereotyping effects. Osuwu-Bempah (1994) found that social workers were more likely to ascribe identity problems to 'black' pupils and prescribe the need for a strong male model than they did to the 'white' pupils. Similarly, Blyth and Milner (1996) undertook an assessment exercise with practising social workers. They were given the following scenario in small groups and asked to make tentative hypotheses about the nature of the problem before the first visit. They all received the same information although the child's name varied:

> N school have referred Darren/Delroy/Shaheen to the service following an assault on a teacher. Darren/Delroy/Shaheen is the eldest boy/girl in a family of five children. S/he is known to the service who investigated his/her poor attendance record at junior school. This was explained by his/her mother as a result of a severe chest infection and the case was closed.
>
> Since starting secondary school, his/her attendance has been patchy, s/he is disruptive and not achieving his/her full potential. His/her friends include one boy/girl who is the most difficult pupil in the class.
>
> An assault was triggered by the class teacher's response to a note delivered by Darren/Delroy/Shaheen, requesting permission for him/her to be off school for a four week family holiday. The teacher said that it would be most unlikely that permission would be granted and Darren/Delroy/Shaheen then 'went wild'.

The group assessing Darren viewed the problem as one of a single mother struggling to bring up a family on a low income. They thought that Darren's behaviour might be due to hyperactivity because of junk food and were worried that he would lose the opportunity of a 'holiday of a lifetime' – probably to visit relatives in Canada. The group assessing Delroy viewed the problem as one of an out-of-control boy, lacking a father figure. They referred to his history of 'violence', although there was none in the scenario. They also suggested that he had written the note himself.

The group assessing Shaheen viewed the problem as one of an overburdened girl in a large two-parent family. They also thought that the family might have unrealistic academic expectations for her. Health was seen as a factor by this group who assumed some deficiency of diet. With regard to the holiday, the group were sure that Shaheen was bound for an arranged marriage in Pakistan and were anxious to avoid this.

Thus each group managed to display stereotyped views around class, race and gender without any supporting evidence. Indeed, so strong were their stereotypes that they found it difficult to believe that they each had the same scenario and they continued arguing about this for some time in the feedback session. They were quite convinced that they were assessing different children, even though they had *constructed* these differences.

This seemed to us to be a dramatic and perhaps unusually marked display of stereotyping so we replicated the experiment with a group of social work students, timing the experiment to follow immediately after a lecture on stereotyping effects. Here, the difference in names led to the students considering that the child might be subject to racist inter- pretations of their behaviour by professionals other than themselves.

We suggest that in new situations, social workers routinely ask themselves 'how is this person similar to others – how might they be categorised?' and then ask 'how are they *different?*'

Attributional bias

All of us wish to make sense of social interactions so that we can control and predict events (Heider, 1958). That is, if we can decide why someone has done something, it will help in deciding our own behaviour towards them, as well as being able to predict what they will do. We are biased towards looking for causes and making inferences (attributions) that are subject to a range of irrational biases (see, for example, Nisbett and Ross, 1980). The attribution process is switched on whenever people attract our attention through the selective atten- tion effects mentioned above, and when events and actions do not meet our expectations and need an explanation that fits with our ideas about the nature of people.

By and large, we attribute our successes to our own efforts and our failures to events outside ourselves. However, we judge other people oppositely. This is called an attributional bias. The first part of this, attributing positive outcomes to stable, personal factors and negative outcomes to unstable, external factors, is called a self-serving bias (see, for example, Miller and Ross, 1975). This is actually a healthy thing because it not only helps us to make sense of unexpected events, but also protects our self-esteem and public image. For example, if we get a cold, we are likely to think this is the result of being surrounded by cold germs at work, whereas if we are the only person at work who escapes getting the cold, we are likely to attribute this to something we did – such as taking vitamin C or not smoking. Perhaps, a little nearer home, the social worker who is named in a child death inquiry will probably see this as resulting from a lack of resources or bad luck, while all other workers will probably be quite sure that their own assessments would have been better.

The tendency to attribute causes oppositely when observing other people is called 'fundamental attribution error'. This arises from over-attribution and defensive attribution, both of which can serve to insulate observers from anxiety. If other people are considered *personally* responsible for their misfortunes, the same fate cannot befall the observer. This means that we are all predisposed to victim blaming – even where the 'victim' is clearly constrained and controlled by situational factors. Thus it can be seen that we have an inbuilt tendency to prefer social work interventions that locate the problem within the subject. It is not only that it is easier to 'work' on the subject rather than social circumstances, it also makes us each feel more individually secure. Thus as we switch from teaching victims of domestic violence to accept responsibility for the perpetrator's actions to challenging abusers (mostly men), we create 'an "us" and "them"' mentality, a delusion which is particularly seductive for therapists working with abuse. This delusion can mask the continuum of abusive behaviour in our own experience and the general community' (Jenkins, 1996, p. 121). To counter this tendency, Jenkins recommends that social workers self-monitor, reflect and de-brief to check against a possible 'inner tyrant', operating from a position of self-righteous superiority.

Sensory distortions

Not only do we make judgements about people as a result of the mental processes outlined above but we also make inferences about people's whole characters simply from the way they look, smell and speak. Our 'cognitive miserliness' may help us to take short cuts in assessment but it is rarely accurate. The most obvious sensory distortion in personal perception is the effect of physical appearance on judgements. Good-looking people are usually ascribed positive personality traits – a factor that belies the saying that beauty is only skin deep. Physical appearance is, of course, the most 'salient' and 'recent' impression we receive. All social workers know of some young, handsome charmer who escaped a realistic assessment of his/her behaviour, but far more serious for social work subjects is the bias against those with unfortunate physical appearances. For example, the rapid increase in the number of exclusions from school shows some evidence that it not necessarily the most badly behaved children who are most frequently excluded – it is the under- or oversized, peculiar looking ones who have little appeal for the hard-worked teacher (Hayden, 1996). And in a society whose people spend a fortune eliminating body odours, smell is important in assessments – the child or old person who smells of stale urine is not likely to be assessed positively for strength of character.

We have mentioned linguistic oppression earlier but there are obvious gender and ethnic biases that operate with regard to *speech* as well as the actual words used. Many apparently natural aspects of men's and women's voices cannot be explained simply in terms of anatomical differences between the sexes but are acquired as speakers learn the cultural norms of feminine and masculine behaviour (Graddol and Swann, 1989). Speech reflects gender divisions, a masculine tone is regarded as the voice of authority. Service users are unlikely to be able to afford the voice-coaching that Margaret Thatcher used to lower the tone of her voice. Indeed, their voices are likely to lack 'authority' as a result of the stress of their circumstances making them more shrill than usual. As we discussed earlier, service users who can conform verbally have been found to be more likely to form positive relationships with assessing social workers (Holland, 2000) but this is an unfair burden to place on service users.

Difficult though it is, social workers can strive to be non-judgmental by asking themselves what characteristics they dislike about a person's presentation and whether a list of positive qualities could be drawn up to counter-balance them. Here too a future focus helps, working out the next small step towards change; giving service users time and opportunity to show some progress.

Interagency distortions and risk assessment

Much of the drive towards interagency meetings as a check against individual errors in assessment work comes from the child protection field, although the notion of the case conference has now become popular in other areas of social work, such as the assessment of risk in probation practice, the identification of children with special educational needs and the management of community care for elderly and disabled people. The case conference is generally thought to be particularly effective in assessing risk (see, for example, Home Office, 1991). We query the wisdom of viewing the case conference as an effective check against individually biased assessment. We do not believe that two heads are necessarily better than one, and we support our argument with generic psychological explanations of group and individual decision-making processes.

Groupthink

One popular explanation of reasons for defective decision-making in groups is the concept of groupthink. This describes decision-making in groups under stress where a group engages in particular types of behaviour. When Janis and Mann (1977) studied several disastrous policy decisions, they found that these behaviours included: shared rationalisations to support the first apparently adequate course of action suggested by an influential group member, a lack of disagreement between group members, and a consequent high level of confidence in the group decision. This concept of groupthink has already been aired in the child protection literature and suggestions for improving case conference performance with reference to making corrections to the symptoms of groupthink have been promoted in training packs (Lewis *et al.*, 1991). However, there are two fundamental problems with the application of correctives. First, the concept of groupthink itself suggests that once a group is subject to its symptoms, it will be too deeply entrenched in its behaviour to see a need for re-evaluation or change. Second, it may be the case that an individual can exert far more influence on the decisional direction of the group due to framing effects.

Group polarisation

Whyte (1989, 1993) suggests that rather than alter the original framing of the problem, a group would be subject to the effects of group polarisation, and this would *accelerate* the tendency to risk or caution of the original framing, group polarisation effects demonstrating that people in a group take a more extreme position than they would as individuals (Moscovici and Zavalloni, 1969). This, suggests Whyte, means that rather than act as a countercheck to any unwarranted optimism, if the decision is framed in terms of losses, the group will commit resources to a course of action initially agreed on by the group, even when it is failing. Group members will bolster this decision by self-justification, such as 'The plan needs more time to work' or 'We need more resources'. The group then has the potential to become so risky that there is always the possibility for a decision fiasco. This group behaviour is not only found in social work assessments of risk. As Leiss and Chociolko (1994, p. 31) comment on industrial risk assessment: 'the significance of an event's probability tends to decrease as conceivable consequences increase, until what is possible becomes more feared than what is probable'.

An analysis of child protection case conference decisions (Kelly, 2000) showed that most child protection assessments are framed in the domain of losses; the *key decision-maker* was the individual social worker who dealt with the initial referral and prepared the report for the case conference; the case conference did not act as a check against this initial assessment (it did, as Whyte predicted, escalate rather than reduce risky decision-making); and that, although individual social workers perceived other case conference members to be more powerful than themselves, these members actually had little influence on the decision.

This does not imply notions of unwarranted optimism or careless assessment work on the part of social workers *per se*. The social psychological theory explaining these effects is universal and there is no evidence that other case conference forums are any more effective in realistically assessing risk (Whyte, 1989, 1993). What it does imply is that an individual social worker would make less risky decisions than a group when a losses frame is applied and that an interagency group can operate more effectively when a gains frame is applied. O'Sullivan (1999) cautions that social situations are complex and uncertain, with sound decisions arising from a process which includes involving service users to the highest feasible level; consultation between *all* the stake-holders; careful framing of the decision situation; and making a systematic choice between options. Even then, the relative lack of influence social workers have over wider social factors can limit what sound decisions alone can achieve.

Prospect theory

Kahnemann and Tversky (1979) offered an explanation of how individuals make decisions that tend towards the direction of risk or caution depending upon whether or not the initial choice is framed in terms of options that involve gains or losses. If the possible options are framed in terms of gains, individuals will be risk-averse, that is they will opt for a certain, although perhaps smaller, gain as opposed to another larger gain that is uncertain or risky. In other words, they will be less likely to gamble or risk losing the certain gain. However, if the options are framed in terms of losses, individuals will be more risk-seeking and will tend to avoid a certain, although smaller, loss in favour of another, larger loss that is uncertain. They will be more likely to risk the gamble, exposing themselves to a potentially greater risk. Positive framing leads to caution, and negative framing to risk-taking. The various options open to social workers are often all unattractive, desired outcomes usually having a low probability and less desirable outcomes having a high one. All the options can usually be framed either positively or negatively, and this will affect riskiness in decision-making.

The principle was demonstrated with a group of 120 delegates attending an international conference on child protection. They were asked to choose between two unattractive options in the following scenario (Kelly and Milner, 1996a):

A known paedophile is about to be discharged from prison after serving the full term of a three-year sentence. He intends to resume a relationship with a previous partner who has six children aged two to sixteen years. She knows that he will not be allowed to live with her and the children but you suspect that he will visit at night. You have devised two child care plans which will secure the safety of the children but both have consequences for the children's relationship with their mother.

Half the group were asked to make a choice between two losses:

- If you choose plan A, four of the children will lose contact with their mother.
- If you choose plan B, there is a third likelihood that none of them will lose contact with their mother and a two-thirds likelihood that all of them will lose contact with their mother.

The other half were asked to make a choice between two gains:

- If you choose plan C, two of the children will remain in contact with their mother.
- If you choose plan D, there is a two-thirds likelihood that none of the children will maintain contact with their mother and a one-third likelihood that all of them will maintain contact.

The odds are identical in both halves of the exercise since plan A and plan C are the same, although framed differently, as are plans B and D. Still, of those making the choice in terms of losses, 100 per cent opted for plan B, avoiding a certain loss but risking a greater one that was uncertain. Of those making the choice in terms of gains, 55 per cent opted for plan C and only 45 per cent opted for plan D (the risky gamble). Those making the decision in terms of trying to avoid a certain loss therefore exposed themselves to the possibility of a greater loss for all the children and were risk-seeking, whereas the other half were more risk-averse, that is cautious.

Many of the dilemmas in social work involve choices between two unattractive options. For example, a social worker is regularly faced with leaving a child in an abusive family or admitting the child to care, with leaving a potentially dangerous offender in the community or recommending he be sent to prison. Similarly, the choice for many frail elderly people is between an unsafe home environment and an old person's home. While respite care and adequate domiciliary services remain underdeveloped, the first option in these examples is highly desirable for the social worker, but, in opting to avoid a certain loss, other possible (uncertain) losses are ignored and risky behaviour sets in (see, for example, Kelly and Milner, 1996b). It is common to hear social workers say that risk-taking is a vital component of good practice, but we maintain that the converse can be true. Cautious behaviour, that is seeking to achieve certain gains, is more likely to lead not only to re-evaluation and contingency plan-making, but also to creative and effective social work.

Unfortunately, social work legislation often encourages risk-seeking behaviour. For example, the Children Act 1989 has no definition of what constitutes the welfare of a child in terms of gains, the criterion for an order being the possible losses to welfare in comparison with a similar child. Social workers are therefore usually faced with choices between losses. To avoid the shift towards risk-taking, they need to reframe options in terms of certain and uncertain gains.

Before leaving prospect theory, social workers, when involved in the management of risky situations, need also to listen carefully to the frames that service users are using. If they are in the domain of gains as they frame their options, they may be less prone to high risk-taking (for example, offending), whereas if they are in the domain of losses, more vigilance is suggested as they may be more prone to gamble on a high risk. So both they and the social worker need to be helped to move into the domain of gains. Solution-focused and narrative approaches facilitate this more than do other types of intervention as they emphasise safety, which is more easily measured than is risk.

Risk assessment and safety approaches

Assessing risk is an impossible task on at least three grounds: child abuse research, for example, demonstrates that it is only possible to predict between 65–80 per cent of known future abuse, with at least 20 per cent of any sample likely to be wrongly thought to be likely to abuse or neglect their children (for an overview, see Corby, 2000); it eludes quantification – for example, is emotional abuse more or less damaging than physical abuse; and, once identified, how can a social worker ever know that it has ceased to exist? Safety approaches avoid these dilemmas by inviting abusive people to take responsibility for their own behaviour. Effective safety plans resulting from this approach have been obtained in the fields of domestic violence (Jenkins, 1990, 1996; Sebold and Uken, 2000), child abuse (Berg, 1994; Turnell and Edwards, 1999), and suspected sexual abuse which is strongly denied (Essex *et al.*, 1996). Briefly there are six practice principles involved in this approach:

1 Jenkins (1990, 1996) comments that we treat those who abuse others with considerable disrespect at the same time as we expect them to learn to show respect for others, therefore, the first step is to treat abusers as people worth doing business with; seeking to identify and understand values, beliefs, and meanings. Turnell and Edwards (1999) say that this does not involve collusion; it is more about being open and honest about any disagreements. Equally important is to issue invitations to the service user to take responsibility for their behaviour rather than challenge them head on. Not only does such challenging lead to a sullen stand-off between social workers and abusers but: 'Acknowledgement [of responsibility for abuse] while preferable, is neither a sufficient nor a necessary condition of safety'. (Turnell and Edwards, 1999, p. 140).

2 Rather than analysing only the 'five per cent' of behaviour that is considered risky, the assessing social worker seeks to identify exceptions to it. Whilst it is useful to know when a person could have behaved abusively but did not, it is even more useful to know when, where, and how the changes/differences happened, what was different about this, and how the abuser understands what they did on those occasions so that they can be encouraged to repeat that behaviour. This creates hope for both social worker and abuser, and may indicate possible solutions.

3 Discovering the abuser's strengths and resources is also important – and recommended in the DoH guidelines (2000c, 1.33). We usually do this by saying something like 'we have talked a lot about what brought you here, can we stop a moment and look at what has gone right?' This shift in focus encourages the abuser to make changes in their behaviour as it is much easier to do *more* of something that is satisfactory than it is to *stop* doing something. Also, at this point, asking the abuser to say what are their good points helps them to regain self respect. They have usually forgotten anything good about themselves as a result of the emphasis on their wrongdoing and, as Jenkins (1996) comments, they cannot be expected to show respect for others if they have no self-respect.

4 A safety goal is a priority; both for the abuser and the abused. Essex *et al.*, (1996), who work exclusively in instances where abuse

is strongly suspected and equally strongly denied, help the family members to construct a safety plan which the alleged abuser must then take responsibility for carrying out. They also add extra safety contingencies for particularly vulnerable family members, such as an ornament which can be moved to alert an adult to a child's fears, whilst Dolan (1998) recommends the social worker leave the abused person with a SAE postcard containing an innocuous message – but the posting of it would alert the recipient to danger. We have found that asking the abuser 'how will I know that x is safe?' is also useful in encouraging that person to take responsibility for their own behaviour. And, of course, the safety plan provides concrete measurable outcomes from which progress towards safety can be achieved.

Where an abuser is unable to suggest any constructive goals or agree a safety plan, it becomes clear that danger is increased and further safety measures are required. Any family safety goal plan needs to include *each* family member's individual goals.

5   Risk estimation is professional knowledge, making it difficult for service users to know what they need to do in order to demonstrate reduced risk. Far easier is the scaling of *safety* (see, for example *Signs of Safety* Scale in Parton and O'Byrne, 2000; *Overcoming Violence Chart* in Milner and O'Byrne, 2002). For example, James was not allowed to have his eldest stepdaughter living with him until he underwent 'anger management' training. When asked how much control he had over his temper, he rated himself at 7 on a 10 point scale (10 being complete control) but his children rated him lower. Interestingly, they rated their sense of safety much higher than he did.

    Scales are also useful in inviting abusers to accept there is risk. For example, asking someone to rate their temper control or fathering ability on a 10 point scale (10 being good enough to close the case and 1 being very little safety), allows for them being overoptimistic in their rating – say nine – but still leave the assessing social worker one point for discussion about possible changes to be made. Our experience is, however, that people are so relieved not to be at 1 that they rarely overestimate their competence.

6   A safety focus is maintained at all times by determining the abuser's motivation and ability to carry out plans before trying to implement them. Here it is useful to use separate 1–10 scales for motivation and ability as we often find that people are well motiv-ated to end their violence but not confident in their ability to do

so. Depending on which is the more problematic, goals are developed to meet this. Turnell and Edwards (1999) also make the point that motivation should be shared between the social worker and service user and that the former has a responsibility to create a context that maximises the likelihood of motivation to make changes. Equally Walsh (1997) finds it important to provide practical support for abusers who are themselves often neglected and impoverished.

Above all, Turnell and Edwards recommend that a safety assessment balances safety and dangerousness; assuming nothing, taking care over judgements, and not expecting everything to work, in order to remain flexible and creative to opportunities for change; that is, being prepared to re-assess continuously.

Recording distortions

For most social workers, recording is a chore that detracts from the real business of social work – the interpersonal nature of the social work relationship. Once having learnt the agency format of records and reports, 'learning the forms and words of a specific discourse' (Rojek and Collins, 1988, p. 613), social workers spend much more time developing their intervention skills. This, we suggest, seriously undervalues the importance of the case file. Prince's study of agency records (1996) found that 'Records actually occupy a "hot seat" in the power relations between social workers, their managers and consultants, and functioned not only as an index of power but also as a bearer of meanings, codes, resources and emotions' (p. 180). Once something is written down, it gains authority. White and Epston (1990) suggest that the invention of the case file enabled individuals to be captured and *fixed* in writing:

> In our world, language plays a very central part in those activities that define and *construct* persons, and if written language makes a more than significant contribution to this, then a consideration of modern documents and their role in the redescription of persons is called for. (White and Epston, 1990, p. 188, emphasis added)

This is particularly important in social work practice since recording has become diagnostic rather than simply factual. As Kagle (1991) comments, the case file is both selective and analytic, but analyses are often retrospective reconstructions of the worker's thinking processes rather than a prospective aid to assessment. As we noted earlier, analyses of case files and case conference minutes reveal evidence of selective use of facts, inaccurate information and 'shaping'. The written word has such power that social workers could usefully re-examine their attitudes towards recording. The process of individualising service users in reports and records should not be allowed to slip into pathologising.

Pathologising the individual arises mainly from an emphasis on the subject of the case file, obscuring the fact that the social work relationship involves two people – the *subject* and the *author* of the document. White and Epston (1990, p. 188) argue that the author has 'a library of terms of description that have been invented by and considered the property of this particular domain of expert knowledge'. This expert knowledge, combined with the invisibility of the author, creates the impression of the possession of an objective and detached view that does not actually exist. For example, adherents of psychodynamic social work practice carefully chart the resistances and manipulations of clients while viewing their own resistances and manipulations as 'therapy'. They are able to bolster a view of the therapy as essentially beneficial and the therapist as rational and scientific through the construction of the subject within their specialised discourse in a way which hides the moral assumptions implicit in it (for a fuller discussion, see Ingleby, 1985). Essential detail is often missing from records; for example, it is not uncommon to read in case files concerning child development issues that a child has 'blossomed', but there seems to be no equivalent that supplies detail about what would be the evidence for 'wilting'. Additionally, the social work discourse is mainly within a micro domain, therefore racism, for example, is a macro concept that is not readily accessible within this:

> It was noteworthy that individual assessments for all clients appeared to be based upon highly individualised descriptions of personality...the probation officer appeared to be creating a certain form of reality which was meant to represent the nature of the offender and the offender's problem. (Denney, 1992, p. 96)

With the introduction of service user access to files, there is also a reluctance to record assumptions, although they remain in the social worker's head. This manifests itself in the form of Chinese whispers in the interagency group or the use of euphemisms in reports, particularly court reports. Euphemisms may seem kinder to the service user but have the disadvantage that they cannot be challenged. They are often nothing more than coded insults: for example, 'He tries his best' actually means 'He has failed'; 'manipulative' means 'S/he will not do what I suggest'. Additionally, euphemisms can have coded meaning for the reader; for example, 'The house is typical of this estate' often means 'This is a filthy house, like most others in the area'.

Reports are particularly prone to distortion as they often have the purpose of persuading the reader to accept a recommendation as well as informing and explaining. This means that reports usually contain either a 'pitch' or a 'denunciation' (Emerson, 1969) that involves the writer in 'recycling the evidence' (Aronsson, 1991). A 'pitch' will attempt to individualise or victimise the subject and will use words such as 'unfortunately' and 'however', which then cast doubt on statements of fact. A 'denunciation' will use similar words but give them a negative connotation. There is no reason why reports should recycle the evidence; a more factual account would leave the reader to make up his/her own mind, and any statements of opinion could be labelled just that (which we have aimed to do in this book, despite the many 'howevers'). For further discussion of linguistically sensitive language, see Pugh (1996).

Conclusion

Thus social psychology tells us that it is not easy to make objective assessments in *any* social situation. And the human tendency to make attributions, develop stereotypes and increase risk-taking in groups is such robust behaviour that exhortations to keep an 'open mind' can be quite worthless. Perhaps we don't keep our minds open at all, although we may sometimes pretend that our judgements are non-judgmental. Not only would it be against our self-interests to do so in terms of our own mental health, but it would also be incredibly time-consuming – and no-one would listen to us when we had done so anyway. Is the ideal of the non-judgmental social worker quite impossible? Is there anything we can do to counter distortions?

Modestly, we would suggest that there is a way forward. First, this would involve removing the interagency group from social work assessments. By all means, consult with all the people in your action/target system, but by no means give them the mandate to make judgements. Accept individual responsibility for your own judgements. This is not to say that the interagency group has nothing to offer the individual social worker in terms of resources and management of the individual decision. Neither is it to say that you need not listen carefully to service users but, at the end of the day, you must state your judgement and note differences of opinion.

Second, be aware of the importance of your first assessment because this will underpin all your subsequent decisions and may hinder the process of evaluation. The only way in which you can reasonably engage in evaluation of your assessments, we suggest, is by ensuring that you have multiple frames at the outset. Consider the maps outlined earlier even where they do not fit comfortably with your theories about people. For example, it will be obvious to the reader that we do not particularly like psychoanalytic explanations of human behaviour as it works against our own self-efficacy efforts, but we include it as a possible truth that we must consider even if we are both more likely to begin with a cognitive explanation of events. These frames need to be written down in terms of possible hypotheses to provide the means by which you actually evaluate your outcomes or else you will engage in the self-justification efforts described earlier.

Third, test each frame by checking your hypotheses against the outcomes by asking the subject of your assessment. Continuous bridging of the gap between assessor and subject will assist this process.

Fourth, check your case files for language usage that pathologises rather than individualises the subject.

Finally, set out your report in a logical order using some adapted version of the headings listed in Chapter 4. These are based loosely on the work of Meyer (1993) and, as the reader will have realised by now, they reflect the layout of this book and mirror the six stages of the process of making assessments.

1 *Define the 'case'*: its boundaries and systemic context.
2 *List the data*: what facts, happenings, oppressions and supports are present.
3 *Weigh the data.* How is the person(s) functioning in the circumstances? How is the balance of strengths and limitations, reactions and resources, affecting the situation? These should be based on your use of social science 'knowledge' (see Chapters 2–5).
4 *Analysis, inference and explanation.* Interpret the interaction between the variables. Make causal connections. Check hypotheses. This should be based on the theoretical maps outlined in Chapters 6–10. A final check should be made against distortions at this point.
5 *Situation definition/summary.* What are the needs, what needs to be and can be done, internal/external change first or both, what workers can the service offer, what are the priorities, what risks are involved, how could safety be increased? These should be informed by the ideas outlined in this chapter.

6 *Recommendations*. What would be the best focus of attention/intervention? What could be attempted? What is the preferred method? What is an alternative method? Is the time frame brief time-limited, episodic or open ended? Who is the best person to take action? What is the expected outcome? What are the criteria for evaluating the outcome? What about cost?

Summary

- Assessments necessarily involve making a judgement that is the responsibility of the individual social worker.
- Objectivity in assessment work is subject to a range of distortions: selective attention, stereotyping, attributional and sensory biases.
- Interagency groups are even more prone to biases than individual decision-makers and do not act as a safeguard against risky decision-making.
- Case recording and report writing practices rarely acknowledge the power of the writer to construct the subjects of social work interventions.
- Language reflects the racial and gender divisions of society, so the language used in reports often reproduces dominant social values.
- Social workers need to build a series of checks into their individual assessments and take responsibility for them.
- A *Signs of Safety* approach concentrates on how to build safety, in collaboration with families, while not ignoring danger.

12

Conclusion

We hope that the comprehensive framework that we have presented will, first, help social workers to be theory conscious at least in their reflections and that, with a clearer idea of how various theories reflect different explanations of human behaviour, they will be encouraged to draw more deliberately on the theoretical maps as they journey towards helpful analyses of situations.

Social workers will continue to approach assessments from their favoured theoretical standpoint, and each theoretical approach has its own usefulness and limitations. The psychodynamic approach, we suggest, offers a considerable analysis of a person's *individual* problems but is severely limited in *social* work practice because it largely ignores important 'weather conditions' such as oppressions to do with sexuality, gender, race and class. Adherents of behavioural approaches claim to be more value-free and rigorous in their assessment of behavioural problems, but the reality is often that this approach is used selectively in assessment work with a tendency to go for a 'quick fix'. Strict behavioural assessments need careful attention to behavioural baselines if the assessment is to yield testable outcomes.

Task-centred approaches to assessment are essentially value-free and non-oppressive as they emphasise service user involvement in the analysis, but there is a danger here that this may be taken as read and that social workers may be lulled into a false sense of security about their abilities to empower service users through this approach. The solution-focused approach to assessment differs from all the others in that it rejects the preoccupation with problems. As such, it has enormous potential for anti-oppressive assessment practice, but it still requires the social worker to undertake a careful analysis and to be disciplined in avoiding the traditional tendency to pathologise or to lean towards psychological reductionism. Much the same can be said of the narrative approach, although it more explicitly addresses oppression and injustice.

188

There is, of course, no reason why all the maps we outline should not be used in making an assessment, as long as the process is carefully and systematically carried out and the competing and contradictory nature of the various approaches is understood.

Second, we hope that practitioners' confidence about the identification, placing and use of theory will enable them to relax with it, in the sense of being comfortable with uncertainty, in such a way that they will seriously listen for service users' views and take time to construct mutual dialogue and engagement despite differences of race, gender, class and age. Indeed, the greater the differences, the more time and care is required for this. We believe that listening to, and engaging with, people's subjective experiences and meanings lies at the heart of effective practice.

What must be emphasised is that assessment is complex, time-consuming and fluid. So our third hope is that practitioners who are better rooted in theory will endeavour to be more research-minded and keep track of the outcomes of their assessments, with a view to being able to identify what they do that is different, either in the process or in the theoretical map chosen, when the outcome is satisfactory. But, of course, good outcomes will never remove all problems from people's lives – our definition of good progress is moving from the stuckness of the same damn thing over and over to the normality of one damn thing after another.

The main hallmark of effective *professional* practice is when theoretical knowledge acts as a basis of professional expertise (Sibeon, 1992) but, as theory informs practice, so practice develops theory. Beresford (2000) points out that there is much more scope for using the theory building of service user movements. Rather than restricting this to direct action and change, it also has much to offer the intellectual basis of practice, policy, teaching and research. We hope, therefore, that practitioners will become less ambivalent about theory, that they will seek to own it rather than abandon it to academics. Commitment to social work values, to caring, to high standards and to effectiveness will involve much thinking as well as doing, and much reflection before and after the doing. Theoretically informed practice in assessment work is more likely to provide a clearer basis for interventions and their evaluation. Perhaps one of the obstacles to the integration of theory and practice is the mystique that sometimes surrounds theoretical discussion. We hope that by focusing on making assessments useful we have been able to cut away some of the mystique and bring theory down to earth, making it more useable in the real world.

For those who are interested in our fundamental orientation, readers will have noticed that our approaches are anti-positivist and that we consider human action to be conditioned or restrained, but not entirely determined, by external factors. People are not passive objects but are 'conscious social actors who play an active part in plotting the course of their lives' (Thompson, 1995, p. 43). But, while we reject positivism, we do not reject all social science – we accept the hermeneutical approach that focuses on the interrelationship between the objective world and social actors, and we accept the critical approach that seeks to integrate this with wider social and political factors. Thus we are very interested in postmodernist issues and in the current growth of literature relating them to social work; see, for example, Parton and O'Byrne (2000) and Milner (2001), which shows how we are particularly attracted to social constructionism and narrative approaches. We agree with Thompson (1995, p. 46) that we need 'to understand not only individual subjectivities but also shared subjectivities in terms of membership of social groups'. Our philosophy is also influenced by existentialism, which is a philosophy of lived experience, of freedom and of responsibility; it does not seek to be prescriptive or to tie people down to specific practices (Thompson, 1992).

Theory on its own is not able to provide ready-made solutions for practice, but it can guide and inform it. Messy uncertainty remains part of reality, and the best we can do is 'continue to struggle through our confusion, to insist on being human', as R. D. Laing used to say. In social work, we are dealing with unique difficulties each day, and we therefore need to carry on what Sibeon (1992, p. 163) calls a 'reflective conversation with the situation'. What we make of situations includes our own contribution to them, and service users can be helped to see this too. This approach embraces uncertainty, encouraging its creative use. It also means there are no guaranteed outcomes, hence the need for evaluating assessments when their outcomes are known. This is a far cry from the mechanistic application of theory or expecting theory to fit perfectly with reality.

Furthermore, in order to embrace anti-discriminatory practice, it is necessary to become aware of how the structure of psychocultural assumptions and biases constrains our view of others and to take action to counteract them when they lead to inequality. In other words, we need to avoid assuming that our theories, social roles and expectations are not problematic for others. Such practice is about seeking to make the best use of the theory that is available, learning how to make it more useful or helpful and learning from our mistakes. To do this, we need to work in partnership with service users, for they are well, if not best, placed to reflect on the usefulness of the partnership. As Trevithick (2000) comments:

This involves moving away from choosing practice approaches that suit our personal preferences and styles, and instead choose ways of working that best meet the needs of service users, or the particular problem presented. This requires that we are more rigorous and creative in the way we approach our work and the relationship between theory, practice and research. (pp. 65–6)

Finally, assessment necessarily involves making a judgement for which social workers need to take responsibility. There are many biases that can shape assessments to desired decisions, and these biases are universal. We do not think that social workers are a special breed whose training makes them any less likely than other mortals to be free from distorting service users' realities. Additionally, we question the ability of multiagency groups to act as a check against inadequate initial assessments and faulty decision-making. What we do consider to be important in assessment activity is the need to emphasise the critical role of the individual social worker's professional judgement. Thus, individual accountability for these judgements, through a series of checks such as routine consumer and interagency feedback, is essential. We realise that making assessments in the way we have detailed will demand much effort at an early stage of the social work process, but we envisage that it will result in improved confidence in professional abilities and help to put the *social* back in social work. At all times, however, seek and keep balance. Like Fisch *et al.* (1983), we see theory as important, and indeed necessary, for practice, yet theory can be over-elaborated or taken too seriously – deified – until it hampers direct observation and the clear interpretation of situations.

References

Aggleton, P. and Chambers, H. (1986) *Nursing Models and Nursing Process*. London: Macmillan.

Ahmad, B. (1990) *Black Perspectives in Social Work*. London: Venture Press.

Arber, S. and Ginn, J. (1991) *Gender and Later Life*. London: Sage.

Aronsson, K. (1991) 'Social interaction and the recycling of evidence', in Coupland, M., Giles, H. and Weimann, J.M. (eds) *Miscommunication and Problematic Talk*. London: Sage.

Audini, B. and Lelliott, P. (2001) *Are There Groups of the Population Sectioned more Frequently Than Others? An Analysis of Mental Health Act Assessment Data*. London: DoH.

Audit Commission (1992) *The Community Revolution: Personal Social Services and Community Care*. London: HMSO.

Audit Commission (1994) *Seen But Not Heard. Coordinating Community Child Health and Social Services for Children in Need*. London: HMSO.

Babuscio, J. (1976) *We Speak for Ourselves – Experiences in Homosexual Counselling*. London: SPCK.

Baldwin, S. (1993) *The Myth of Community Care: An Alternative Neighbourhood Model of Care*. London: Chapman & Hall.

Bandura, A. (1969) *Principles of Behaviour Modification*. New York: Holt, Rinehart & Winston.

Bandura, A. (1977) *Social Learning Theory*. Englewood Cliffs, NJ: Prentice Hall.

Barber, J.G. (1991) *Beyond Casework*. London: Palgrave Macmillan/BASW.

Barker, V. (1994) *Promoting Partnerships Through Consultation*. Lyme Regis: Russell House.

Barr, V. (1987) 'Change in Women' in S. Ernst. and M. Maguire (eds) *Living with the Sphinx*. London: Women's Press.

Barrett, D. (1997) *Child Prostitution in Britain*. London: The Children's Society.

Barrett, D. and Mullenger, N. (2000) 'Conclusion', in Barrett, D. with Barrett, E. and Mullenger, N. (eds) *Youth Prostitution in the New Europe. The growth in sex work*. Lyme Regis: Russell House Publishing.

Bateson, G. (1977) *Steps to an Ecology of Mind*. New York: Ballantine Books.

Beck, A.T. (1967) *Depression: Clinical, Experimental and Theoretical Aspects*. London: Hoeber.

Beck, A.T. and Tomkin, A. (1989) *Cognitive Therapy and Emotional Disorders*. London: Penguin.

Bee, H. and Mitchell, S. (1985) *The Developing Person*. London: Harper & Row.

Beresford, P. (2000) 'Service Users' Knowledge and Social Work Theory: Conflict or Collaboration', *British Journal of Social Work*, 30:489–503.

Beresford, P. and Croft, S. (1993) *Citizen Involvement: a practical guide for change*. Basingstoke: Palgrave Macmillan.

Berg, I.K. (1994) *Family-Based Services: A Solution-Focused Approach*. New York: Norton.

Berg, I.K. and Miller, S.D. (1992) *Working with the Problem Drinker*. New York: Norton.

Berg, I.K. and Reuss, N.M. (1998) *Solutions Step by Step: A Substance Abuse Treatment Manual*. New York and London: Norton.

Berne, E. (1964) *Games People Play*. New York: Grove Books.

Berne, E. (1978) *A Layman's Guide to Psychiatry and Psychoanalysis*. London: Penguin.

Blair, M. (1996) 'Interviews with black families', in Cohen, R. and Hughes, M. with Ashwort, L. and Blair, M. (eds) *Schools Out: The Family Perspective on School Exclusions*. London: Family Service Units and Barnardo's.

Blaug, R. (1995) 'Distortion of the face to face: communicative reason and social work practice', *British Journal of Social Work*, 25(4), 423–39.

Blyth E. and Milner J. (1990) 'The process of interagency work' in Violence Against Children Study Group, *Taking Child Abuse Seriously*. London: Unwin Hyman.

Blyth, E. and Milner, J. (1995) 'Young black people excluded from school'. Paper presented at Current Developments in Child Care: Linking Practice with Research. Leeds: Leeds University.

Blyth, E. and Milner, J. (1996) 'Black boys excluded from school: race and masculinity issues' in Blyth, E. and Milner, J. (eds) *School Exclusions: Interprofessional Issues for Policy and Practice*. London: Routledge.

Bocock, R. (1983) *Sigmund Freud*. London: Tavistock, Ellis Horwood.

Bowlby, J. (1964) *Child Care and the Growth of Love*. London: Penguin.

Bowlby, J. (1982) *Attachment and Loss*. London: Hogarth Press.

Bowlby, J. (1988) *A Secure Base: Clinical Implications of Attachment Theory*. London: Routledge.

Bowlby, J. and Parkes, C.M. (1970) 'Separation and loss within the family', in Anthony, E.J. and Koupernik, C. (eds) 'Growing points of attachment theory and research' *Monographs of the Society for Research in Child Development*, 50(1–1), 3–35.

Boykim, W. and Toms, F.D. (1985) 'Black child socialisation: a conceptual framework', in McAdoo, H.P. and McAdoo, J.L. (eds) *Black Children: Social, Educational and Parental Environments*. London: Sage.

Braye, S. and Preston-Shoot, M. (1992) *Practising Social Work Law*. London: Palgrave Macmillan.

Braye, S. and Preston-Shoot, M. (1995) *Empowering Practice in Social Care*. Buckingham: Open University Press.

Brayne, H. and Martin, G. (1993) *Law for Social Workers*. London: Blackstone.

Bridge Child Care Consultancy Service (1995) *Paul. Death through neglect*. London: Islington Area Child Protection Committee.

Bruner, E. (1986) 'Ethnography as narrative', in Turner, V. and Bruner, E. (eds) *The Anthropology of Experience*. Chicago: University of Illinois Press.

Bruner, J. (1990) *Acts of Meaning*. Cambridge, MA: Harvard University Press.

Buchanan, A. (1999) *What Works for Troubled Children? Family Support for Children with Emotional Behavioural Problems*. Wiltshire County Council: Barnardo.

Burnard, P.A. (1991) 'Method of analysing interview transcripts in qualitative research', *Nurse Education Today*, 11, 461–6.

Burns, D.D. (1992) *Feeling Good*. New York: Avon.

Burr, V. (1995) *An Introduction to Social Constructionism*. London: Routledge.

Burton, S., Regan, L. and Kelly, L. (1989) *Supporting Women and Challenging Men. Lessons from the Domestic Violence Intervention Project*. Bristol: The Policy Press.

Campbell, J. and Oliver, M. (1996) *Disability Politics*. London:Routledge.

Caplan, G. (1961) *An Approach to Community Mental Health*. London: Tavistock.

Carter, E.A. and McGoldrick, M. (1980) *The Family Life Cycle and Family Therapy; A Framework for Family Therapy*. New York: Gardner Press.

Cavanagh, K. and Cree, V. (eds) (1996) *Working with Men. Feminism and Social Work*. London: Routledge.

Challis, D. and Davies, B. (1986) *Care Management in Community Care*. PSSRU: University of Kent at Canterbury.

Challis, D., Chessum, R., Chesterman, J., Luckett, R. and Taske, K. (1990) *Case Management in Social and Health Care*. Canterbury: PSSRU, University of Kent.

Channer, Y. (1995) *I am a Promise. The School Achievement of Black African Caribbeans*. London: Trentham Books.

Chapman, T. and Hough, M. (2001) *Evidence-based Practice: A Guide to Effective Practice*. London: H.O.I.P.

Cigno, K. (1998) 'Cognitive-behaviour Practice' in R. Adams, L. Dominelli and M. Payne (eds) *Social Work: Themes, Issues and Critical Debates*. Basingstoke: Palgrave Macmillan.

Cigno, K. and Bourn, D. (1998) *Cognitive-behaviour Social Work in Practice*. Aldershot: Ashgate.

Clark, H., Dyer, S. and Hansaran, L. (1996) *Going Home: Older People Leaving Hospital*. London: Polity Press in conjunction with the Joseph Rowntree Foundation and Community Care Magazine.

Clifford, D. (1994) 'Towards an anti-oppressive social work assessment method', *Practice*, 6(3), 226–38.

Cockburn, C. (1991) *In the Way of Women. Men's Resistance to Sex Equality in Organisations*. Basingstoke: Palgrave Macmillan.

Connell, R.W. (1987) *Gender and Power*. Cambridge; Polity Press.

Coombes, M.A. (with Sedgewick, A.) (1998) *Right to Challenge: the Oxfordshire Community Care Project Rights' Project*. Bristol: Policy Press and the Joseph Rowntree Foundation.

Corby, B. (1993) *Child Abuse: Towards a Knowledge Base*. Milton Keynes: Open University Press.

Corby, B. (2000) *Child Abuse. Towards a Knowledge Base*. 2nd edn. Buckingham, Philadelphia: Open University Press.

Cordery, J. and Whitehead, A. (1992) 'Boys don't cry: empathy, collusion and crime', in Senior, P. and Woodhill, B. (eds) *Gender, Crime and Probation Practice*. Sheffield: Pavic.

Coulshed, V. (1988) *Social Work Practice: An Introduction*. Basingstoke: Palgrave Macmillan.

Coulshed, V. and Orme, J. (1998) *Social Work Practice – An Introduction*. 3rd edn. Basingstoke: Palgrave Macmillan.

Crain, W.C. (1985) *Theories of Development: Concepts and Applications*, 2nd edn, Eagleswood Cliffs, NJ: Prentice Hall.

Dale, P., Morrison, T. and Waters, J. (1986) *Dangerous Families: Assessment and Treatment of Child Abuse*. London: Tavistock.

Dale, P., Davies, M., Morrison, T. and Waters, J. (1983) 'A Family Therapy Approach to Child Abuse: Countering Resistance', *Journal of Family Therapy*, 5, 117–45.

Dalrymple, J. and Burke, B. (1995) *Anti-oppressive Practice. Social Care and the Law*. Buckingham: Open University Press.

Davies, D. (1999) 'Homophobia and heterosexism', in Davies, D. and Neal, C. (eds) *Pink Therapy: A Guide for Counsellors and Therapists Working with Lesbian, Gay and Bisexual Clients*. Buckingham, Philadelphia: Open University Press.

Davies, M. (1981) *The Essential Social Worker: A Guide to Positive Practice*. London: Heinemann.

Davies, M. (1997) (ed) *The Blackwell Companion to Social Work*. Oxford: Blackwell.

Davis, A. and Ellis, K. (1995) 'Enforced altruism or community care', in Hugman, R. and Smith, D. (eds) *Ethical Issues in Social Work*. London: Routledge.

Davis, A. Ellis, K., and Rummery, K. (1997) *Access to Assessment: Disabled People's Experience of Assessment for Community Care Services*. York: Policy Press.

Dearden, C. and Baker, S. (1995) *Young Carers: The Facts*. Sutton: Community Care.

Denman, G. and Thorpe, D. (1993) 'Participation and patterns of intervention in child protection in Gwent'. *A Research Report for the Area Child Protection Committee, Gwent*. Lancaster: University of Lancaster.

Denney, D. (1992) *Racism and Anti-Racism in Probation*. London: Routledge.

Dermer, S.B., Hemesath, C.W. and Russell, C.S. (1998) 'A feminist critique of solution-focused therapy', *American Journal of Family Therapy*, 26: 239–250.

Derrida, J. (1973) *Writing and Difference*. Chicago: Chicago University Press.

de Shazer, S. (1985) *Keys to Solution in Brief Therapy*. New York: Norton.

de Shazer, S. (1988) *Clues: Investigating Solutions in Brief Therapy*. New York: Norton.

de Shazer, S. (1991) *Putting Difference to Work*. New York: Norton.

de Shazer, S. (1993) Verbal communication, at Glasgow conference, Solutions in Brief Therapy.

de Shazer, S. (1994) *Words Were Originally Magic*. New York: Norton.

Devore, W. and Schlesinger, E.G. (1991) *Ethnic-sensitive Social Work*. New York: Macmillan.

Dobash, R.E. and Dobash, R.P. (1992) *Women, Violence and Social Change*. London: Routledge.

Dobash, R.E., Dobash, R.P., Cavanagh, K. and Lewis, R. (2000) *Changing Violent Men*. London: Sage.

Doel, M. and Marsh, P. (1992) *Task Centred Social Work*. London: Ashgate.

DoH (1988) *Protecting Children: A Guide for Social Workers Undertaking a Comprehensive Assessment*. London: HMSO.

DoH (1990a) *Community Care in the Next Decade and Beyond: Policy Guidance*. London: HMSO.

DoH (1990b) *Child Abuse: A Study of Enquiry Reports 1980–1989*. London: HMSO.

DoH (1995a) *Child Protection: Messages from the Research*. London: HMSO.

DoH (1995b) *Looking After Children*. London: HMSO

DoH (1998) *Modernising Mental Health Services: Safe, Sound and Supportive*. http:/www.doh.gov.uk/nsf/mentalh.htm

DoH (1999a) *Framework for the Assessment of Children in Need and their Families*. Consultation Draft. London: DoH.

DoH (1999b) *Me, Survive, Out There? New Arrangements for Young People Living in and Leaving Care*. London: DoH

DoH (2000a) *No Secrets. Guidance on developing and Implementing Multi-agency Policies and Procedures to Protect Vulnerable Adults from Abuse*. London: DoH.

DoH (2000b) *Safeguarding Chidren Involved in Prostitution. Supplementary Guidance to Working Together to Safeguard Children*. London: DoH.

DoH (2000c) *Framework for the Assessment of Children in Need and their Families*. London: DoH.

DoH (2001) *National Services Framework for Mental Health Modern Standards and Service Models*. http:/www.doh.gov.uk/nst/mhexecsum.htm

Dolan, Y. (1998) *Beyond Survival. Living Well is the Best Revenge*. Workshop held at Brief Therapy Practice, Institute of Child Health, London, 2–3 July.

Dryden, W. and Mytton, J. (1999) *Four Approaches to Counselling and Psychotherapy*, London: Routledge.

Dryden, W. and Yankma, J. (1993) *Counselling Individuals – A Rational Emotive Handbook*. London: Whorr.

Durrant, M. (1993) *Creative Strategies for School Problems*. Epping, NSW Australia: Eastwood Centre.

Ellis, A. (1962) *Reason and Emotion in Psychotherapy*. New York: Lyle Stuart.

Emerson, D. (1969) *Judging Delinquents*. Chicago: Aldine.

Epstein, L. (1988) *Helping People: The Task Centred Approach*. Columbus, OH: Merrill.

Epston, D. (1998) *Catching up with David Epston: a collection of narrative-based papers, 1991–1996*, Adelaide: Dulwich Centre Publications.

Erikson, E.H. (1948) *Children and Society*. Harmondsworth: Penguin.

Erikson, E.H. (1977) *Childhood and Society*. London: Granada.

Erickson, M.H. (1959) *Hypnotherapy: An Exploratory Casebook*. New York: Irvington.

Evans, J. (1995) *Feminist Theory Today*. London: Sage.

Everitt, A., Hardiker, P. and Littlewood, J. (1992) *Applied Research for Better Practice*. London: Palgrave Macmillan.

Essex, S. Gumbleton, J. and Luger, C. (1996) 'Resolutions: working with families where responsibility for abuse is denied', *Child Abuse Review*. 5: 191–201.

Fawcett, B., Featherstone, B., Hearn, J. and Toft, C. (eds) (1996) *Violence and Gender Relations Theories and Interventions*. London: Sage.

Featherstone, B. and Trinder, L. (1997) 'Familiar Subjects? Domestic Violence and Child Welfare', *Child and Family Social Work*, 2: 147–159.

Field, P.A. and Morse, J.M. (1985) *Nursing Research: The Application of Qualitative Approaches*. London: Croom Helm.

Fisch, R., Weakland, J.H. and Segal, L. (1983) *The Tactics of Change*. New York: Jossey Bass.

Fisher, D.J., Himle, J.A. and Hanna, G.L. (1998) 'Group behavioural Therapy for Adolescents with Obsessive-Compulsive Disorder', *Research on Social Work Practice*, **8**(6): 629–36.

Fisher, J. and Goceros, H. (1975) *Planned Behaviour Change*. New York: Free Press.

Forster, N. (1994) 'An analysis of company documentation', in Cassell, C. and Symon, G. (eds) *Qualitative Methods in Organisational Research*. London: Sage.

Forsyth, D.R. (1986) *Social Psychology*. Monterey, CA: Brooks Cole.

Foucault, M. (1972) *The Archaeology of Knowledge and the Discourse of Language*. New York: Pantheon.

Foucault, M. (1973) *The Birth of the Clinic*. London: Tavistock.

Foucault, M. (1980) *Power (Knowledge)*. New York: Pantheon.

Foucault, M. (1988) 'Technologies of Self' in L. Martin., H. Gutman. and P. Hutton (eds) *Technologies of Self*. Amherst: University of Massachusetts.

Fraiberg, S. (ed.) (1980) *Clinical Studies in Infant Mental Health*. London: Tavistock.

Freeman, J., Epston, D. and Lobovits, D. (1997) *Playful Approaches to Serious Problems*. New York and London: Norton.

Freire, P. (1972) *Pedagogy of the Oppressed*. Harmondsworth: Penguin.

Freud, A. (1936) *Ego and the Mechanisms of Defence*. New York: International Universities Press.

Freud, A. (1968) *Ego and the Mechanisms of Defence*, 2nd edn. London: Hogarth Press.

Freud, S. (1937) 'Constructions of analysis, vol. 23', in Strachey, J. (ed.) *The Standard Edition of the Complete Psychological Works of Sigmund Freud*. London: Hogarth Press.

Furman, B. and Ahola, T. (1992) *Solution Talk*. New York: Norton.

Gilligan, C. (1982) *In a Different Voice*. Cambridge, MA: Harvard University Press.

Gilligan, S. and Price, R. (1993) *Therapeutic Conversations*. New York: Norton.

Glaser, B. and Strauss, A.L. (1969) *The Discovery of Grounded Theory: Strategies for Qualitative Research*. Chicago: Aldine.

Glass, N. (2001) 'What Works for Children – the political issues', *Children and Society*, **15**(1): 14–20.

Goldberg, E.M., Gibbons, J. and Sinclair, I. (1985) *Problems, tasks and outcomes: The Evaluation of task-centred casework in Three Settings*. London: Allen & Unwin.

Goldman, A.I. (1970) *A Theory of Human Action*. Englewood Cliffs, NJ: Prentice Hall.

Gorey, K.M., Thyer, B.A. and Pawluck, D.E. (1998) 'Differential Effectiveness of Prevalent Social Work Practice Models: A Meta-Analysis' in *Social Work*, **43**(3): 269–278.

Graddol, D. and Swann, J. (1989) *Gender Voices*. New York: Norton.

Hall, C.S. (1954) *A Primer of Freudian Psychology*. London: New English Library.

Halliday, M.A.K. (1978) 'Antileagues' in M.A.K. Halliday (ed.) *Language as Social Semiotic: the social interpretation of language and meaning*. London: Arnold.

Hanmer, J. and Statham, D. (1988) *Women and Social Work*. London: Macmillan.

Hanson, B. and Maroney, T. (1999) 'HIV and Same-Sex Domestic Violence', in Leventhal, B. and Lundy, S.E. (eds) *Same-Sex Domestic Violence. Strategies for Change*. London: Sage.

Haralambos, M. and Holborn, M. (1990) *Sociology: Themes and Perspectives*. London: Unwin Hyman.

Harris, T.A. (1970) *I'm OK – You're OK*. London: Pan.

Harrison, H. (1995) 'Child assessment and family support.' Paper given at conference Assessing the Needs of Individual Children, 31 October. London: National Children's Bureau.

Hayden, C. (1996) 'Explaining exclusion from primary school: an analysis of the reasons behind the rise in the recorded primary school exclusions in the early 1990s'. PhD Thesis. Portsmouth: University of Portsmouth.

Hayes, N. (1984) *A First Course in Psychology*. London: Edward Arnold.

Hayes, N. (2000) *Foundations in Psychology*, 3rd edn. London: Thompson Learning.

Hearn, B. (1995a) *Child and Family Support and Protection. A Practical Approach*. London: National Children's Bureau.

Hearn, J. (1995b) 'Imaging the Imaging of Men' in B. Featherstone and A. Wernick (eds), *Images of Aging: Cultural Representations of Later Life*. London: Routledge.

Heider, F. (1958) *The Psychology of Interpersonal Relationships*. New York: John Wiley & Sons.

Hilsenroth, M.F., Ackerman, S.F. and Blagys, M.D. (2001) 'Evaluating the Phase Model of Change During Short-Term Psychodynamic Psychotherapy', *Psychotherapy Research*, 11: 29–41.

Holland, S. (2000) 'The Assessment Relationship: Interaction between Social Workers and Parents in Child Protection Assessments', *British Journal of Social Work*, **30**, 149–163.

Hollis, F. (1964) *Social Casework: A Psychosocial Therapy*. New York: Random House.

Home Office/DoH/Department of Education and Science/Welsh Office (1991) *Working Together under the Children Act 1989: A Guide to the Arrangements for Inter-Agency Cooperation for the Protection of Children from Abuse*. London: HMSO.

Home Office/Department of Health/Welsh Office (1995) *National Standards for the Supervision of Offenders in the Community*. London: Home Office Probation Services Division.

Home Office (1997) *Management and Risk Assessment in the Probation Service* London: Home Office.

Home Office (2000) *National Standards For the Supervision of Offenders in the Community*. London: Home Office.

hooks, bell (1991) *Yearning*. London: Turnaround.

hooks, bell (1993) *Sisters of the Yam: Black Women and Self-Recovery*. London: Turnaround.

Howe, D. (1995) *Attachment Theory for Social Work Practice*. Basingstoke: Palgrave Macmillan.

Huberman, A.M. and Miles, M.B. (1994) 'Data management and analysis methods', in Denzin, N.K. and Lincoln, Y.S. (eds) *Handbook of Qualitative Research*. London: Sage.

Hudson, B.L. and Macdonald, G.M. (1986) *Behavioural Social Work: An Introduction*. Basingstoke: Palgrave Macmillan.

Hughes, B. (1993) 'A model for the comprehensive assessment of older people and their carers', *British Journal of Social Work*, **23**(4), 345–63.

Hughes, B. and Mtezuka, M. (1992) 'Social work and older women: where have older women gone?', in Langan, M. and Day, L. (eds) *Women, Oppression and Social Work: Issues in Anti-Discriminatory Practice*. London: Tavistock/ Routledge.

Hugman, R. and Smith, D. (1995) *Ethical Issues in Social Work*. London: Sage.

Hussain, N. (1996) 'An investigation of the placement arrangements made for children and young people "looked after" in relation to cultural and religious origins'. Dissertation. Department of Behavioural Sciences, University of Huddersfield.

Ingleby, D. (1985) 'Professionals as socialisers: the "psy complex"', in Spitzer, S. and Scull, A.T. (eds) *Research in Law, Deviance, and Social Control*. New York: Jai Press.

Iveson, C. (1990) *Whose Life? Community care of Older People and their Families*. London: Brief Therapy Press.

Jacob, F. (2001) *Solution Focused Recovery from Eating Distress*. London: B.T. Press.

Jacobs, M. (1999) *Psychodynamic Counselling in Action*. London: Sage.

Janis, I.L. and Mann, L. (1977) *Decision Making*. New York: Free Press.

Jenkins, A. (1990) *Invitations to Responsibility*, Adelaide: Dulwich Centre Publications.

Jenkins, A. (1996) 'Moving Towards Respect: A Quest for Balance' in McClean, C., Carey, M., and White, C. (eds) *Men's Ways of Being*. Boulder, Colorado: Westview Press.

Jones, E. (1932) 'The early development of female sexuality', *International Journal of Psychoanalysis*, 8, 459–63.

Jones, W. (1994) 'Research expertise in the World Bank', in Walford, G. (ed.) *Researching the Powerful in Education*. London: University College London Press.

Jordan, B. (1990) *Social Work in an Unjust Society*. Hemel Hempstead: Harvester Wheatsheaf.

Jordan, J. (1989) *Moving Towards Home. Political Essays*. London: Virago.

Kagle, J.D. (1991) *Social Work Records*. Belmont, CA: Wadsworth.

Kahneman, D. and Tversky, A. (1973) 'On the psychology of prediction', *Psychological Review*, **80**, 237–51.

Kahneman, D. and Tversky, A. (1979) 'Prospect theory: an analysis of decisions under risk', *Econometrician*, 47, 263–91.

Kahneman, D. and Tversky, A. (1982) 'The psychology of preferences', *Scientific American*, 136–42.

Katz, I. (1996) *The Construction of Racial Identity in Children of Mixed Parentage: Mixed Metaphors*. London and Bristol, Pennsylvania: Jessica Kingsley Publishing.

Kelly, L. (1994) 'The interconnectedness of domestic violence and child abuse: challenges for research, policy and practice', in Mullender, A. and Morley, K. (eds) *Children Living with Domestic Violence. Putting Men's Abuse of Children on the Child Care Agenda*. London: Whiting & Birch.

Kelly, N. and Milner, J. (1996a) 'Decision-making in child protection practice: the effectiveness of the case conference in the UK'. Paper presented at ISPCAN Eleventh International Congress on Child Abuse and Neglect. University College, Dublin, 18–21 August.

Kelly, N. and Milner, J. (1996b) 'Child protection decision-making', *Child Abuse Review*, 5(2), 91–102.

Kelly, L., Wingfield, R., Burton, S., and Regan, L. (1995) *Splintered Lives. Sexual exploitation of children in the context of children's rights and child protection*. Ilford: Barnados & Child Abuse and Woman Studies Unit, University of North London.

Kelly, N. (2000) *Decision Making in Child Protection Practice*. PhD thesis, Huddersfield: University of Huddersfield.

Kemshall, H. (1996) *Reviewing Risk: a review of research on the assessment and management of risk and dangerousness – implications for policy and practice in the probation service*. London: Home Office Research and Statistics Directorate.

Kemshall, H. (1998) *Risk in Probation Practice*. Aldershot: Ashgate.

King, N. (1994) 'The qualitative research interview' in C. Cassell and G. Symons (eds) *Qualitative Methods in Organisational Research*: A Practice Guide. London: Sage.

Kline, P. (1972) *Fact and Fantasy in Freudian Theory*. London: Methuen.

Kohlberg, L. (1968) 'The child as a moral philosopher', *Psychology Today*, 2, 25–30.

Kral, R. (1989) *Strategies that Work: Techniques for Solution in the Schools*. Milwaukee, WI: Brief Family Therapy Centre.

Lawrence, M. (1992) 'Women's psychology and feminist social work', in Langan, M. and Day, L. (eds) *Women, Oppression and Social Work. Issues for Anti-Discriminatory Practice*. London: Routledge.

Leiss, W. and Chociolko, C. (1994) *Risk and Responsibility*. Quebec: McGill-Queen's University Press.

Letham, J. (1994) *Moved to Tears, Moved to Action. Solution Focused Brief Therapy with Women*. London: BT Press.

Leventhal, B. and Lundy, S.E. (eds) (1999) *Same-sex Domestic Violence. Strategies for Change* (London: Sage).

Lewis, A., Shemmings, D. and Thoburn, J. (1991) *Participation in Practice – Involving Families in Child Protection: A Training Pack*. Norwich: Social Work Development Unit, University of East Anglia.

Lewis, J. and Utting, W. (2001) 'Made to Measure? Evaluating Community Initiatives for Children. Introduction', *Children and Society*, 15(1):1–4.

Lindow, V. (2000) 'User Perspectives on Social Work', in R. Davies (ed) *The Blackwell Encyclopaedia of Social Work*. Oxford: Blackwell.

Lockwood, R., and Ascione, F.R. (1998) (eds) *Cruelty to Animals and Interpersonal Violence. Readings in Research and Application*. West Lafayette, Indiana: Purdue University Press.

Logan, S.L. *et al.* (1990) *Social Work Practice with Black Families*. New York: Longman.

London Borough of Lambeth, (1985) *Whose Child? The Report of the Panel of Enquiry into the Death of Tyra Henry*. London: HMSO.

Lymbery, M. (2001) 'Social Work at the Crossroads', *British Journal of Social Work*, 31, 369–84.

Mac an Ghaill, M. (ed.) (1996) *Understanding Masculinities*. Buckingham: Open University Press.

Macdonald, A. (1997) 'Brief Therapy in Adult Psychiatry – further outcomes', *Journal of Family Therapy*, 19(2): 213–222.

Macdonald, G. (1998) 'Promoting evidence-based practice in child protection', *Clinical Child Psychology and Psychiatry*, 3(1): 71–85.

Macdonald, G. (2000) 'Evidence Based Practice', in M. Davies (ed.) *The Blackwell Encyclopaedia of Social Work*. Oxford: Blackwell.

McGuire, J. (1995) (ed.) *What Works: Reducing Re-offending. Guidelines from Research and Practice*. Chichester: Wiley.

McNay, M. (1992) 'Social work and power relations', in Langan, M. and Day, L. (eds) *Women, Oppression and Social Work Issues in Anti-Discriminatory Practice*. London: Routledge.

Mackinnon, C. (1987) *Feminism Unmodified: Discourses on Life and Law*. Cambridge, MA: Harvard University Press.

Macleod, M. and Saraga, E. (1988) 'Challenging the orthodoxy: towards a feminist theory and practice', *Feminist Review*, 28, 16–56.

Marshall, J. (1981) 'Pansies, perverts and macho men: changing conceptions of male homosexuality', in Plummer, K. (ed.) *The Making of the Modern Homosexual*. London: Hutchinson.

Marshall, W. (1996) 'Professionals, children and power', in Blyth, E. and Milner, J. (eds) *School Exclusions: Interagency Issues for Policy and Practice*. London: Routledge.

Maslow, A.H. (1954) *Motivation and Personality*. New York: Harper.

Masson, H. and O'Byrne, P. (1984) *Applying Family Therapy*. London: Pergamon.

Maturana, H. and Varela, F. (1987) *The Tree of Knowledge: Biological Roots of Human Understanding*. Boston: New Science Library.

Mayer, J.E. and Timms, N. (1970) *The Client Speaks: Working Class Impressions of Casework*. London: Routledge & Kegan Paul.

Maynard, M. and Purvis, J. (1995) *Researching Women's Lives from a Feminist Perspective*. London: Taylor & Francis.

Mead, G.H. (1934) *Mind, Self and Society*. Chicago: Chicago University Press.

Meredith, B. (1993) *The Community Care Handbook: The New System Explained*. London: Age Concern.

Messerschmidt, J.W. (2000) *Nine Lives. Adolescent Masculinities, the Body, and Violence*. Boulder, Colorado: Westview Press.

Meyer, C. (1993) *Assessment in Social Work Practice*. New York: Columbia University Press.

Miller, D.T. and Ross, M. (1975) 'Self-serving biases in the attribution of causality: fact or fiction?' *Psychological Bulletin*, 82, 213–8.

Miller, J. Baker (ed.) (1973) *Psychoanalysis and Women*. Harmondsworth: Penguin.

Mills, C. Wright (1943) 'The professional ideology of social pathologists', *American Journal of Sociology*, 49, 165–80.

Mills, C. Wright (1970) *The Sociological Imagination*. London: Oxford University Press.

Milner, J. (1993) 'A disappearing act: the differing career paths of fathers and mothers in child protection investigations', *Critical Social Policy*, 38(13), 48–68.

Milner, J. (1996) 'Men's resistance to social work', in B. Fawcett *et al.* (eds) *Violence and Gender Relations: Theories and Interventions*. London: Sage.

Milner, J. (2001) *Women and Social Work. Narrative Approaches*. Basingstoke: Palgrave Macmillan.

Milner, J. and O'Byrne, P. (2002) *Brief Counselling: Narratives and Solutions*. Basingstoke: Palgrave Macmillan.

Morgan, D.L. (1998) *The Focus Group Guidebook*. London: Sage.

Morgan, G. (1986) *Images of Organisations*. London: Sage.

Morris, J. (1998) 'Creating a Space for Absent Voices: disabled women's experience of receiving assistance with daily living' in Allot, M. and Robbs, M. (eds) *Understanding Health and Social Care. An Introductory Reader*. London: Sage.

Moscovici, S. and Zavalloni, M. (1969) 'The group as polariser of attitudes', *Journal of Personality and Social Psychology*, 12, 125–35.

Mukherjee, S. and Martin, J. and Mnentz, G. (1991). 'The Key to Success', *Community Care*, 9–15, December 26.

Mullender, A. (ed.) (1999) *We Are Family. Sibling relationships in placement and beyond*. London: British Agencies for Adoption and Fostering.

Mullender, A. and Morley, R. (1994) (eds) *Children Living with Domestic Violence: Putting Men's Abuse of Women on the Child Care Agenda*. London: Whiting and Birch.

Murray Parkes, C. (1986) *Bereavement*. London: Tavistock.

Neill, J. (1989) *Assessing Elderly People for Residential Care: A Practical Guide*. London: National Institute for Social Work.

Newburn, T. (2001) 'What do we mean by evaluation?', *Children and Society*, **15**(1):5–13.

Nice, V. (1988) 'Them and us: women as carers; clients and social workers', *Practice*, **2**:(1), 58–73.

Nisbett, R.E. and Ross, L. (1980) *Human Inference: Strategies and Shortcomings of Social Judgement*. Englewood Cliffs, NJ: Prentice-Hall.

O'Hagan, K. and Dillenburger, K. (1995) *The Abuse of Women Within Child Care Work*. Buckingham: Open University Press.

O'Hanlon, B. (1995) *Breaking the Bad Trance*. London conference.

O'Hanlon, B. and Beadle, S. (1994) *A Field Guide to Possibility Land*. Omaha: Possibility Press.

O'Leary, E. (1996) *Counselling Older Adults. Perspectives, Approaches and Research*. London: Chapman & Hall.

O'Sullivan, T. (1999) *Decision Making in Social Work*. Basingstoke: Palgrave Macmillan.

Olsen, M. (1984) *Social Work and Mental Health*. London: Tavistock.

Osuwu-Bempah, J. (1994) 'Race, identity and social work', *British Journal of Social Work*, 24(2), 123–36.

Packman, J., with Randall, J. and Jacques, N. (1986) *Who Needs Care? Social Work Decisions about Children*. Oxford: Basil Blackwell.

Parad, H.J. (1965) *Crisis Intervention: Selected Readings*. New York: FSA of America.

Parton, N. (1985) *The Politics of Child Abuse*, Basingstoke: Palgrave Macmillan.

Parton, N. (ed.) (1996) *Social Theory, Social Change and Social Work*. London: Routledge.

Parton, N. and Marshall, W. (1998) 'Postmodernism and discourse approaches to social work' in R. Adams, L. Dominelli and M. Payne (eds) *Social work: Themes, Issues and Critical Debates*. Basingstoke: Palgrave Macmillan.

Parton, N. and O'Byrne, P. (2000) *Constructive Social Work*. Basingstoke: Palgrave Macmillan.

Pavlov, I.P. (1960) *Conditional Reflexes: An Investigation of the Psychological Activity of the Cerebral Cortex* (translation). New York: Dover Publications.

Payne, M. (1991) *Modern Social Work Theory*. Basingstoke: Palgrave Macmillan.

Payne, M. (2000) *Narrative Therapy; an introduction for counsellors*. London: Sage.

Pearson, G., Treseder, J. and Yelloly, M. (1988) *Social Work and the Legacy of Freud*. Basingstoke: Palgrave Macmillan.

Penfield, W. (1952) 'Memory mechanisms', *AMA Archives of Neurology and Psychiatry*, **67**, 178–98.

Piaget, J. (1977) *The Origin of Intelligence in the Child*. Harmondsworth: Penguin.

Pincus, A. and Minahan, A. (1973) *Social Work Practice: Model and Method*. Itasca, IL: Peacock.

Pinsof, W.M. (1994) 'An overview of integrated problem solving therapy', *Journal of Family Therapy*, 16(1), 103–20.

Pocock, D. (1995) 'Searching for a better story', *Journal of Family Therapy*, 17, 149–74.

Pozatek, E. (1994) 'The problem of certainty', *Social Work*, 29, 396–404.

Prince, K. (1996) *Boring Records? Communication, Speech and Writing in Social Work Records*. London, Bristol: Jessica Kingsley.

Pugh, R. (1996) *Effective Language in Health and Social Work*. London: Chapman & Hall.

Read, J. (2000) *Disability, the Family and Society. Listening to Mothers*. Buckingham: Open University Press.

Reder, P., Duncan, S. and Gray, M. (1993) *Beyond Blame: Child Abuse Tragedies Revisited*. London: Routledge.

Reid, W.J. (1963) 'An experimental study of the methods used in casework treatment'. Doctrinal dissertation. New York: Columbia University Press.

Reid, W.J. (1978) *The Task-Centred System*. New York: Columbia University Press.

Reid, W.J. (1992) *Task Strategies*. New York: Columbia University Press.

Reid, W.J. and Epstein, L. (1972) *Task-Centred Casework*. New York: Columbia University Press.

Reid, W.J. and Shyne, A. (1969) *Brief and Extended Casework*. New York: Columbia University Press.

Reimes, S. and Treacher, A. (1995) *Introducing User Friendly Family Therapy*. London: Routledge.

Renzetti, C.M. (1992) *Violent Betrayal. Partner Abuse in Lesbian Relationships*. London: Sage.

Renzetti, C.M. and Lee, R. (1993) *Researching Sensitive Topics*. London: Sage.

Rich, V. (1977) *Of Woman Born: Motherhood as Institution and Experience*. London: Virago.

Richards, J. (1980) *The Sceptical Feminist*. London: Routledge.

Richards, M. (1987) 'Developing the content of practice teaching', *Social Work Education*, 6(2).

Richards, S. (2000) 'Bridging the Divide: Elders and the Assessment Process', *British Journal of Social Work*, 30, 37–49.

Richmond, M. (1917) *What Is Social Care Work?* New York: Russell Sage.

Robson, C. (1993) *Real World Research*. Oxford: Basil Blackwell.

Rojek, C. and Collins, S. A. (1988) 'Contract or con trick revisited. Comments on the reply by Corden and Preston-Shoot', *British Journal of Social Work*, 18, 611–22.

Rorbaugh, J.B. (1981) *Woman: Psychology's Puzzle*. London: Abacus.

Rose, N. (1985) *The Psychological Complex: Psychology, Politics and Society in England 1869–1939*. London: Routledge & Kegan Paul.

Rutter, M. (1981) *Maternal Deprivation Reassessed*. London: Penguin.

Sainsbury, E. (1970) *Social Diagnosis in Casework*. London: Routledge & Kegan Paul.

Sampson, A., Smith, D., Pearson, G., Blagg, H. and Stubbs, P. (1991) 'Gender Issues in Inter-Agency Relations: Police, Probation and Social Services', in P. Abbott and C. Wallace (eds) *Sex, Gender and Care Work: Research Highlights in Social Work*. London: Jessica Kingsley Publishing.

Sawicki, J. (1991) *Disciplining Foucault: Feminism, Power and the Body*. London: Sage.

Schaffer, H.R. (1990) *Making Decisions about Children*. Oxford: Basil Blackwell.

Schwartz, A. and Goldiamond, I. (1975) *Social Casework: A Behavioural Approach*. New York: Columbia University Press.

Scott, D. (1998) 'A Qualitative Study of Social Work Assessment in Cases of Alleged Child Abuse', *British Journal of Social Work*, 28, 73–88.

Sebold, J. and Uken, A. (2000) *Treating Domestic Violence Offenders*. Audio Tape available from: Brief Family Therapy Centre, P.O.Box 13736, Milwaukee, Wisconsin, 53213–0736.

Segal, L. (1997) *Slow Motion, Changing Masculinities, Changing Men*. London: Virago (revised edition).

Seligman, M.E.P. (1992) *Helplessness: On Depression, Development and Death*. New York: Freeman.

Sheldon, B. (1982) *Behaviour Modification, Theory, Practice and Philosophy*. London: Tavistock.

Sheldon, B. (1995) *Cognitive-Behavioural Therapy, Research, Practice and Philosophy*. London and New York: Routledge.

Sheppard, M. (1995) *Care Management and the New Social Work. A Critical Analysis*. London: Whiting & Birch/Social Care Association (Education).

Sibeon, R. (1992) *Towards a New Sociology of Social Work*. Aldershot: Avebury.

Sinclair, I., Parker, R., Leat, D. and Williams, J. (1990) *The Kaleidoscope of Care: A Review of Research in Welfare Provision for Elderly People*. London: HMSO, for National Institute for Social Work.

Sinclair, R., Garrett, L. and Berridge, D. (1995) *Social Work and Assessment With Adolescents*. London: NCB.

Skinner, B.F. (1953) *Science and Human Behaviour*. New York: Macmillan.

Skinner, B.F. (1958) 'Reinforcement theory', *American Psychologist*, 13, 94–9.

Smale, G. and Tuson, G., with Brehal, N. and Marsh, P. (1993) *Empowerment, Assessment, Care Management and the Skilled Worker*. London: National Institute for Social Work.

Smale, G., Tuson, G., Ahmad, B., Darvill, G., Homoney, L. and Sainsbury, E. (1994) *Negotiating Care in the Community*. London: HMSO, for National Institute for Social Work.

Social Services Inspectorate. (1991) *Getting the Message Across. A Guide to Developing and Communicating Policies, Principles and Procedures on Assessment*. London: HMSO.

Spence, M.F. (1995) 'Finding a healthy path through racism and sexism', *Social Work Education*, 14(4), 106–13.

Spender, D. (1985) *Man Made Language*. 2nd edn. London: Routledge & Kegan Paul.

Stanley, N. (1999) 'User-Practitioner Transactions in the New Culture of Community Care', *British Journal of Social Work*, 29, 417–35.

Stanley, L. and Wise, S. (1991) 'Method, methodology and epistemology in feminist research process', in Stanley, L. (ed.) *Feminist Praxis: Research, Theory and Epistemology*. London: Routledge.

Steward, I. and Joines, V. (1999) *TA Today; A New Introduction to TA*. Nottingham: Lifespace Publishers.

Strand, P.S. (1997) 'Towards a Developmentally Informed Narrative Therapy', *Family Process*, 36, 325–39.

Strean, H.F. (1968) 'Casework with ego-fragmented parents', *Social Casework*, April.

Strom-Gottfried, K. (1999) *Social Work Practice. Cases, Activities, and Exercises*. Thousand Oaks, London, New Delhi: Pine Forge Press.

Stuart, R.B. (1974) 'Behaviour modification: a technology for social change', in Turner, F.J. (ed.) *Social Work Treatment*. New York: Free Press.

Sugarman, L.(1986) *Lifespan Development*. London: Methuen.

Sutton, C (2000) *Child and Adolescent Behaviour Problems*. Leicester: The British Psychological Society.

Tamasese, K. and Waldegrave, C. (1996) 'Culture and Gender Accountability in the "Just Therapy" Approach', in C. Mclean., M. Carey. and C. White (eds) *Men's Ways of Being*. Colorado and Oxford: Westview Press.

Thoburn, J., Lewis, A. and Shemmings, D. (1995) *Paternalism or Partnership? Family Involvement in the Child Protection Process*. London: HMSO.

Thompson, N. (1992) *Existentialism and Social Work*. Aldershot: Avebury.

Thompson, N. (1993) *Anti-Discriminatory Practice*. Basingstoke: Palgrave Macmillan.

Thompson, N. (1995) *Theory and Practice in Health and Social Welfare*. Buckingham: Open University Press.

Thompson, N. (1997) *Anti-Discriminatory Practice*. Basingstoke: Palgrave Macmillan (second edition).

Thompson, N. (1998) *Promoting Equality: Challenging Discrimination and Oppression in Human Services*. Basingstoke: Palgrave Macmillan.

Thyer, B. (1998) *Handbook of Social Work Practice*. Chichester: J. Wiley

Thyer, B. (2002) *Handbook of Social Work Research*. London: Sage

Trevithick, P. (2000) *Social Work Skills. a practice handbook*. Buckingham, Philadelphia: Open University Press.

Trepper, T. S. and Barrett, M. J. (eds) (1986) *Treating Incest*, Binghamton, NY: Haworth Press

Tunstill, J. (1993) 'Local authority policies on children in need', in Gidden, J. (ed.) *The Children Act 1989 and Family Support*. London: HMSO.

Turnell, A. and Edwards, S. (1999) *Signs of Safety: A Solution and Safety Orientated Approach to Child Protection Casework*. New York: Norton.

Vennard, J., Sugg, D. and Hedderman, C. (1997) *The Use of Cognitive Behavioural Approaches with Offenders: Message from the Research Unit*. London: Home Office.

Walford, G. (1994) 'A new focus on the powerful', in Walford, G. (ed.) *Researching the Powerful in Education*. London: University College London Press.

Walker, N. (1987) *Crime and Criminology*. Oxford: Oxford Paperbacks.

Walsh, F. (1999) 'Partner Abuse' in Davies, D. and Neal, C. (eds) *Pink Therapy. A guide for counsellors and therapists working with lesbian, gay and bisexual clients*. Buckingham, Philadelphia: Open University Press.

Walsh, T. (ed) (1997) *Solution Focused Child Protection – towards a positive framework for social work practice*. Dublin: University of Dublin, Trinity College, Department of Social Studies, Occasional Paper No. 6.

Ward, E. (1984) *Father–Daughter Rape*. London: Women's Press.

Wasserman, S.L. (1974) 'Ego psychology', in Turner, F.J. (ed.) *Social Work Treatment*. New York: Free Press.

Webb, S. (2001) 'Some Considerations on the Validity of Evidence-Based Practice in Social Work', *British Journal of Social Work*, 31, 57–79.

Werner, H.D. (ed.) (1970) *New Understandings of Human Behaviour*. New York: Association Press.

Westwood, S. (1990) 'Racism, black masculinity and the politics of space', in Hearn, J. and Morgan, D.H.J. (eds) *Men, Masculinities and Social Theory*. London and Winchester: Hyman, 55–71.

Westwood, S. (1996) 'Feckless parents. Masculinities and the British state', in Mac an Ghaill, M. (ed.) *Understanding Masculinities*. Buckingham: Open University Press.

White, M. (1988) 'The externalizing of the problems and the re-authoring of lives and relationships', *Dulwich Centre Newsletter*, Summer: 3–21.

White, M. (1991) 'Deconstruction and therapy', *Dulwich Centre Newsletter*, 3.

White, M. (1993) 'Deconstruction and therapy', in S. Gilligan and R. Price (eds) *Therapeutic Conversations*. New York & London: Norton.

White, M. (1995a) *Re-authoring Lives: Interviews and Essays*, Adelaide: Dulwich Centre Publications.

White, M. (1996) Conference on narrative work. Doncaster.

White, M. and Epston, D. (1990) *Narrative Means to Therapeutic Ends*. New York: Norton.

White, V. (1995b) 'Commonality and Diversity in Feminist Social Work', *British Journal of Social Work*, 143–56.

Whyte, G. (1989) 'Groupthink reconsidered', *Academy of Management Review*, 14(1), 40–56.

Whyte, G. (1993) 'Decision failures, why they occur and how to prevent them', *Academy of Management Executive*, 5(3), 23–31.

Wilgosh, R., Hawkes, D. and Marsh. I. (1993) 'Session two and beyond', *Context*, 17, 31–3.

Williams, F. (1993) 'Women and Community' in Borat, J., Pereira, C., Pilgrim, D., and Williams, F. (eds) *Community Care. A Reader*. Basingstoke: Palgrave Macmillan.

Wise, S. (1995) 'Feminist ethics in practice', in Hugman, R. and Smith, D. *Ethical Issues in Social Work*. London: Sage.

Wittgenstein, L. (1980) *Remarks on the Philosophy of Psychology.* Oxford: Blackwell.

Wright, K., Haycox, A. and Leadman, I. (1994) *Evaluating Community Care Services for People with Learning Difficulties.* Buckingham: Open University Press.

Yapko, M. (1988) *When Living Hurts: Directives for Treating Depression.* New York: Brunner/Mazel.

Zeig, J.K. (1985) *Ericksonian Psychotherapy. Volume 1: Structures.* New York: Brunner/Mazel.

Index